Table Of Contents

Below the Water Line

When the wind stopped blowing,
Thought we made it through another one.
When the wind stopped blowing,
Thought I'd be home with the rising sun.
But then the water came on in and it changed everything,
In just that moment in time.

That's when my life fell below the water line,
That's when my life fell below the water line,
When the water came in, it didn't leave me a thing,
But trouble on my mind.

Lyrics excerpted from "Below the Water Line," written by Paul Soniat, a self-taught musician from New Orleans, Louisiana. Available at: www.paulsoniat.com.

Just an Ordinary Day

Saturday, August 27, 2005

THE POOL WATER is bathtub warm, and the sky is postcard-perfect, clear and blue.

Thirteen-year-old Samantha floats on a raft near me. My daughter has carefully positioned herself with her arms extended by her sides and her chin tilted up toward the sun. Since school started last week, her tan has faded and she is determined to preserve it. She lies perfectly still; her only movement is the subtle rise and fall of her chest as she breathes.

A major hurricane named Katrina lurks just a few hundred miles away, out in the Gulf of Mexico, but we are not concerned. Landfall predictions are still uncertain, and I'm expecting that this hurricane will turn to the east or west and spare New Orleans, just like all of the hurricanes in the past forty years have done.

I take notice when I come in from the pool, turn on the television, and see the satellite image showing that Katrina has increased in intensity, and is now bigger than the state of Texas. Even so, the hurricane watch area extends all the way from western Louisiana to the eastern edge of the Florida panhandle. Anything can happen with this hurricane at this point.

Late in the afternoon, New Orleans Mayor Ray Nagin calls for a voluntary evacuation. He says he's adhering to the state's evacuation plan, and will not order a mandatory evacuation until thirty hours before Katrina's expected landfall so that people living in low-lying surrounding areas can leave first and avoid gridlocked escape routes.

My eleven-year-old son calls and tells me he's ready to be picked up from his friend Colin's house. On the stoop outside their house, Colin's father asks if we are evacuating, and I tell him my plan is to watch the news and The Weather Channel and then decide. If Jim Cantore shows up in New Orleans, then we're going to skedaddle, since he always seems to broadcast from the bulls-eye of a storm. Colin's father says he plans to see how things look in the morning. And I have jury duty on Tuesday, I tell him. Can't miss that!

My son John and I make a quick stop at Breaux Mart on the way home. Cars circle the parking lot, competing for the few open spaces. The store is clogged with people, and many shelves already are bare. I dispatch John to see if there are any hamburger buns still on the shelf. He reports back that just a few packages remain and like a fisherman, proudly holds up his catch. I see a few scattered packages of ground beef lying in a refrigerator case, and speed up to get there before anyone else does.

There's nervous chatter in the long checkout line as people debate hunkering down or getting on the road. Older folks recall evacuating in '92 after Hurricane Andrew blasted across southern Florida, and then entered the Gulf of Mexico and headed toward Louisiana. Andrew made landfall as a category 3 hurricane a couple of hours west of New Orleans, so we dodged that bullet. Hurricane Alberto in '94 looked like it was headed for New Orleans, but veered off to the Florida Panhandle. And no one could forget evacuating for Hurricane Ivan last year and the arduous, tortuous process that was.

With ample time in the checkout line, many evacuation stories are told, eliciting nods of recognition from the people standing in the adjacent lines. We know all too well what it was like to batten-down the house, creep north along the interstates, spend a sleepless night out, and return a day or two later to sunny, intact New Orleans to start reversing the process. "Here we go again," another "hurrication," seems to be the sentiment of many in line. A number of people say they're waiting to see how things look in the morning.

It's inconceivable that a major hurricane is headed this way. The sky is clear, the air is still, and the sunset is spectacular. Buddy, our 80-pound yellow Lab, takes a leisurely swim in our pool while we eat dinner on the patio. It's just another ordinary day.

All evening long, we wear down the television remote jumping from station to station. We, too, have decided to see how things look in the morning, knowing that a lot can happen in twelve hours. I'm still predicting that fateful turn that hurricanes take at the last minute, the turn that produces a collective sigh of relief from the people in their initial path.

We watch evacuation footage and see that even with the contraflow on the interstate this year, it's no better than last September when about half of the people in New Orleans evacuated for Hurricane Ivan. Despite six lanes of traffic all heading westward, the traffic on Interstate 10 does not move at all. People are standing beside their cars, an impromptu and odd social gathering of sorts. Good thing we didn't leave tonight, I tell my husband, Rich. We'd be stuck out there on the highway in the dark. I can't imagine our family—two adults, two kids, and two dogs—inching along the interstate all night.

John plops down on the couch and announces that it would be fun (fun?) to evacuate at night. He tells us he would bed-down in our car, tell the dogs goodnight, and go to sleep. Rich raises his eyebrows. He knows our two kids would be squabbling before we back out of the driveway. And there's no telling how Buddy and John's 12-pound Jack Russell Terrier, which he named Jack, would handle a long car ride. We have trouble driving around the neighborhood with our dogs, and with our kids for that matter.

A news announcer casually mentions that Pat Sajak and Vanna White, who are in town taping New Orleans-themed episodes of *Wheel of Fortune,* have cut production short and are leaving. The "Wheelmobile" and eight tractor trailers of equipment are being readied for departure. It is the first time in its thirty-year history that the long-running game show cancels taping.

I silently pray that Katrina weakens and changes course, but the latest information indicates that this hurricane is strengthening and coming our way. Local weatherman Bob Breck pronounces that "the water will be so high that you'll be on the roof with the cockroaches!"

Around 10 p.m., we are surprised to see Mayor Ray Nagin back on TV. He looks just as surprised to be on TV; earlier today, he said he would issue his next statement in the morning. The mayor says he received a phone call from Louisiana Governor Kathleen Blanco, who in turn had received a call from the National Hurricane Center Director. The news is not good. As Nagin puts it, "Ladies and gentlemen, this is not a test. This is the real deal."

Where R U Going 2 Go?

Sunday, August 28th

THE HOUSE PHONE is ringing as I'm packing fruit in a cooler. It's my friend Becca in Oregon calling me at 4:30 a.m. her time.

"Are you up?" she asks.

"We've pretty much been up since yesterday."

"You're not staying, are you? It sounds really bad." I can hear the worry in her voice.

I tell her that we've been through this so many times now, and every time it's predicted to be bad, the hurricane veers off and we're fine. I'm expecting the same with Katrina. I tell her we're headed to Houston, where I've reserved a hotel room for the next couple of days.

"We decided to go to Houston because it's easy to get to, plus they have a ton of hotel rooms. And Rich's brother lives there. He offered to have us stay with him, but he and Dana are going to have his son Alex and his family there, and they're in a townhouse, so I just went ahead and booked us a hotel room." I tell Becca that we should be on the road in the next hour.

"Oh my God, Lisa, you be careful and let me know when you get to Houston," she says.

A friend who has kids the same ages as ours calls to ask if we're leaving. She's got her kids eating up the ice cream that's in her freezer. It's seven in the morning.

My mother, who lives in upstate New York, asks why we haven't left yet. My two sisters, who live near my parents, are watching The Weather Channel and need assurance that we are evacuating and not being stupid by trying to "ride it out."

Rich's partner in his general surgery practice, Bobby, is covering for the practice for the weekend, and calls to say he's given a report on their hospitalized patients to Joe, who is heading the hospital hurricane team. East Jefferson General Hospital is one of two parish (county) hospitals and will remain open. Bobby and his wife Sharon are headed to Atlanta.

With one eye on the TV, I continue packing up food and the phone rings again. Rich's cell phone rings. My cell phone rings. Samantha's cell phone, with its superbly annoying ring tone, rings. I try to keep the conversations short because I have lots to do and too little time. Everyone wants us to "report in" to them once we get to Houston, but I'm now worried that we won't even be able to get out of New Orleans with all of these phone delays.

Rich tells me to just not answer the calls. I tell him that to not answer them will get people worrying about us, so we should answer but keep things brief. It's day one, hour one and we're already arguing about something.

A friend of ours who lives in earthquake country in

California calls and simply says, "You better get your asses out of there." Rich's cousin Marcie in Atlanta, who has been in contact with relatives in Miami, tells us that Katrina surprised everyone there. Windows blew out of high-rise buildings and there is extensive damage. This news worries me a little since I somehow had gotten the impression that Katrina simply passed over southern Florida.

The TV in the living room is now making a loud, beeping sound. There's a message scrolling across the bottom of the screen that says that evacuation is mandatory. It's the first-ever mandatory evacuation for New Orleans. Katrina now has our full attention.

I glance around the house and ask Rich to take photos with my purple Cool Pix camera. We'll be needing them for the insurance adjuster if this hurricane is as bad as predicted. Open the freezer, I direct him. Take a photo of what we have in there. Go into each room and take photos from different angles, so we can document what we have there. Put the table and chairs by the pool into the garage. Get the white rockers from the front porch and bring them inside the house so they don't float or fly away. Bring in the rest of the stuff from outside, like the garbage cans. And don't forget the doormats.

Our house flooded in what is commonly referred to as the "May '95" flood, so I know what I should take, what I should protect, and what I should just leave alone. Although we live in the New Orleans suburb of River Ridge five feet above sea level, our house flooded with two feet of water. The flood, which took New Orleans by surprise, was caused by an unexpected rainstorm that dumped thirteen inches of rain in about an hour. Canals in our neighborhood drain water to Lake Pontchartrain, but in the spring of 1995, construction work was being done on the Soniat Canal at the end of our street. With the canal obstructed, the rainwater had nowhere to go except inside people's homes. The May '95 flood shut down the city for two days, caused $3.1 billion in damage, and left six people dead.

The May '95 flood wiped out any record of the first year of John's life and the first three years of Samantha's. The birth videos, photo albums of birthday parties and holiday gatherings, and framed wedding and baby pictures—all gone. It taught me that everything else was just "stuff"—non-essential, replaceable, material goods. And like most families in America, we had way too much stuff.

The thought of going through another flood now, just ten years later, leaves me shaking my head in disbelief. Hurricanes bring wind damage too, and I shudder at the thought that our house could be completely destroyed within the next few days.

I make one last run through the house. I notice John's second grade painting on the wall of the dining room and start pulling all of our kids' artwork from the walls. I double bag the pieces in plastic, put the artwork in plastic storage bins, and place the bins high on my closet shelf, with fluffy comforters stuffed around them. The valuables that we must leave behind are now safe and protected.

The kids have woken up, and I hand them each a small sports duffle bag. I tell them that they can bring whatever will fit in the bag, and they need to bring their school backpacks too, so they won't get behind on their homework. It's Sunday and I'm thinking that there won't be school on Monday and Tuesday, possibly into Wednesday, to allow for what I'm expecting to be a slow and painful evacuation and slow and painful return.

Samantha's bag is overflowing with clothes when she comes downstairs. She has packed a hairbrush, toothbrush, underwear, two bathing suits, two tops, two pairs of shorts, and four very dressy dresses. Where in the world does she think she's going?

John's bag zips up just fine and he's obviously planning to spend only one night out. He's packed a toothbrush, a shirt, a pair of shorts, his baseball glove, and Sharky, a stuffed animal long ago acquired at Sea World. No underwear.

I send him back upstairs as the phone continues to ring. Callers tell us how frustrating it has been trying to reach us. They suspect the phone lines and cell towers are jammed, and they probably are.

I hear Rich on the phone talking to friends and relatives, reassuring them that we're evacuating. He downplays Katrina's intensity—now predicted to be a category 5 hurricane. I hear him talk about how he's lived in New Orleans all of his life, and how so many hurricanes appear to be headed this way but then veer away.

We've never evacuated for a hurricane before. The fact that evacuation is mandatory makes me nervous. We know we need to get out of "harm's way," a term now very popular with the Bush administration. I estimate that we will be on the road for at least ten hours, although the trip to Houston normally takes about six. I hear on the TV that a million people are expected to evacuate. I then think of the worst case scenario, being stuck on the road even longer, and start packing Rich's Ford Expedition with:

- 4 bagels smeared with cream cheese
- 1 box of crackers
- 1 40 ounce jar of creamy peanut butter
- 1 jar of strawberry jam
- ½ box of Cheerios
- 10 pint sized bottles of water
- 6 juice pouches
- 2 bottles of Diet Pepsi
- 6 plums
- 4 bananas
- 2 oranges
- 1 bag of Keebler Chips Deluxe Rainbow cookies with "chocolate in every bite"
- 1 bag of dog food and 2 dog bowls
- 2 pillows and 1 small blanket
- 1 container of wet wipes

I shove the plastic folder that contains our important papers under the front seat, and put the little box containing my Hartwick College nursing pin, gold charm bracelet, silver locket, and my "good" earrings in the glove compartment.

I snap some photos of my Tahoe, parked in the driveway in the place with the fewest trees, and walk to the street to get some shots of the house and yard. We've covered six of the nine French doors on the front of our house with plywood and would have covered more, but six sheets of plywood was the maximum anyone could buy.

I check the back yard one last time to see if we missed anything. Our house sits on an acre of land, and both the back and front yards are filled with live oaks, pine and pecan trees, azalea bushes, and heirloom Old Blush climbing roses in full bloom. I wonder what our property will look like upon our return.

Rich is jogging around the front yard with the two dogs in an attempt to tire them out. He's positioned their crates in the back of the SUV, and it looks like we're ready to go.

Evacuating is an adventure for the kids, and they're already excited about the very good possibility of school being cancelled this coming week. They've only been in school for eight days. Samantha has just started eighth grade, and John just moved up to middle school and sixth grade.

Samantha is standing by the car door, her slender thumbs pecking away on her cell phone. John comes up beside her to get in, and Samantha body slams him into the side of the SUV for no apparent reason. It's going to be a long ride to Houston.

My cell phone rings, and it's my mother wanting to know why her precious grandchildren are still in New Orleans.

I'm at the front door, wondering if we have forgotten anything. Nothing that I can think of, except maybe paper towels. I tuck a roll under my arm, set the burglar alarm and lock the door, and head to Rich's SUV.

We are still rolling out of the driveway when Samantha puts on her headphones, turns on her portable CD player, and announces that she is not to be disturbed until we get to Houston.

John yells good-bye to the house, and Rich and I just look at each other. In all likelihood, everything will be just fine, and we'll be home again in a day or two.

I read *People* magazine with Angelina Jolie and her new

baby Zahara on the cover. We're inching along the road, and we're less than a mile from our house when John asks for a bagel. Then Samantha wants one, then Rich, and then I eat one too. Rich says he thought that almost everyone had left by now, but clearly the roads are packed.

After an hour, we're about three miles from home and have another three miles to go before we reach Interstate 10 and the contraflow lanes heading west. At this point, the cars have stopped inching forward, and we are gridlocked on Williams Boulevard.

Rich's Expedition rides fairly high off the ground, so I've spent a lot of time peering down into the cars next to us. There is a predictable pattern; drivers impatiently tap on the steering wheel and adjust the radio, the front passengers attempt to make calls on their cell phones, and children play little Nintendo games in the back seat. About half of the cars have what appears to be an older relative and/or a pet or two.

The kids are no longer "having fun" on this outing, and my right arm is roasting from the sun beaming down. I take a section of the Sunday paper, which I plan to read next, and put it up on the window. I show Samantha how to "hang" the paper by opening and closing her window and soon she, too, has a papered window to block the intense sun.

Rich fiddles with the radio. All of the stations repeat the order to evacuate and traffic reports confirm what we've suspected, that all routes north and west are now at a standstill. Gas is in short supply everywhere. Announcements are made about stations that still have gas, and a few minutes later, we hear that these stations are now closed.

The dogs are unusually quiet and Rich asks John to check

on them, to make sure they're still alive back there. The dogs appear to be doing fine. Another thirty minutes pass.

The opposite side of Williams Boulevard has been desolate all morning. Now, we see a few cars zooming toward us. Then, a few more fly by, and a few more after that. We finally realize that cars in our stopped lanes of traffic are turning around.

If there's one thing I can't stand, it's sitting idle, going nowhere. Any forward motion would be preferable in this unbearable 90-plus degree weather.

A reporter for local television station WWL is flying around New Orleans in a helicopter, and describes fairly smooth sailing on Interstate 10 going *east.* Rich and I look at each other once again. John tells us that we should go east and go to the beach in Florida.

Rich swings the SUV out of the line of cars, and we turn around and head south on Williams Boulevard. In less than ten minutes, we're back at our house because Samantha has to pee and it's on our way east anyway. We get the dogs out of their confining crates and let them run around for a few minutes. On the way out of the house, I grab a Rand McNally *Atlas of the United States* from the shelf in my office, and we pile back into the SUV.

Once again, we yell good-bye to the house, but this time we really mean it.

We sail to downtown New Orleans. We're driving perpendicularly to the traffic, all attempting to head north. As we pass the Superdome, it looks like hundreds, if not thousands of people are trying to get in there. There is no shade around the cement monstrosity, and heat from the pavement is making little waves as it rises.

"I thought the Dome was supposed to be medical or last resort only," I recall.

"I did too. Boy am I glad that I'm on the C-team," Rich replies.

At Rich's hospital, staffed mostly by physicians in private practice, a hurricane staffing list is assembled each year with A, B, and C teams. The A-team is comprised of physicians who report to the hospital prior to a hurricane, the B-team relieves the A-team after the hurricane has passed, and then the C-team comes in to relieve the B-team. The physicians on each of the teams are rotated each year, and many volunteer for A-team duty because they can bring their families and pets with them to the hospital, and are therefore assured to have a safe place with a generator in which to wait out, or ride out, a storm.

"Holy cow," I say as I look backward as we pass the Superdome. "That line to get in goes all the way down Poydras. There's no way that all of those people are medical or last resort only!"

We are on the elevated portion of the interstate and look down on the French Quarter, the Municipal Auditorium, and the above-ground cemeteries. The streetcars have stopped running. A few minutes later, we encounter the first slowdown of traffic. We previously were traveling 40-50 mph and now creep toward the high rise, the elevated part of the interstate that rises over the Industrial Canal just east of downtown New Orleans.

The fast food places are boarding up and many have

"closed" signs. The few that are open have long lines of cars in the drive-thru.

My sister Erica calls. "Jim Cantore is in New Orleans," she announces. "So you know it's gonna be bad."

We are not alone in heading east. Other people apparently have decided to head in this direction, and many appear to not know exactly where they are headed. Cars slowly pass us, with maps spread out across the dashboard and fingers pointing here and there. At the side of the road, a group of people lean over a map that covers the hood of a car.

Samantha is getting increasingly frustrated as she tries to call her friends but keeps getting busy signals. I call Rich's brother in Houston and amazingly get through after a few attempts, and tell him that we're no longer headed to Houston, and are now on our way to Florida. It soon becomes clear that calls to and from the 504 New Orleans area code do not go through, and that calls to other area codes go through, some easily and some after several attempts. Samantha then discovers that text messages can be sent and received without any problem.

Text messages in 2005 were short and sweet because the numeric keypad had to be used (the number 2 button was pushed three times for the letter C). Consequently, text messages also required texting "shorthand," so Sam sent, and received, numerous "Where R U going 2 go?" messages.

"Claire's going to Baton Rouge," Sam announces.

"Sarah's going to her grandpa's in Tuscaloosa," she adds. "Chloe's trying to get to Pineville."

"Ellie says they've been on the road since 4 a.m., and

everything was fine until Grandmother had diarrhea in the car," she adds.

We continue east on I-10, going five to sometimes fifteen miles per hour. We make it to the twin spans, 5½ mile-long bridges that cross the eastern portion of Lake Pontchartrain, the second largest salt water lake in the United States. Although the twin spans consist of two lanes in each direction, there are three lanes of cars and trucks going east and none going west.

"Why aren't they contraflowing here?" asks Rich. "There's not a single car on those lanes over there." He bangs his head on the steering wheel.

I wonder if the bridge will hold up under all this weight. It's probably never had a packed lane of cars driving on the right shoulder in addition to cars and trucks driving on the two lanes of the bridge. Cars are overheating too, and many have shut off the air conditioning and opened the windows. We do the same.

We are out over the lake and the wind has picked up considerably. It cools us off a bit, and the kids remark that there are waves in the lake. On a normal day, the lake is calm and there are dozens of sailboats in this area, but today there are none.

My friend Cheryl, who's like a sister to me, calls and asks where we're going. I tell her that we've had to change our original plan because of the gridlocked traffic heading west, and that we are now headed east. She shudders at the thought of us going through the Gulf Coast to get to the Florida panhandle. She asks, "What if it turns east?" She tells me that earlier in the week, she booked four rooms at a motel in Brookhaven, Mississippi, 170 miles due north of New Orleans.

"Three of the rooms are for our neighbors, but I'm not sure if Debbie's going to take one of them. She thinks this thing is headed right up the mouth of the river and will keep going north right through Brookhaven. She's thinking of going further north, and she's supposed to call me back by two to let me know what she's doing. If she doesn't want the room, it's yours, and even if she does take it, just come. Four adults, four kids, and four dogs in one room won't be bad for one night. It'll be fun! And I've got three bottles of wine with us."

"Should we go to Brookhaven?" I ask Rich as we continue creeping east.

"Florida will be better, since like she said, Brookhaven is due north of New Orleans. I want to get as far away from this thing as possible."

"How far do you think we'll need to go in Florida in order to find a hotel room?" I ask.

"We'll just have to keep driving until we find a place."

I then remember that an oncology nurse friend of mine recently moved to Destin. "If we get in a bind, I'm sure Connie will let us stay at her house overnight."

We're starting to see arms come out the windows of the cars, turning containers over to empty yellow liquid that quickly steams on the hot pavement. John finds this highly entertaining. Some pour water into their containers afterward, a primitive sort of "flush" I imagine. Courteous travelers bolt from their cars, run over to the shoulder of the interstate, and empty their containers onto the grass instead of the pavement.

A woman in the car next to ours empties a bucket onto the pavement between her car and ours.

"OH MY GOD, WHAT IS THAT SMELL?" Samantha asks as her eyes open and she sits up straight.

"Pee pee," John informs her.

"Pee?" she asks, incredulous. "Pee?" she asks again, this time leaning forward to address the question to me.

"Yup." Rich and I answer in unison.

We all close our windows and run the air conditioning for a few minutes.

"Sam, stop it!" John says.

"Move over."

"Move over? You have most of the space here already. Stay on your side." John draws an imaginary line down the middle of the back seat.

"Mom," Sam calls. "John won't move over."

You have plenty of room, I tell her. No she doesn't, she replies. The back seat battle is now going full throttle, and I wonder if people in the cars next to us can hear our kids behaving badly.

People ride by sitting in a motor boat pulled behind a truck.

The temperature gauge inside our car shows that it is 104 degrees outside, and up ahead of us is a pickup truck with at least a dozen men, women, and children sitting in the back of the truck. Some are perched along the sides of the back and others sit low in the bed of the truck. Four men ride backwards, their legs dangling from the tailgate. Like the people sitting in the motor boat, they too are riding along beneath the blazing sun and *they are not complaining.* I am about to try to convey this to our children, but fortunately, the point has already been well-taken. Both of our kids are sitting up straighter, they are on their "own side" of the back seat, and they are silent.

After what seems to be an eternity, we reach the I-10 and I-59 split just east of Slidell.

I-59 is contraflow only, so traffic is headed north in all four lanes. We plan to continue going east on I-10 until we see the "closed" signs and Mississippi State Police cars blocking those lanes. We are forced to go north on I-59. We were not expecting this.

"You would think this would have been announced on the radio," says Rich.

I pull out my atlas and turn to the "Mississippi" page to see what cities and towns line Interstate 59 to the north. There's Hattiesburg, Laurel, Meridian, and then I-59 enters Alabama. I turn to the "Alabama" page. There's the town Cuba (Cuba?), then Tuscaloosa and Birmingham. Another option is that we could go east when we get to Meridian, and head south to the beach in Florida. Rich and I ponder how long this circuitous route would take, and wonder if we'd make it there with gas being in such short supply.

"We should have left earlier," I tell Rich.

"Yeah, but we didn't."

"If we left at six like I wanted to, instead of eight, we'd be there by now."

"Where?"

"Houston or near there. We left too late. We should have left earlier," I tell him again.

"But we didn't," he reminds me.

"But we should have left earlier. We should have," I say again.

"But we didn't leave at six, did we? Your mother and sisters kept calling and you kept yapping with them. I had to do everything to get the car ready. And you made me haul in all of the patio furniture. And then I had to bring all sorts of stuff upstairs. *And double bag in black plastic bags, and then put it in a bin, and make sure the lid is on tight!"* he says in a voice mocking my own. Thank goodness the kids are now watching *The Lion King* DVD and have headphones on.

A rest stop is ahead and we all need a break. Rich and I stopped talking to one another several miles back.

Samantha and I sprint to the restroom. We've refused to pee in the car or in the bushes by the side of the interstate and really have to go. John thought it was fun to pee in the car, and peed in a plastic water bottle so often that we had to take it away from him.

I hear Sam gagging in the adjacent stall and tell her to breathe through her mouth, an old nursing school trick. The toilet paper has been long gone, and I hand her a few tissues under the wall of the stall.

We make a quick exit. I have hand sanitizer in my purse and squirt it all over our hands. We wipe our sticky feet on the grass.

The people walking around the rest area look beaten down and worn out already. A few ask how long others have been on the road. "Since early morning" is the most frequent answer, and although it's mid-afternoon, we're not even 50 miles from New Orleans. On our way to the car, I notice that the vending machines have been emptied out. We walk the dogs for a few minutes, and get back into Rich's SUV. We've eaten about half of the food and have six bottles of water left.

"That bathroom was deplorable," I announce.

"What's deplorable mean?" asks John.

"Crap and pee and wet toilet paper all over the floor. Stinky. Poop on the side of one of the toilets. No paper towels. Faucet handles that don't work. Someone may have puked by the door…" Rich trails off when John says "Yeah, yeah, yeah, okay, I get it."

I try to call my sister Erica, and after several repeated attempts, I am able to get through to her 518 area code in upstate New York. I ask her to go on her computer and find motels that are located along I-59 in Mississippi. Ten minutes later, she sends me a text message that lists several numbers.

I spend the next hour dialing and redialing numbers. When I finally get through to the third motel on the list, I am told for the third time that they do not have any available rooms. I ask the desk clerk if she knows if there are rooms available at any of the motels in the area. She tells me they're awful. I tell her that I don't care if they're nice or not, we just need a roof over our heads.

"They're all full," she drawls slowly.

I attempt to call other motels on my list. It takes eight to ten tries before I get through, and I am often placed on hold when I do get connected. My frustration is mounting. We have nowhere to go and it is getting late in the day. I begin to think hurricane evacuation shelter, here we come.

I check the *Atlas* to see where we are in relation to Brookhaven, where my friend Cheryl has booked four rooms. If we keep going north on I-59, we can head northwest on State Route 42, and then go west on State Route 84.

"I think we should go to the motel where Cheryl and Wayne and their boys are staying," I tell Rich as we continue to inch our way north on I-59. Rich agrees. After many attempts, I call my sister and tell her our plan, and give her the motel's name and phone number. Erica says she'll let everyone in the family know where we are.

We pass a car with a flat tire. In order to get to the spare, they've stacked suitcases, blankets, pillows, and grocery bags by the side of the road. We travel along next to a car in which a woman is making sandwiches—while driving. We are moving along agonizingly slowly.

It's odd to be driving on the "wrong side" of the interstate. We look to the right and see the cars on the northbound lanes start moving faster, and see cars from our side drive across the grassy median to merge into the other lanes. However, shortly after making the move, the northbound lanes also come to a crawl.

The fast food restaurants now have signs saying "closed" and "closed—out of food." There's also one that says "Closed for the Bitch."

It's 2 p.m., and people are getting testy and starting to drive on both the right and left shoulders of the interstate. We now have eight "lanes" heading north. The kids encourage Rich to join the shoulder-riders but he says no way, although I can tell he's tempted. Before long, eight lanes of cars are heading north, all going at a snail's pace.

Rich's temples flare out when he's stressed or super tired. They're flaring now. He's also grinding his teeth.

"We can get off 59 and get on 11, which parallels 59 but might not be as slow," I tell him. He's had it with contraflow and the interstate, so we take the next exit to cross over to Highway 11.

The movie finishes, and Sam starts her homework. It feels good to go thirty miles per hour. Although there are tons of cars on the country road, the traffic is at least moving.

John soon announces that he feels sick, which usually means that he's going to barf in about a minute or so.

"Of course you feel sick, you idiot," Sam informs him. "You ate half of the bag of cookies."

Rich tells Samantha she is so compassionate, and gives John permission to throw up on his sister. We stop so John can get some air. It's starting to get windy and after a few minutes of walking around in the grass by the side of the road, John says he feels better.

We stop at a gas station that has no gas, and John spends twenty minutes in the spic-and-span restroom. Rich buys a bunch of Slim Jim's, his comfort food in times of distress, and gobbles them down.

We continue on the back country road and eat peanut butter and jelly on crackers. It's getting dark when we stop by the side of the desolate road to give the dogs some water and let them out of their crates. The wind has picked up and dirt swirls upward, stinging our eyes.

When Rich opens the tailgate of the Expedition to get the dogs back into their crates, Buddy unexpectedly jumps up as Rich is looking down to release the leash from Buddy's collar. Buddy practically knocks Rich out. Rich recoils and hollers in pain. The area around his left eye swells and begins to turn black and blue.

On the outskirts of Brookhaven, a gas station is open—and has gas! Although it's six bucks a gallon, we fill up the Expedition. We've used three quarters of a tank just to get here.

We arrive at the motel in Brookhaven at 8:10 p.m. We've been on the road just over twelve hours and are only 120 miles north of our house. The motel is right off of I-55, which runs north from New Orleans to Brookhaven to Jackson and then on to Memphis. From the parking lot, I can see that I-55 is still packed with cars creeping north. The Cracker Barrel restaurant across the street is jammed with cars, many of them double parked. We are too exhausted to eat, and I tell the kids that I'll take them to the Cracker Barrel in the morning for a nice, big breakfast.

Cheryl is sitting on the balcony outside of her second floor room and yells to us as we get out of the SUV.

"Where's the wine?" asks Rich.

"What happened?" she asks Rich, pointing to his eye.

"We duked it out in the car," I tell her.

"No really," she says as she comes closer. "What happened? Your eye is almost swollen shut!"

Cheryl tells us that Debbie is fearful that Brookhaven is not far enough north, so we have a room for the night. Although we've done nothing but sit in the car all day, we're all exhausted, and I'm relieved to have a room.

The motel is two stories tall and shaped like the letter "U," with an in-ground pool area in the center. It's an old-fashioned kind of motel, painted teal blue, with no elevator, and doors all opening to the outside.

We get the room key and move everything from the SUV into our first floor room. It's a standard room with two beds, musty dark green carpet, and towels so thin that you can see right through them.

"Looks like somebody was murdered in the bathtub," Rich announces. I use the few remaining wet wipes to clean the sink, tub, and toilet.

We walk the dogs, feed them in our room, and take them outside again. Our kids have met up with Cheryl and Wayne's two boys, and they're out exploring. We go to Cheryl's room on the second floor in the mid-section of the "U" of the motel to find her husband Wayne fixated on The Weather Channel.

Cheryl opens her cooler and asks, "Who wants red and who wants white?"

Her neighbor, who has a room next door, calls for a toast, and with her plastic cup raised high, says, "Lord, give me coffee to change the things I can, and wine to accept the things I can't." Amen, we all say.

We sit on the edge of the beds as Wayne flips through the channels. Newscasters are already predicting the death toll. I walk out onto the balcony to call my mother, but only hear, "Due to the hurricane, your call cannot be completed as dialed."

We round up the kids and herd ours to our room. Samantha decides to bathe when she realizes that there's nothing worth watching on TV. She is miffed that "her shows" have been pre-empted for hurricane coverage. We put the dogs in their crates, and I tuck John into the bed next to

Sam. The satin edging on the thin green blanket is partially ripped off, but the sheets appear clean.

Samantha is fervently using her cell phone to text message her friends, and gives Rich and me a crash course on how to write and send a text message. We've never text-messaged before. We later learn that voice calls consume significantly more bandwidth than text messages, which explains why voice calls were not going through and text messages generally were able to be sent and received before hurricane Katrina struck and while the cell towers were still standing.

At 11 p.m., weather reporter Jim Cantore is broadcasting from Gulfport. Phew, I tell Rich, the guy is in Mississippi, so New Orleans is going to be just fine.

DAY 2

Monday, August 29th

MY CELL PHONE rings at 4:12 a.m. and it's our home security system company calling, saying that the alarm at our house is going off. The woman tells me she's going to send the police out to our house.

"You're kidding, right?" I ask her.

No, she tells me, she'll get the police right out there. The lilt of her accent makes me suspect that she's somewhere far away, like India. I just finished reading Thomas Friedman's book *The World is Flat* and ask where she's calling from. She hedges, saying that she's calling on behalf of our security company, whose headquarters are in Dallas. I tell her about Katrina and tell her to forget about calling the police.

I am now wide awake. I lie in the darkness, trying to fall back asleep, but my mind races. Did a window at our house break and cause the alarm to go off? Is the roof peeling off? Is water filling our house and tripping the door alarm sensors? Or was it just a power surge and everything's fine?

At daybreak, wind is whistling around the door of our

motel room. I pull back the curtain on our window and see tree branches swaying in the distance. A paper bag dances by. I call my mother and am surprised to be able to get through to her. She's watching The Weather Channel and tells me things are very bad in New Orleans, even though the major brunt of the storm is still not expected for hours.

I turn on the TV but mute the sound, and see deserted New Orleans streets, boarded up storefronts, and swinging traffic lights. The wind in New Orleans has definitely picked up.

Gradually, more light enters our room and Rich and the kiddies start to stir. Samantha has had at least sixteen hours of sleep in the past twenty-four hours, but says she needs more. Rich and I let Buddy and Jack out of their crates, snap leashes to their collars, and head outside.

The dogs do not like howling wind. I keep one hand on Jack's leash and use the other to keep my hair from blowing into my eyes as we start to walk across the parking lot. Leaves and trash cartwheel beside our feet. Jack, with his head just inches above the ground, does not like this at all. He is shaking and lets out a high pitched cry. I bring him back inside our motel room, where he promptly pees on the carpet.

Rich and I head out again, this time taking only Buddy. I look across the street and see that the Cracker Barrel is now closed and boarded up, and its parking lot is empty. The traffic light still works, but is swinging wildly in the wind.

Cheryl is sitting outside of her second floor room, drinking from a coffee cup. She gives us a wave like a queen waving to her subjects. "It's agony to wait," she says. "I just want this to be over with." Don't we all.

We congregate in Cheryl's room because the motel's breakfast room and lobby have been overtaken by stranded motorists who could not get any further up I-55. It's wall-to-wall people in there, and I am so grateful to Cheryl that we had a room for the night.

Breakfast for the kids is a granola bar or Pop Tart, and a glass of water from the tap. In our group, we have three men, four women (one woman's husband is in Iraq), eleven children ages 8-15, and six dogs named Bear, Max, Buddy, Jack, Duke, and Piglet. All of the adults forego eating anything.

The kids are sent off to their rooms to do homework, and Cheryl's son Greg goes out on the balcony to practice his saxophone. Wayne flips through the channels on the TV, and we hear that there are 10,000-30,000 people in the Superdome, which sparks a discussion about how do they not know how many are in there? We then see that the Superdome roof is starting to peel off.

Rich calls Joe, the surgeon covering his practice, learns that East Jefferson General Hospital has water in its lobby, and loses the call. The hospital is three blocks from the south shore of Lake Pontchartrain. High winds have likely blown lake water into the streets and hospital.

I'm startled when my cell phone rings. It's my sister Erica, who says that she's so relieved that Katrina is not as bad as predicted. When Hurricane Katrina made landfall at 5 a.m. near Buras, Louisiana, it was downgraded from a category 5 storm with wind speeds of 175 mph to a category 3 with wind speeds of 125 mph. We chat about the wind and rain, and I tell my sister that we'll likely be headed home tomorrow. We'll have some branches and maybe a tree or two down, but that should be it.

The lights have been flickering on and off all morning, and the power goes out at 10:30. The air conditioners churn to a stop and it's eerily quiet, except for the howling of the wind. After a few minutes, a hard rain starts. Wayne picks up the phone in the room and says the line is dead.

I go to check on our kids, who are learning how to play poker in the semi-darkness of the adjacent room where Cheryl's neighbor is staying and all of the kids have gathered. They seem to be doing just fine, so I go back to Wayne and Cheryl's room.

After a few minutes, a cluster of kids appears at the door, saying they're bored and there's nothing to do.

"Y'all could be sitting in a car stuck on the side of the interstate right now, so quit complaining. Find something to do!" orders Cheryl's neighbor as she waves them away. The kids retreat to the room next door.

There's very little conversation among the adults. None of us wants to speculate on what may be happening back home. Every few minutes, Wayne gets up from his perch on the bed farthest from the window and walks outside.

After his fourth trip in and out, he says the wind is now gusting.

Another batch of kids comes into our room, announcing that they're roasting and sweating, and are absolutely going to die from boredom.

"Y'all could be in an evacuation shelter right now, so quit complaining. Get outta here and go find something to do!" says Cheryl's neighbor as she points to the door. "I didn't think we'd lose power here," she adds. "Aren't we like two hundred miles from the Gulf?"

"This is worse than being in labor," says another of Cheryl's neighbors as she fans herself with the plastic "Do Not Disturb" card. "I can't believe how hot it is, and how slowly time is passing."

Wayne jiggles the window, but finds that it does not open. "You should have cranked the AC way up to cool this room off before the power went out," he tells his wife.

"Like I'm supposed to know that the power was going to go out?" Cheryl replies.

"You should have figured on it going out."

"And why didn't *you* figure on it going out?"

"Because you had me doing everything else." Wayne mimics Cheryl's voice. "Take out the trash, make up the beds, tidy up the room, take the dogs out, feed the dogs, move the cooler."

One of Cheryl's neighbors says she's going to check on her kids and make them some lunch, and we have a mass exodus from the room.

The lunch choices for our family are:

- Peanut butter on a plastic spoon
- Peanut butter on a very soft, and now brown banana
- Peanut butter on Keebler Rainbow Deluxe cookies with chocolate in every bite

After we've eaten, I tell the kids to do their homework, and John creates a makeshift desk on top of the HVAC by the window. Samantha sits on a bed and says she can hardly see. Do your homework and stop complaining, I tell them. I've kept a journal for years, and pull it out to add the most recent events. I write "home tomorrow" and put six exclamation points after this entry.

Tomorrow can't come fast enough. I am so hot and sweaty that I can't stand it.

Everything in our room—the bedspreads, the chair seat, even the roll of toilet paper in the bathroom—is damp. We've had the door open since the power went out, and the air is moist and heavy. Rich and I sit cross-legged on our bed for lack of anything better—or anything else—to do. The dogs are up on the bed and circle around us. There is dog hair and dog drool everywhere.

"Do you think we'll have maid service today?" asks Rich.

Rich disappears and I find him sitting in his SUV, with the AC and radio on. It's mostly static interrupted by a few intelligible words. The control panel on the dash shows that it's 94 degrees outside and it must be 100% humidity. I see several people in their cars, ears tilted toward the radio's speakers. I then hear the crackle of a breaking limb, and see a large branch fall from the top of a pine tree and land with a thud.

Water is sloshing onto the walkways in front of the motel rooms. The wind drives the rain horizontally and I walk with hands over my face to shield it from the sting of the raindrops.

Rich and I and the other adults reconvene in Cheryl and Wayne's room.

"Tell Cheryl that I'm going to the van to see if I can hear anything on the radio," Wayne tells me, even though he has to pass by the chair by the door where Cheryl is sitting.

Cheryl looks over at me and says, "Tell Wayne to go fuck himself."

Cheryl tells me that their lunch consisted of Goldfish and

leftover celery and carrot sticks. She snaps open a Tupperware container and offers me a limp stalk of celery.

Cheryl's dogs are pacing and whining as the rain continues to steadily fall and the wind howls. We hear a window blow out and suddenly everyone is yelling "the kids!" in unison. We bolt toward the open door as someone says, "Stay away from the windows!"

The older group of our kids is on the floor of the room next door, playing the card game "Spoons" with an assortment of plastic knives. The younger group is on one of the beds and has cards spread out all over. A few other kids from who-knows-where have joined them, and frantic parents soon appear to collect them. We race with our kids to our room on the first floor, our feet drenched from the ankle deep water on the walkway.

Buddy and Jack are acting a lot like Cheryl's dogs now, whimpering and whining and turning in circles. We're in the room no more than a minute when we hear a second window blow out.

It's dark in the room despite it being mid-afternoon, and the rain and wind are intense. Twenty minutes later, we hear the roar of a freight train coming closer and hear people screaming. I grab the kids by their shoulders and propel them toward the back of our room. Rich herds the two dogs into the bathroom. We put the dogs and the kids in the tub and crouch down against the flimsy door.

It's hot. It's humid. And it's dark. Time ticks by slowly as we silently sit and listen to the wind howl and parts of the motel blow away.

At one point we hear the crack of a big limb, followed by

lots of "pops" as smaller tree branches snap. Pop, pop, pop. Like popcorn in the microwave.

"Thank God this motel is surrounded by concrete and no trees are close to the building," says Rich.

We venture out of our hideaway an hour later, and both dogs immediately pee on the already damp carpet.

The motel parking lot has been transformed. We can no longer see where the parking lot ends and the surrounding grass begins. There is water everywhere, and only the chain link fence around the motel pool is visible. The pool is somewhere under that murky water. Big pine trees have toppled onto some of the cars and trucks parked at the edge of the lot. It looks like every single tree has been stripped of its leaves. Branches are down everywhere, and leaves and garbage skate across the water. The water ripples with every wind gust. Drenched curtains float out of blown-out windows. The first floor on the other side of the motel is filling with water.

The water outside our motel room door begins to seep in. After a few minutes, I feel water squishing around my toes as I walk around the room in my sandals. It's beastly hot and none of the motel windows can be opened.

Small groups begin to gather as people tentatively venture outside. So far, no one has been injured and all of the pets, lord only knows how many of them, apparently are all right.

"I just heard on the car radio that there's seven feet of water in Metairie," a man says.

Another says, "The roof collapsed at the Dome and Slidell is gone. Gone!"

Cheryl and Wayne live in Slidell, on the northeast shore of Lake Pontchartrain. It's an area prone to flooding. Cheryl turns her back and slowly walks away in stunned disbelief.

We rally around her and tell her that this is an unconfirmed report, that we don't even know who the guy is that's saying this.

We head back to our rooms as darkness begins to take over the motel and a slow, steady rain begins to fall. Rich takes the umbrella and leashes the dogs for one last outing for the day. They absolutely will not pee or poop in the flooded parking lot or on the flooded grassy areas around the motel, so Rich walks them around the motel and up the I-55 embankment.

I take the desk chair and sit by the doorway in the dimming light and look at *People* magazine again, its pages all rippled from moisture. I now notice the State Farm ad about disaster planning that has the tagline "Life doesn't always go as planned." How very true.

We have not heard a peep about how our neighborhood, River Ridge, has fared. We flooded in 1995, so it would stand to reason that we would flood again now, in 2005. I physically shudder at the thought of repairing a flooded house once again, and start making dinner.

"Peanut butter again?" asks Sam. "We're not having peanut butter for dinner, are we? Are you kidding?" She looks at me as if I've lost my mind.

"Or you can have Cheerios," I tell her.

I feed the kids peanut butter on the last of the cookies, and pour the dry dog food into bowls. It looks tempting.

"Mommy, do you hear me? Mom!"

"What?"

John is standing by the sink, toothbrush in hand. "The faucet doesn't work."

I try both handles. Nothing. Samantha emerges from the toilet and tub area to the sound of a gurgling toilet.

"The toilet's not flushing," she announces.

I tell Rich that the water's out and that we have two bottles of water and one juice box left. And a third of a jar of peanut butter and some Cheerios. That's it.

A few minutes later, there's a knock at our open door and it's the older woman from two doors down. In her hand are two pieces of ham, starting to glisten green.

"For the children," she says.

I thank her profusely. She explains that the ham has been in a cooler so it's safe to eat. I'm not so sure, and toss it in the trash can as soon as she leaves. Buddy immediately gobbles it up and lives through the night.

Rich has set up the DVD player for the kids and they watch *The Lion King* for the third time in two days. They're sweaty, and wipe their faces with hand towels as they watch the movie and drink the last of the water and juice.

I walk along the walkway outside our room, with no particular destination in mind. What's happening to us is so surreal that it can't really be happening. What are we going to do? Where are we going to go?

I duck under the stairwell and lean against the soda machine, sobbing. I know I have to pull myself together, but I cannot. I slide down the wall, and crouch near the floor, and cry for ten minutes straight. I use the hem of my shirt to wipe my eyes and nose, and head back to our room.

I go back to my perch at the doorway and look out at the motel. All of the doors are wide open and the rooms are lit by flashlight or candlelight.

I write in my journal that I'm 47 years old and I'm going to bed hungry for the first time in my life.

The DVD battery depletes midway through the movie. Rich tells the kids his old standby story, which the kids never tire of hearing, about a little girl and boy riding on the Orient Express and going to the buffet to eat. The buffet is endless, and Rich names every item.

"There is macaroni and cheese, spaghetti and meatballs, and chicken fingers," he says. Rich typically names about two dozen things, and the kids usually nod right off when Rich gets to the last item, which is always Baked Alaska.

"Shut up about the food," I hiss. "You're making me hungry. Have those kids play checkers or something. Or have 'em look out the window of the damn train." I flip over so that my back is to him, and try to think of anything but food.

Rich continues on with his story. "And then they went to the dessert station. There is a big fountain dripping with chocolate, and there are big bowls of strawberries...and marshmallows...and pretzels for dipping." Rich is speaking more slowly, which helps the kids drop off to sleep. "There is a big, big table with cherry strudel...and Krispy Kreme donuts...and Brennan's bananas foster...and Commander's Palace bread pudding soufflé...and coffee ice cream."

It occurs to me that Rich is now naming all of my favorite desserts. I give him a hard shove in his ribs with my elbow. "You're a shit, you know that? A real shit," I tell him.

"And then the boy and girl see the Baked Alaska!" he says as he ends the story.

My little redhead is asleep in his undies, on top of the covers. John has never had trouble going to sleep and really likes to sleep. When he was in kindergarten, he came home one day asking if he could go to night kindergarten, as it was becoming just too difficult to get up in the morning.

Last summer, when he was ten, he and Samantha went to a local day camp. On the last day, Sam bounded to the car with a fistful of ribbons. John proudly showed me his sole blue ribbon with "Best Rester" written with a swirl in silver ink.

John lies idle with his stuffed animal Sharky securely tucked under his arm while Samantha flops like a fish.

"It's really hot in here," she tells us. "I can't sleep."

Rich tries his cell phone, and then mine, and then Samantha's, repeatedly but to no avail.

The general noise around the motel begins to quell, and flashlights and candles are extinguished in some of the rooms.

At 10:30 p.m., a man yells "fire!" and pandemonium ensues on the other side of the motel. People emerge from the surrounding rooms with their flashlights. A man is trying to scoop up water from right outside his door, where is it still ankle deep. There's a race to the pool to fill motel trash cans and plastic bags with water. It is pitch black between our section of the motel and the other side. I shine our flashlight toward the commotion, but the beam of light only gets as far as the chain link fence around our side of the pool. I squint and look for smoke or flames, but I don't see any. The fire apparently was quickly snuffed out, and life as we knew it, returned to normal.

Samantha is still tossing and turning when I lie back down on the bed next to Rich. We lie there like soldiers, on our backs, awake and staring up at the popcorn ceiling. I imagine that most of the people in this motel are lying like this right now. And many are three or four to a bed made for two.

Rich whispers, "Lisa?" and I immediately answer with "What?"

"I didn't know if you were awake or not," he says.

"I'm awake."

"What are you thinking about?"

"That this isn't really happening. It can't be happening. It's like we're in some weird, really bad movie."

"I wish it was a movie and we'd wake up and everything would be fine."

"I know, this is like a horror movie. I mean, this is really unbelievable. Unfathomable. I cannot wrap my head around it."

Rich squeezes my hand. "Before you get going down that road, let's wait and see how things look in the morning."

"Okay," I tell him, "so the movie we're in is *Sleepless in Brookhaven* then?"

"That would work. Or *It's a Wonderful Life: the Remake.*"

"*Singing in the Rain: the Remake.*"

"Some Like it Hot: the Remake."

"On the Waterfront: the Remake."

"Gone with the Wind: the Remake."

We are giggling so hard that Samantha asks what's going on.

"Daddy said something funny. Try to get some sleep honey."

Rich whispers, "It's so fuckin' hot in here."

"Tell me about it."

"What are we going to do if our house is gone?" he asks.

"Don't say that. We don't know anything about River Ridge yet. Go to sleep."

I am so hungry that I think about going out to Rich's SUV to find French fries that I know for sure are under the seats and perfectly preserved. There might be some dropped M & Ms there too. It could be a buffet bonanza.

"I am so hungry," I whisper to Rich.

"Go eat some cereal," he tells me.

I refuse; it's for the kids in the morning, in case the Cracker Barrel doesn't open. They'll just have to eat the cereal, even though they've said they're sick of Cheerios. I'm now using the top bed sheet not as a cover, but as a sweat wipe. I've never sweated this much, not even in a sauna.

"Hey Rich, did you ever think we'd end up like this? Lying here half-naked in a fleabag motel filled with dog pee, with no air conditioning, no food, no phones, no water, and no good information about what's going on? Is this really happening to us?"

DAY 3

Tuesday, August 30th

GRAY LIGHT PEAKS into our room. I don't remember falling asleep, but I must have at some point. I need to orient myself to my surroundings. It's a feeling I've had many times when I've traveled for work, and have woken up in hotel rooms and have had to ask myself where I am. It takes only a moment for me to remember. I'll never forget this motel.

I then wonder what day it is. Our usual routine is disrupted and this is no vacation. I have to backtrack in my mind to determine if it's Monday or Tuesday. It's easy to lose track of time when the hours creep by and daytime blends into nighttime. It's Tuesday, jury duty day. Guess that's scratched.

I look over at Rich. He's already awake and looks back at me with his eyes bug-eyed wide open, although his left eye is not as wide as his right eye because of the swelling from his black eye.

"You know the expression 'I didn't sleep a wink'? That would be me," he says.

There is enough light for me to see that Samantha and John both have glistening skin and swollen, cracked lips. Cheryl is at the door and says that the motel owner has made coffee—coffee!!—on his charcoal grill now that the winds have died down, and asks if I would like to go get some. I'm immediately thinking of using that grill of his to boil street water for our kids to drink.

Cheryl says that her ice chest is full of melted ice water, and we scoop up our empty water bottles to refill them in her room. We bring them back to the kids, and I wake them up to drink a few sips. They miraculously fall back asleep before I leave the room. Rich has the trash can in his hands and says he's going to the pool for water to flush the toilet.

Cheryl and I walk through varying depths of water to cross over to the motel lobby.

"Are you and Wayne talking yet?" I ask.

"Nope," she replies with a snort. "Maybe in a year or two. He is so bad with stress."

I tell her how Rich and I didn't talk for hours when I got on him for not leaving sooner.

"Things like this bring out the worst in us," she says as she wipes the sweat from her face.

"Greg got a text message saying that Salmen High School in Slidell is now a morgue," she adds. "This is really awful."

"No kidding. The worst part is not knowing what's going on. It is so frustrating to not have power and not be able to get a radio station."

The motel lobby is abuzz with speculation about how New Orleans and the Gulf Coast fared with Hurricane Katrina. By the looks of things way up here in Brookhaven, only a very few are cautiously optimistic about things back home.

Much of the conversation centers on food and water supplies. Not only are the nearby restaurants, grocery stores, and gas stations closed, they're also either severely damaged or inaccessible because of flooding and storm debris. And they don't have power.

"We thought we'd be fine," says Cheryl's neighbor. "I had no idea we'd already go through a case of water bottles and almost all of our food."

"We had enough for the car ride," says her other neighbor. "We never thought the power would go out *here.*"

We're all down to very little, if anything, in terms of food and water. What little we have is reserved for the kids.

A man walks in, sees the big coffee vat, and says, "I can't fuckin' believe there's coffee!"

The motel owner, busy wiping the counter, smiles and says, "I need to put that on our brochure."

Rich comes in and has the nerve to ask if there's decaf. Several people ask what the hell happened to his eye. Rich's eye is still immensely swollen and has turned dark blue.

We sip weak but delicious coffee, and hear that New Orleans is terribly bad and we won't be able to go back there for days to weeks. We're hoping it's not as bad as people are making it sound. We hear that Lakeside Mall is gone. Gone! Someone says that the Southern Yacht Club is on fire, but firemen cannot get through the standing water to get to it.

I overhear conversations as I walk around the lobby. It's like the game "Telephone" gone wild. New Orleans is totally gone! This really was the big one and there's nothing left there! No one will ever be able to go back there!

Cheryl's next door neighbor says that our kids will have great college essay material. Cheryl and I are not amused.

A recurring report is that after making landfall near Buras, Katrina crossed the Breton Sound and Lake Borgne and made landfall again near Slidell. People are saying that Slidell, where Cheryl and Wayne and their boys live, has been destroyed. This news is too much for Cheryl to bear, and I find her outside furiously dialing her nearly dead cell phone.

"What are you doing?"

"Calling my mom to see if my brother's okay." He stayed behind in Slidell as everyone else evacuated. And her mother has been dead for six months.

In the brighter daylight, Cheryl looks 70 years old despite being in her mid-40s. "Cheryl," I tell her, "Your mom died a few months back. She's not going to answer."

"I have to find out how my brother is," she replies as she continues to punch at her phone.

There is no cell service. I walk Cheryl back to her room and return to ours.

I pass my "crying spot" under the stairs and am surprised to see a woman there, weeping. She looks up and says, "Don't mind me. This is just so hard to take."

Rich has the dogs leashed and we head outside with them. The kids have been given the directive to each drink an entire bottle of water before we get back. The sun is starting to peek through the overcast, and it's no longer drizzling.

A family in bathing suits stands at the side of the pool filled with murky water, swishing water up under their chins and armpits.

"Oh my God," says Rich. "We're in Calcutta."

We walk the dogs around the back of the motel and hear

noise on the interstate. On top of the embankment, the dogs pee as bulldozers push downed trees and debris from the roadway. They're clearing the northbound lanes.

Rich astutely notes that Buddy, our 80-pound Lab, has not pooped in three days. Neither has he, he adds. Twelve-pound Jack, on the other hand, has produced a good amount of diarrhea, including a few bursts on the carpet in our motel room. The Sunday paper was used to scoop up as much as we could and cover the rest.

We walk back toward the motel and find the motel owner outside at his grill, flipping sausage patties. There's a swarm of people around him, watching the patties cook.

Although Rich and I haven't eaten anything since noontime yesterday, and didn't eat much then, I'm reluctant to eat those sausage patties. I mentally calculate when they would have thawed, and it seems to me that way too much time has passed for the unrefrigerated patties to be safe to eat. Especially in 90-plus degree weather.

We join the group at the grill and it's confirmed that the interstate northbound lanes, with less storm debris than the southbound lanes, are being cleared.

Rich looks at me and says, "We should leave."

"Where are we going to go?"

"North. We have a full tank of gas and can go at least 200 miles."

Cheryl and Wayne declare us crazy when we tell them of our plan. They've decided to stay in Brookhaven for now, for fear of getting stuck somewhere on I-55. Cheryl is pretty much a zombie, not having slept at all, and worried sick about her brother. She's furiously fanning her face with a section of folded-up newspaper.

"Can we swap food before you go?" she asks.

We trade a nearly empty box of Cheerios for 62 Gold Fish crackers.

Rich and I pack up the SUV and notice that Buddy and Jack look sad and resigned. Maybe they're just tired but no, this is a different look, one that suggests that they too understand what's going on.

John's stuffed animal Sharky has pretty much stayed under his left arm the entire time in Brookhaven, and John makes sure that Sharky has a good spot in the back seat. He pats Sharky on the head and says, "Everything's going to be okay. We're going on an adventure!"

Sam is brushing her sweat-drenched hair and I'm studying the Rand McNally *Atlas* "Mississippi" page as we pull out of the parking lot.

We get on the I-55 northbound lanes and attempt to find a coherent radio station. It's nothing but static, so we turn off the radio. The air conditioning feels fantastic and within a few minutes, both kids are fast asleep in the back seat. I plug Rich's cell phone into the car charger and repeatedly try calling my mother, sisters, Rich's brother, and anyone I can think of. No service. Text messages also do not go through.

"Keep your eyes peeled for a McDonald's or a gas station or *anything*," Rich says. "I'm starving."

"Me too." I glance out the window and see nothing but continued destruction, trees down, and roofs blown off. I look around my seat for old forgotten French fries and maybe a rogue juice box that fell into a crevice in the SUV. There's nothing.

"So where are we going?" I ask Rich as I study the map.

"Dunno. Maybe Memphis? They've got to have power and normalcy up there."

Memphis looks to be about 250 miles north.

"Then what?" I ask.

"I don't know. We need to see what's going on in New Orleans." Rich turns the radio on again and searches for stations, but still nothing.

"What if it's as bad as they say in New Orleans?"

"Then we're screwed," he replies.

We have to drive slowly. Downed trees and debris have been pushed aside to make a drivable space on the interstate. In some places, we weave around downed trees, and the cleared path takes us onto the adjacent grass at the side of the road.

After driving for half an hour, we see trucks driving toward us. We edge over to the shoulder of the interstate to allow a convoy of power company trucks from Tennessee to continue southward. We give a little wave to each of the drivers. The last truck stops.

"How's it look south of here?" the driver asks.

"It's like this down to Brookhaven. One lane. It's slow going."

"The bulldozers were in Brookhaven this morning, going south" I add. "Where did you come from and how are the roads?"

"Memphis. Left this morning right at six and there's been a lot of debris on the road all the way from Jackson. Jackson to Memphis is clear."

"How far up is it before there's power?" I ask.

"As best I recollect, there's no power until up north of Batesville." We're 200 miles from Batesville. My eyes widen with the thought that a huge swath of the United States is without power.

"Where are you headed?" my husband asks.

"Covington, Louisiana." Covington is across Lake Pontchartrain, about 40 miles north of downtown New Orleans. "We were supposed to be headed to New Orleans, but then they said it's destroyed and there's no point going down there now."

Rich and I press on northward in stunned silence. He tries the radio again, and I try the cell phones again, but still no service. Our sleeping kids look like grimy little angels. I wished I brought more wet wipes with us.

I look at the map of the United States in the *Atlas*. If New Orleans has been wiped out as reported, then we need to go somewhere else. But where? And for how long?

So we need a house, jobs, and a school. And bedding, and dishes, and clothes, and furniture, and everything else we've essentially taken for granted all our lives.

Rich's temples are flaring and he's grinding his back teeth.

"We could go up to Memphis and I could do locum tenens work. I get a ton of emails looking for surgeons to fill in while docs are out on vacation or medical leave," he says.

"And I could keep doing the nursing education programs that I've been doing. I can do those from anywhere since I can easily fly out of whatever city we end up in. We can figure something out for the kids if we're both gone at the same time."

"We should get an apartment, not a house," Rich announces.

"Maybe we should go to upstate New York. My parents

could watch the kids while we're gone, and they have good public schools there. My mother would spoil them to death, which isn't such a bad thing, considering what they've been through with this."

Samantha rouses and asks if we're going to Grandma's. We're not sure, we tell her, we're figuring out our options. She says she's really hungry and asks if we can stop for lunch. Preferably Red Lobster.

"There's no power, honey, so no Red Lobster. I'm sorry," I tell her.

We drive up I-55 looking for signs that the power is on in the gas stations and little towns by the side of the interstate. There's nothing but darkness and everything remains closed.

Samantha, who is now fully awake, lifts her left arm and sniffs. "OH MY GOD," she declares. "I stink! Really bad! I need a shower. I must have a shower," she tells us. Her shower will have to wait.

I'm finally able to get a radio station. Static is fairly constant, and we strain to hear what is being said, like the old days when people gathered around the radio, their ears close to the speakers. We first hear that thirty-five people swam out of the emergency command center in Biloxi in Mississippi, and are now in the courthouse there. The Treasure Bay casino, a barge that looks like a pirate ship, is up on the beach. The Hard Rock Café casino and hotel, scheduled to open in September, is "half-destroyed" but its two-story tall guitar still stands. In nearby Gulfport, the Grand Casino barge has washed ashore and is blocking Highway 90.

The reporter states that Hurricane Katrina did more damage to the area than Camille, which claimed 144 lives in August 1969. A woman named Mrs. Jenkins is interviewed by the reporter and says that the water came in "fast and furious." She and her husband crouched in their attic for seven hours, and this morning found that most of the houses that once lined the beach are simply gone. Even houses that withstood Camille are now nothing but slabs. She adds that "people are in a daze," that everyone is "shell-shocked" by the devastation.

This news is unbelievable. Damage along the Gulf Coast was expected, but this much? Unfathomable. I retrieve my journal and start writing, partly to capture this information, but also to keep me busy and distract me from thinking the worst about our family's future.

I turn the radio volume louder when the reporter says that there is now Marshall Law in New Orleans.

"What's that?" our kids ask. Rich and I attempt to explain.

One million homes are without power across the South. The death toll is 55 so far. The damage is estimated to exceed 26 billion dollars.

"Where do they get those numbers?" asks Rich. "Why not 25 billion or 27 billion? It's ludicrous that they have any idea at all about the extent of the damage, let alone how much it will cost to repair."

Katrina, now a tropical depression, is in southern Ohio. Heavy rain falls there, and there are reports of Katrina-spawned tornadoes across eastern Georgia.

New information from New Orleans has come in, and the reporter informs us that the water is rising in the city. Water is reported to be as high as fourteen feet in some areas.

Rescue teams look for survivors and use axes to chop through the roofs of houses.

The reporter on the radio announces that Dave Benson at WLOX has sent a message via the Internet that says there is catastrophic damage on the Gulf Coast, and downtown Bay St. Louis is "gone."

I shake my head, trying to picture what the area must look like. I know that "gone" means gone, as in entirely gone. Nothing remains.

We briefly are able to tune into 870 AM, a New Orleans station. We hear that there is a second breach in the Industrial Canal levee.

"Second?" Rich and I say in unison. We are stunned.

People are walking in waist-deep water to I-10 to get to the Superdome. There is an unconfirmed report that the I-10 twin spans have washed away. We then hear a shuffle of papers, and the reporter asks anyone with flat bottomed boats to go to the intersection of Airline Highway and the Earhart Expressway in Metairie, a staging area for rescue operations. Water is rising throughout the city, and the reporter says that officials are unsure exactly where it is coming from. They suspect the 17th Street Canal in Metairie may be overflowing.

It takes us three hours to get to Jackson, 50 miles north of Brookhaven. At a closed gas station just off the interstate, we're able to refill our water bottles. Katrina's path of destruction extends through this area. Roofs have been stripped of their metal sheeting, street signs are twisted, and none of the traffic lights are working since there is no power.

Half an hour later, at least twenty utility company vehicles and a dozen Army Hummers pass us going the opposite direction. We hear on the radio that levees have been breached—they are not overtopping—and large sandbags are being dropped from helicopters. Louisiana Governor Kathleen Blanco says that "the devastation is greater than our worst fears."

Water in many parts of New Orleans continues to rise. Patients in Tulane Hospital are being moved to higher floors, and there are reports of bodies floating in the water. There is now no air conditioning in the Superdome and the bathrooms there are "malfunctioning."

The kids are whiney from hunger. It is mid-afternoon and 31 Goldfish apiece for breakfast have not sustained them. The fast food restaurants by the side of the interstate are dark and empty. I keep hoping that even without power, something—*anything*—will be open so we can get something to eat.

As we make our way north, we listen for updates on the radio. None are good. We still have not heard specific mention of different parts of the city, including River Ridge where we live. We hear that Slidell, where Cheryl and Wayne live, has sustained major damage and I pray that Cheryl's brother is alive and well. Almost every news item starts with the words, "We have unconfirmed reports that…."

The doomsayers are already on the radio. Gas will soon cost over three dollars a gallon! Food will become scarce! National unemployment will skyrocket! Elderly people in the northeast will die this winter because they won't be able to pay their heating bills, all because of Katrina.

It's dusk when we get to Batesville, Mississippi, 150 miles north of Jackson. We're about 200 miles from our starting point in Brookhaven. It feels like we've spent days in the car. I'm starting to think about spending the night in the car at the side of some road when I see lights—lights!—up ahead.

"Oh my God, lights!" I yell.

The kids sit up straighter and Rich lets out a sigh of relief.

"Do you see a Red Lobster sign?" asks Samantha hopefully.

"No," says Rich, "Let's go see what's open." He's accelerating and we're now doing 80 mph.

We peel off the interstate and find a Popeye's and Wendy's across the street from one another.

"I want Popeye's!" squeals Sam.

"I want Wendy's," yells John simultaneously.

"I'll take either one," I add.

Rich looks in the rearview mirror at the kids. "I am never ever in my life going to do this again, but I am going to go through the Popeye's drive-thru for Samantha, and then we'll go over to Wendy's and go in and eat and use the restrooms. We can get a couple of burgers for the dogs there too."

Life is normal here. People are in their cars, driving to the bank or the grocery store. People sit in restaurants and wait by bus stops. Delivery trucks go by. The scene is surreal to me. I want to stop and shake these people, and ask them if they know what is happening in New Orleans and along the Mississippi Gulf Coast. I want to slap them and ask them if they care.

We get mild chicken strips for Sam, and they're practically gone by the time we do a U-turn and wait for a light in order to reach the Wendy's across the street. I tell Sam to slow down. Rich says, "Don't swallow a chicken bone."

"They're strips," says Samantha through a mouth jammed with food.

John is skipping into Wendy's as Rich checks on the dogs in back. We look like a vagabond family in our now dirty, sweat-scented clothes, and when Rich and his black eye walk in behind us, people in line actually move away from us. Feeling rejected by humanity is a new feeling for me.

I tell the kids to go to the restroom and wash their hands real good.

We order so much food that the teen at the register narrows his eyes as he punches in our order. We're getting the "are you sure you can pay for all this" look. He keeps glancing over his shoulder toward his manager.

We take our forty-dollar dinner and sit down at a table in the back, so as to not embarrass ourselves any further or make others uncomfortable. I can see people giving us the "I bet they live in their car" look. And look at that guy with the black eye, he's probably a drug dealer! It must be meth by the way they're eating!

I feel the sting of other people's stares. I really didn't think we looked or smelled all that bad, but apparently we did, because a man came over and slipped Rich twenty dollars and said something about knowing about hard times. Rich adamantly refused to accept the money, and explained that we were from New Orleans and had just spent two harrowing days in a motel in Brookhaven without power, water, or much food. The man pressed the money into Rich's hand and said that after all he's heard about New Orleans on the news, we should take it.

We make a speedy exit from Wendy's. John burps loudly on the way out.

No one has ever given us a "hand-out" and we are embarrassed and uncomfortable about it. We are the ones who give to others, not the other way around. Being a recipient of pity is a new and foreign experience for us.

Buddy and Jack wolf down the hamburgers, and Rich says he's going to walk the dogs around the Wendy's parking lot.

Samantha is unusually quiet but says, "No, daddy, no. Those people will see us." Even she is embarrassed. I was hoping that what went on in Wendy's didn't register with our kids, but apparently it did.

We head back toward the interstate and see a sign with an arrow to the left for "Oxford" and an arrow to the right for "Memphis and Jackson."

"Oxford or Memphis?" asks Rich. He casually adds that he doesn't have any plans for the next few days, so he could go either way. This cracks me up because before we evacuated, Rich had one of the most regimented schedules of anyone I know. He left for the hospital every day at the stroke of seven, and now, because of Katrina, he has no place that he needs to be.

"Maybe we should go to Oxford," I say. "We might have more of a chance of finding a place to stay since it's off the beaten path. And with Ole Miss being there, there should be a bunch of motels since it's a pretty big university."

"Do you think they have power there?" Rich asks.

"I would think so since it's east of here. And if not, we'll just keep going on up to Memphis from there." I run my finger along the map and look at the mileage legend. "Memphis is only 90 or so miles northwest of Oxford."

We drive the 25 miles to Oxford as the sun begins to set. John keeps saying that he's just eaten the best dinner he's ever had in his whole entire life.

I tell the kids not to get their hopes up about having a motel room for the night. We're a family and we stick together in hard times as well as good times, and if we have to sleep in the car for a night, it won't kill us. Think of what the people in the Superdome are going through right now, I tell them. We have it good.

We see a "no vacancy" sign at the first motel. My heart sinks. We drive on as I wonder how many motels are in Oxford. Perhaps this was not the best decision.

Rich optimistically notes that Oxford has power. Still no cell service, but there's power.

The Comfort Inn does not have a sign about availability, so I tell the kids to cross their fingers as we pull under the canopy by the entrance. Rich reaches for his door handle, but Samantha asks him to stay inside the SUV, and let mom go in since it looks like he's been in a big fight and they might turn us away if they see him.

How sad is this? Rich is an upstanding citizen and look at him now. When we were driving, John said Rich looked like a "hobo," which led to a discussion about what exactly a hobo looks like. John said a hobo is somebody who wears dirty clothes, has dirty hair, is scruffy, and lives by the railroad tracks. John's description matches how Rich looks at the moment. And the big black eye doesn't help.

I pull my limp hair behind my ears, straighten my clothes, and fold my arm over the Wendy's ketchup stain on my shirt as I walk into the motel office. Please, please, please dear God let there be a room available.

Moments later, I am elated and run to the SUV to tell my family that we have a room! And because of the hurricane evacuation situation, pets are welcome. We later find out that they're not actually welcome—the motels are grudgingly accepting them because they don't want the bad press associated with refusing them.

The hobo in the family walks the dogs on the grassy expanse behind the motel. It's dark, but the parking lot lights illuminate the area.

Sam and John take showers and use up all of the towels, but I don't care. It feels so good just to sit in an air-conditioned room with the lights on.

The now-famous Hurricane Katrina satellite image is shown again and again on TV as the newscasters talk about the immense size of the storm. Hurricane Katrina maintained category 3 strength well into Mississippi, finally losing hurricane strength more than 150 miles inland near Meridian, Mississippi. Seeing the map on TV makes me realize that we experienced a category 3 hurricane at our motel in Brookhaven, 60 miles south of Meridian and right in Katrina's path. No wonder we lost phone service, power, and water there.

The reporter announces that President Bush has cut his vacation short by two days to return to the White House. CNN airs footage of dramatic roof top rescues. People of all shapes and sizes are being hoisted up in baskets to helicopters. The death toll is now 70. The water is twenty feet deep in some parts of New Orleans and 80% of the city is now under water.

I'm in my catatonic TV-watching and journal-writing state with Rich sitting next to me at the end of the bed. He starts grinding his back teeth, says "I can't watch this," and heads to the shower.

New video clips arrive at the news stations and are shown

on national television. People wading through thigh-deep murky water are asked why they didn't leave before the hurricane struck. The answer to the reporter's question is always the same: "I didn't have nowhere to go."

The reporters cut to new footage sent in by citizen journalists. These videos show wind destruction and massive flooding. Red Cross relief trucks sit in at least four feet of water. People are stranded on the elevated portions of the interstate. Gas is leaking throughout the city, and in one video clip, a fire burns, although the building clearly has several feet of water around it.

An aerial shot of Lakeview shows glistening red, blue, and greenish colors in the floodwater around a home. It's clearly an oil slick and who-knows-what-else in the water. However, Governor Kathleen Blanco says, "I do not think the water is toxic. It's just, you know, water."

The kids want Nickelodeon, so I switch the channel. Rich attempts to make calls from his cell phone, but there is still no service. He tries the motel phone but hears that he's unable to complete his call as dialed when dialing the New Orleans 504 area code. I try my sister Erica in upstate New York and am able to get through. She says, "Thank God you're all right" as soon as she hears my voice, and her voice quivers as we talk. I learn that everyone has been worried about us. She tells me that messages are being posted on Craigslist about people trying to locate their loved ones, and that some messages seek information on the extent of damage in different parts of the city. However, no one has yet provided a reply to information requests about River Ridge, where we live.

I get into the shower and can't believe how good it feels.

My white washcloth turns murky brown when I scrub the floodwater residue from my ankles and feet.

I walk over to the sink, shake out my wet hair from the towel around my head, and stare into the mirror. Dark circles have appeared under my eyes and my face looks drawn, like I've been frowning all day. My skin is pale and my eyes are bloodshot from the tears I've shed during the past few days. The tears start coming again now, as I contemplate what life will be like for us and our beloved city of New Orleans. But this can't be. It can't be true that most of New Orleans is under water. It's impossible that so many people are being rescued from attics and rooftops. Certainly people can't be *dead* from this hurricane. Of course there is damage, but is it really as bad as they say it is?

I can't seem to get out of the denial loop. My thoughts go round and round in a circle, all with the same result. *This can't be happening.* And more importantly, this can't be happening *to us.*

DAY 4

Wednesday, August 31st

WE'RE AWAKE PRETTY much all night because both John and Samantha have diarrhea. My prayer that they would alternate in needing the toilet was answered, and we didn't encounter a time when both needed to go simultaneously. We're all worn out and tired when we wake up.

I let the kids' clothes fall to the ground last night wherever they dropped them, so I pick them up this morning to fold them. They'll be wearing them again.

The pockets of John's shorts are bulging. I scoop out a few French fries from one front pocket, and half of a children's hamburger from the other, carefully wrapped in Wendy's paper. Squirreling away some food for another day apparently.

Rich and I take the dogs out and discuss our next step. We can stay at the Comfort Inn only one more night because the motel is sold out for people coming in for an Ole Miss football game. The first thing we need to do, I tell Rich, is find a laundromat.

We go back to the room, get the kids up, and choose the dirtiest of our clothes to wash and the cleanest to wear. We each have three outfits that consist of shirts and shorts. Two for the laundry, and one to wear today.

I put the clothes in a pillowcase from the motel room and toss it into the SUV. I meet up with Rich and the kids in the breakfast room.

"Look, Mom!" John yells. "A real waffle and not one that comes out of the toaster!"

We pile our plates high, and enjoy every bite. Although we smell much better than last night, we still get a few stares our way. Especially Rich and his black eye, which has now turned an even darker blue.

We check on the dogs in their crates in our motel room, and make our way to the Washboard Coin Laundry. Samantha is a tad overdressed for a laundromat; she's wearing one of the four party dresses she's brought with her so that her entire everyday wardrobe can be washed. We load the washer and take a short drive to Courthouse Square. The Oxford Courthouse is its namesake and focal point.

The streets running east to west through Oxford are named for United States Presidents in chronological order from Washington to Cleveland, and we park on Van Buren Avenue. As soon as we emerge from the SUV, Samantha spots one of her teachers walking on the square. Howard has a son in Samantha's grade, so we know the family as well.

Howard tells us that he and his family are leaving to drive up to his wife's parent's home in Connecticut. He'd gotten a call this morning from a physician friend who had just been airlifted by helicopter off of the Tulane Hospital roof. The friend described flying over our kids' school, and where

Howard teaches, and saw that it was inundated by several feet of water.

"The school's gone," Howard says.

"And you made us do our homework, Mom," says John. "Ugh."

Howard's wife comes out of one of the shops and asks me how our kids are processing all of this. Hers are not doing well, she tells me.

Despite repeated efforts, Howard has not been able to get in touch with anyone from the school, and tells us that he read online that 80% of New Orleans is under water. This concurs with what I heard on CNN.

Rich and John go back to the laundromat to put the clothes in the dryer, and Samantha and I go shopping in the cute stores on the square. Samantha finds a bathing suit on a sale rack, and when I see her posing in the mirror outside of the curtained dressing room, I can tell she wants it. Although it's marked down to only $16, for the first time ever, I pause and wonder if this is something we now can afford. There is so much uncertainty about our home, Rich's work, and the kids' school. Is there anything left to go back to? If the school has flooded, we can pretty much assume that our house has flooded.

I flashback to ten years ago, when our house was filled with murky water and nothing on the first floor was salvageable. I can't begin to imagine going through that again, and take the bathing suit to the cash register at the front of the store. I have a bad feeling about this journey we're on, and Sam deserves to have a moment of happiness.

I use a credit card to pay for the bathing suit, and tell myself I'm just not going to worry about our credit card bill right now. Samantha now has three bikinis, three shirt/shorts sets, and four dressy dresses in her wardrobe.

"I think we need a computer," I tell Rich. "We can find jobs, a place to live, and at least get in touch with people via email since the phones don't work."

We go to the Oxford Wal-Mart and buy a basic laptop computer, underwear, and sneakers from China. My still-soaked leather sandals and the smelly, squishy Nikes that Rich and the kids have been wearing need to go.

With new shoes on our feet, we head to a coffeehouse with a free Internet sign. As we're walking in, John pulls a napkin-wrapped biscuit from his pocket, looks up at me, and says, "Snack."

Internet access back in 2005 was not what it is today. We buy hot chocolate for the kids and get the access code. It takes forever for the computer to come on, and we patiently wait as it connects to the coffeehouse's Wi-Fi. Rich hogs the computer first, and reads emails from friends and relatives aloud to me. Everyone is worried and praying for us, and wants us to report back to them as soon as possible. Send a mass email I tell Rich, as he slowly pecks at the keys.

I keep trying to use Rich's phone and my cell phone. It occurs to me that with a 504 area code cell phone, and being out of the 504 area code geographic area, I can call area codes other than 504 but cannot call a 504 area code number, and no one can call our phones because they have 504 area codes.

Rich slides the laptop over to me, and I check my email. I send one message to my friend Becca in Oregon and ask her to disseminate it to mutual friends. I later learn that she sent it to everyone in her address book, so that explained why I started receiving prayer and concern messages, and even offers of places to stay, from people who do not even know me.

I see that President Bush is flying over New Orleans today, and read a blog post by a CNN reporter who wrote that I-10 east from Gulfport to Biloxi is covered by more refuse than can be imagined. "There are stoves, there are refrigerators, there are basketballs, there are sinks…literally the kitchen sink," on the interstate.

Samantha gets the laptop next to "IM" (instant message) her friends on MySpace. She learns that Allain has been cooped up in a shelter in Mississippi and is "going insane." Her summer camp friends, many of whom live in Houston, tell her to come to Houston.

"Well, that might be where we go," I tell her, since that's where we were originally headed. "I just received two emails saying that your school might open an extension school in Houston for kids from New Orleans."

"That would be good," says Rich. "We've already paid the tuition, I guess they'd have the same teachers, and the kids would have friends there."

We return to the Comfort Inn with our clean clothes, and I stop at the front desk to see if we can extend our stay. I'm hoping people coming in for the Ole Miss game have changed their plans; however, life appears to be rolling on as usual for everyone in the country except us folks along the Gulf Coast. The motel is completely booked for the weekend.

We need to be out of the motel in the morning, so I get the Rand McNally *Atlas* from the car and open it to the place where the entire country is spread over two pages. I study the route to Houston.

Rich and the kids are walking the dogs, and it's the first time I've been alone since we left New Orleans four days ago. I turn on the television, and hear that the Internal Revenue Service has extended tax filing until October 31st for people affected by Katrina. Rich has a private practice and I work as an independent contractor, so we're among those who pay estimated taxes quarterly. I have to think for a moment, what day is today? I've lost count. So this means that instead of having to pay our taxes on September 15th, the IRS has given us an additional six weeks. But wait a minute, if we're not working, and we don't know how long we won't be working, then how are we going to pay our taxes? Or pay the light bill?

So we need to figure out A, where we will live; B, where we will work; and C, where the kids will go to school. The trifecta of Major Life Decisions.

As I continue watching the news, I quickly rule out any possibility of returning to New Orleans. Even if by some miracle our house is still standing, the kids' school has flooded so there's no school, as in NO SCHOOL. The buildings are gone and we need to find a new school for the kids. I want them to get back to a normal routine as soon as possible.

Samantha will easily adapt to a new school. She has tons of friends, makes friends easily, and is generally at ease in new and unfamiliar situations. She'd rather have a hundred friends than one good friend. John, however, is somewhat shy and not as comfortable in new situations. John has a small group of close friends. He's the opposite of Sam; he'd rather have one good friend than a hundred friends.

Most of the shots on the TV news are from helicopters, and show massive areas of flooding up to one-story rooftops.

The on-the-ground shots show the deplorable conditions inside the Superdome.

The newscaster takes calls from viewers. "Oh, it's just awful down there! Those poor people! Where is the Red Cross? Where is the National Guard? Where is everybody?" the caller asks.

Another caller says we should be ashamed that this happened in America. In America!

The newscaster cuts to a screen shot listing relief organizations and ways to donate. I call my sister with the map of the United States open on my lap.

"We need to be out of here first thing in the morning," I tell her.

"Where are you going to go?" Erica asks.

"I'm thinking Houston. The kids' school is supposedly setting up an extension school in Houston since a lot of the kids are in Houston now. At least that's what people are saying in emails. I don't know if that'll happen because it's also sounding like people are scattered all over the place. This is their third day out of school, and some of the parents are already finding new schools for their kids. Apparently a lot of schools, even the private ones, are taking in Katrina kids."

"You should see what's going on even around here. My friend Linda said she'd go stay with her mom so you and Rich and the kids can move into her house up here. For as long as you need to. You could come here too, we'd make room for you. The principal at Whitney's school called me to say he'd heard I had a sister in New Orleans, and he would welcome your kids with open arms. Karla's church is already collecting donations, and she said you could stay with her."

"That is so nice," I say, fighting back the tears. I tell her how our cousin Virginia in New Mexico sent me an email inviting us to stay with her on her ranch. And she said pets are most welcome.

"So where are you going to go?" Erica asks again.

"I think Houston, only because of the school situation. It's also a big enough place that we should be able to get an apartment I would think."

"How are you on money?" she asks.

"I have four hundred in cash in my purse."

"I was asking about money long-term," she says. I'm so conditioned to thinking minute by minute and day to day now. I cannot process thinking about the future.

"We're good…I think…I hope. We've been saving for a rainy day ever since we had our rainy day ten years ago with the '95 flood. We have flood coverage and have homeowner's too, to cover wind damage, so we should be covered. Of course, if the house is totally destroyed, then we're screwed."

"Maybe that would be a good thing, though, if the entire city is destroyed. I mean, who's going to go back there? Can anyone even go back there?" she asks. "That floodwater looks nasty. There must be chemicals in it. And isn't it saltwater too, from the Gulf, so won't that corrode everything?"

"Probably so," I agree. This is getting to be too much to think about. I look down at the map and see that the quickest, and easiest, way from Oxford, Mississippi to Houston, Texas is straight down to New Orleans and then west to Houston. Going through New Orleans is not an option, so we'll need to take I-55 down to I-20 west, drive over to Shreveport on I-20, and then take country roads down to Nacogdoches and on into Houston. I make 100 mile marks on a piece of notepaper from a pad by the motel phone, and slide the paper along our route. It looks to be a 700-mile trip.

Shreveport is around the half-way point. "Erica, see if you can get on your computer and find us a pet-friendly motel around Shreveport. You might have to make calls, too, to see if they'll take Buddy because a lot of motels take only small dogs. Buddy weighs around eighty pounds." She's eager to do whatever is needed, and I tell her I'll call her back in thirty minutes.

"Nothing pet-friendly is available. I'm still looking," she says when I call.

Rich and the kids come back from walking the dogs.

"Mom," says Samantha, stomping her feet. "John made us stop at the vending machine and Dad let him get a Snickers."

"So what? What's the big deal?" I ask her.

"He's already chubby, and now he's gonna get *fat*!"

"He's not chubby. He's hungry." As soon as I say this, I wonder if he's really hungry or just storing up food again. Something is going on in that little eleven-year-old mind of his that I can't quite figure out.

I tell Rich and the kids that Erica is working on a motel for us for the following night and it's a long way away, so we should go eat some dinner somewhere—not Wendy's or Popeye's says Rich—and get some sleep because it's going to be a long drive tomorrow.

I call Erica before we head out to eat, and she says she's made a reservation for us for two nights, in case we need more than one night, at a pet-friendly motel on the outskirts of Bossier City, just south of Shreveport.

We find a little Italian place in Oxford, with cloth napkins and "real plates" as the kids call them. The host at the door picks up the menus and brings us to a table at the back, near the kitchen. He hands Rich a menu and says, "I hope you won the fight."

Rich looks puzzled for a moment. "Your black eye," I tell him. We've all gotten used to it by now, but when people see it for the first time, they all seem to have something clever to say.

I enjoy just sitting here, reading the menu. Before Katrina, we ate out fairly often and I took those meals for granted. It's been so long since I've had a "nice meal" and it feels like a special occasion. Rich orders a glass of Merlot and tells the server to just bring the bottle.

We gorge on salad, pasta, and bread and butter. Real butter. We even share a dessert, even though we are all stuffed.

"You never know when we'll eat again!" exclaims John as he scoops up the last bite of the tiramisu and scrapes his spoon across the plate.

We groan as we walk to the car, and groan some more when we take Buddy and Jack for a walk. The dogs do not want to go back into their crates and prefer to sit on our beds instead. Samantha and John fight about where each will sleep. The walls of our motel room are closing in.

I turn the TV on to escape from the turmoil around me and am immediately jolted by the turmoil in New Orleans. The chaos on the streets has worsened and there is mass confusion.

Louisiana Governor Kathleen Blanco is the guest on *Larry King Live.* She has little to say; it is clear that she is still in shock and denial, like the rest of us. She reacts to the statistic that one million people are now homeless by saying it is "fathomless" and "mind-boggling."

Aaron Brown hosts a CNN special, and remarks that there is no place for people to go. He too, cannot fathom what it must be like to be a refugee in your own hometown. He shakes his head after showing video clips of people sitting on the elevated portions of the freeway, surrounded by water. Along the Gulf Coast and in New Orleans, rescue workers are searching houses and putting markings on houses to identify where the dead are. "What a grim task," he observes.

It's impossible to fall asleep, so I go to the motel lobby and write in my journal for about an hour. I glance at the TV in the lobby. A nurse inside Charity Hospital in New Orleans has called CNN and says that hundreds of patients and staff are trapped there, they have run out of medical supplies and diesel to run the generators, and only three people have been rescued from the hospital so far.

When I go back into our motel room, I find Samantha splayed across the bed, and I have just enough space to lie on my back beside her. I still can't sleep and study the ceiling. The dogs refuse to be kenneled and lie beside our beds. I hear their panting, the jingle of their rabies tags on their necks, and the occasional growl when someone walks past our room.

Light shines in through the gap in the window curtains and I see that Rich, too, is lying face up, eyes wide open. John is curled up in a ball on the other side of Rich, and appears to be sleeping.

All night long, questions circle in my mind. Where will we live? For how long? Can we ever return to New Orleans? Do we even want to?

DAY 5

Thursday, September 1st

THE CNN MORNING news reporter asks New Orleans Mayor Ray Nagin if there are too many cooks in the kitchen in New Orleans. Nagin is talking to the reporter via phone, and the tone of his voice suggests that he is frustrated and bewildered. He says that rescue efforts have been tremendous, but New Orleans has a rising water situation. The reporter says that Nagin knew the hurricane was coming, so why the confusion? Nagin replies that this is an unprecedented event, and that he is sick and tired of the finger pointing. He adds, "Batteries have run out, phones are not working. It's hard to understand the devastation and challenges unless you are here. The people in the Superdome are hot and hungry. We've had our hands full."

I jot notes into my journal. I've turned into a court reporter of sorts, trying to capture what's being said as it is being said. It keeps my mind off thinking about things, and with all of the commotion and conflicting information that abounds, helps me sort out fact from fiction. Some of what we heard in Brookhaven, such as the Southern Yacht Club burning down, turns out to be true. Other early reports, such as extensive gunfire in the Superdome, are now disputed.

CNN proceeds to show new footage of the rising floodwaters, and notes that CNN journalist John Zarella has become part of the story. Thirty CNN employees are now stranded in New Orleans as "the bowl is filling up." Zarella says, "This is what everyone has talked about for years. It's the worst case scenario. And it's happening now."

CNN broadcasts an aerial shot of prisoners in orange jumpsuits sitting on a highway ramp, surrounded by guards with shotguns, both on the highway and in a boat in the water below.

I'm such a news junkie now that I read news on the computer while simultaneously watching the news on TV. CNN's Jim Spellman posts in his blog, "I don't think I really have the vocabulary for this situation," and describes how "thousands and thousands and thousands of people" have spent the night sleeping on the streets and sidewalks near the Convention Center, and are hopeful that a boat or bus is coming for them. "Probably the most disturbing thing," he writes, "is that people at the Convention Center are starting to pass away and there is simply nothing to do with their bodies. There is nowhere to put them."

News reports continue with accounts of looting and violence. The medical evacuation of patients is complicated by other people in New Orleans wanting to get out. According to reports, people are storming the evacuation buses and helicopters and compromising patient and staff safety.

A major topic of discussion is why so many people stayed in New Orleans when there was a mandatory evacuation order to leave. While many had no way to get out, there also were a number of people in New Orleans who were determined to stay. Several families we know vertically evacuate; they stay in hotel rooms in New Orleans that are on the third floor or higher and "ride out" approaching hurricanes. Others we know "hunker down" and take shelter in their homes. These people prepare to ride out the hurricane and endure its aftermath. They have a large food supply, a sufficient water supply, and run generators to power air conditioners and refrigerators.

The ill, the elderly, young children, and babies are especially vulnerable to the heat and poor living conditions that occur in the aftermath of a hurricane. The TV is filled with these images now. People push an old woman on a mattress across a flooded street. Lethargic, diaper-less babies are held in mothers' arms. These images make me want to turn away, but I cannot. I still cannot fathom that what I see is real, and that it is happening in the city in which I live.

All of the news channels are now reporting the flooding that is taking over New Orleans. As Katrina passed over the city on August 29th, rising water in the Industrial Canal caused the flood gates to leak and allowed water to enter the neighborhoods on either side of the I-10 high rise. Storm surge, which had been predicted to be as high as thirty-five feet, pushed against the Mississippi River-Gulf Outlet levee (MR-GO or "Mister Go" as locals refer to it), causing sections of it to collapse. Water from Lake Borgne then swept through the wetlands and entered the neighborhoods in St. Bernard Parish.

Witnesses reported that sections of the 17th Street Canal

levee were leaning toward the Lakeview side, and later in the day on the 29th, several of the canal wall panels broke and released water into Lakeview, Gentilly, the mid-city area of New Orleans, City Park, Carrollton, and parts of Old Metairie. Other parts of Metairie, called New Metairie by locals, have flooded because of unstaffed pumping stations. It's alleged that the pumps were not turned on. Eastern New Orleans has flooded as a result of the mile-long storm surge along Lake Pontchartrain. Water topping the Orleans Avenue Canal pours into City Park and Gentilly.

We take the dogs on a long walk to tire them out before our long ride, and get on the road around ten. We make a quick stop in Batesville for gas, snacks, and wet wipes, and head south on I-55. Batesville to Jackson, where we'll pick up I-20 and head west, is 150 miles. I'm hoping to get to Monroe, Louisiana on this tank of gas. It's highly unlikely that the Jackson area has power restored, so gas pumps in that area won't be working. Shreveport is about seven hours away, so including a stop for lunch and stops along the way, we should arrive at our motel around dinnertime.

It's a clear sunny day, and there is a surprising amount of traffic on I-55, going in both directions. A number of cars with magnetic "disaster relief" signs pass us on the southbound lanes. Red Cross trucks, utility trucks, and several large U-Hauls head south with us.

A text message arrives from Cheryl. She's on her way to San Antonio, but still has not heard from her brother.

I call my sister Erica, and she tells me that there are now numerous messages on Craigslist about how different parts of New Orleans fared, and there are two messages saying that

River Ridge did not flood. However, aerial photos of New Orleans on the Internet show extensive flooding, and she can't tell from these photos if the water stops in the Elmwood area or engulfs our neighborhood. She says that people are buying houses in Baton Rouge sight unseen. Rich and I have been using our computer to check emails and read the news, and I'm surprised to learn that updates are being posted on places like Craigslist.

The traffic is moving along at 60-65 mph and then suddenly, for no apparent reason, we're down to 20 mph for several minutes. At one point, we come to a complete stop, and never learn why we stopped. The flow of traffic picks up, slows down, and picks up again. We are not making good time, and I wonder how late it will be when we get to Shreveport.

We're doing around 60 mph again when a Jeep a few cars in front of us pulls into the left lane to pass a truck pulling an empty flatbed trailer. The Jeep clips the trailer, which fishtails the trailer, causes the cars behind to crash, and sends the Jeep careening off the interstate, flipping several times.

It's all unfolding so quickly and we are so close, but somehow Rich takes the shoulder and gets our car to stop in the grass without us getting hit or hitting someone else. We're still hearing tires screeching and the bam! of cars piling up when I toss Samantha my phone and tell her call 911 and say that there's a big accident about ten miles north of Grenada, southbound lanes.

"I've never called 911 before," she says. "Call it now," I tell her.

Rich and I, along with an unusually big bald guy who appears out of nowhere, run to the overturned Jeep, which is smoking and hissing. A young man is hanging upside down.

No one else is in the Jeep, and Rich reaches in to turn off the ignition. I see the big guy look at Rich's face and quickly explain that the black eye happened a couple of days ago, not in the crash today, and no it wasn't a fight. Rich and Big Guy release the seat belt, drop the man into their arms, and gently pull him from the Jeep.

"Don't move him!" yells a man who has run up.

"Gotta move him, man, this Jeep looks like it's gonna blow," says Big Guy.

I see that Rich has stabilized the young man's neck and is directing Big Guy on how to extricate our patient from the vehicle. I grab his legs as he's pulled out, and we carry him forty or so feet away. The man who advised us not to move him is now following us and screaming, "You are not supposed to move him! You can paralyze him! I took a first aid course and I know this! I am going to report you to the American Red Cross!"

Just as he finishes his tirade, the Jeep lets out an incredibly loud, menacing hiss. The man does not say another word.

People are running toward us with thick, wooly blankets. It is high noon and 90-plus degrees. No, no, no I tell them, we don't need to cover him. We need clean cotton cloths, like towels or even T-shirts—anything—to stop the bleeding. One guy on the sidelines looks around at the others, pulls off his shirt, and hands it to me. A woman gives me a tiny metal First Aid kit containing Band-Aids, antibiotic cream, and two gauze squares.

Our patient looks to be about 18-20 years old. Rich is at the man's head, checking his pupils, and checking for a pulse. Big Guy appears to know what he's doing, which surprises me, because he really does resemble Mr. Clean in the commercials on TV. We're all sweating bullets and I tell the blanket-bearers to hold them up to block the sun.

They seem pleased that they can do something important, and shield us from the sun's burning rays. Rich nods affirmatively that our patient has a pulse, and Big Guy and I keep pressure on places that are bleeding.

It feels like forever, but we hear a siren in the distance, and then another. The State Police, fire trucks, and ambulances arrive. There's so much commotion amid the wrecked cars and trucks that it occurs to us that they might not be aware that one of the most seriously injured people is way over here in the grass. One of the blanket holders must be reading my mind, because he sprints over to a State Trooper and motions him toward us.

The Trooper asks if the guy is alive. Yes, we tell him, he's alive but he's not responsive. Get the paramedics over here and maybe a helicopter to get him out of here, please? Instead, he reaches into the young man's pants pocket as Rich, Big Guy, and I share quizzical looks. He pulls out a cell phone, flips it open, and scrolls through the contact list. "Good, he's got grandma in here," he says and walks off to place the call.

The paramedics arrive with a backboard and take over the care of our patient. They recognize the need to get him to the hospital quickly, strap him down on the board, and carry him toward an ambulance. People who have instantly come together out of nowhere now disperse.

I stand up in the grass and feel blood drip down my legs. Rich and Big Guy have rivets of blood running down their arms and legs as well. Big Guy uses his forearm to wipe the sweat from his forehead, but as soon as he does, he says, "That was dumb." His face is now streaked with blood.

It turns out that Big Guy is an RN who works in the intensive care unit at Touro Infirmary in New Orleans. When the Trooper writing the report hears that a doctor and two RNs just happened to be the first people on the scene, he says, "That kid is the luckiest son-of-a-bitch around."

Wiping the blood on my legs does nothing to remove it, and just smears it around even more. Our kids' eyes are wide as saucers when they see us. Samantha's mottled face tells me she's been crying, and it looks like John may have been crying too.

"You're okay!" yells Samantha as she jumps from the back seat to hug me, but backs away when she sees the blood. "We saw the steam and heard noises, and thought you blew up!"

John has gotten out of the SUV on the other side and hugs Rich. "When we saw the blankets being held up, I thought they put up a screen around your bodies, like they do on TV," says John. "Did they die?"

"Nope, it was one guy and he's alive," says Rich.

We stand by the back of Rich's Expedition and use the wet wipes to clean off the blood on our legs. The blood on my shirt has blended with the Wendy's ketchup stain from two nights ago. We're offered ice cold bottles of water by kind strangers, gratefully accept them, and hand them to Sam and John, who need them more than we do.

We get back in the SUV and learn that the kids are nearly roasted from having the engine shut off. Both were too scared to turn it on for air conditioning, and in our haste to get to the overturned Jeep, Rich and I never thought about it. At least the kids had the good sense to open up their doors.

"I've never had to call 911 before," says Samantha, as she chokes back her tears. She tells us how the operator told her it was very, very bad for kids to call 911 as a prank. I tell Sam that I'm so proud of her for calling 911 and getting help for the young guy. She may well have saved his life.

"The lady operator said, 'honey, how old are you?' and I said thirteen. I told her just what you told me to tell her. She kept saying 'you're doing good honey' and 'stay on the phone with me.' And then when they started putting blankets up, I couldn't talk, and she kept asking 'what's the matter honey, what happened' and kept asking if I was all right, but *I couldn't talk, Mommy, I couldn't talk!"* Samantha is crying so hard. We haven't left the side of the road yet, so I open her door and scoop her up in my arms. She finally calms down, and I see that some of the blood from my shirt has rubbed off on hers.

We sit and wait as the tangled mess of cars is cleared. One lane is finally clear and glass crunches under our tires as we inch onto the roadway. I have blood under my fingernails, and tell Rich we need to stop at the first gas station so we can wash up.

We get off at the next exit, which is the exit for Grenada, and I'm relieved to see a blue hospital sign. Maybe the kid in the Jeep got here fast enough and survived.

The sink bowl in the gas station restroom turns pale pink when I wash my hands. I change my clothes and throw my bloodied shorts and shirt into the trash. Despite blotting my white day-old sneakers with wet paper towels, streaks of blood still cover them.

The gas station is open, but signs indicate that the gas is for incoming utility crews only. I see an LE Myers Company electrical construction truck from St. Louis at the pump and go up to the driver to thank him for coming in to help. When I tell him I'm from New Orleans, he says, "I'm so sorry, ma'am."

It's already two in the afternoon, and we've traveled less than 60 miles on our 400 mile journey. Rich washes up and comes out with water for me and Icees for the kids. I ask how he's doing and he says fine. He eats an entire can of Pringles.

We get back on the road as the kids slurp the frozen Icees, made just the way they like them, cherry mixed with raspberry. I see a school bus dropping off kids, and wonder where our kids will go to school. Things seem so normal here, and I feel like an alien from another world that has been dropped into this perfect world. I look up from my journal writing to see a large American flag, flying at half-staff, and feel the tears running down my cheeks.

We go through a McDonald's drive-thru for "linner," lunch and dinner, and eat as we make our way south. The southbound traffic on I-55 continues to be stop-and-go, all the way down to Jackson.

We see truck after truck heading toward the Gulf Coast. I think about the men and women who have left their families behind in order to come in to help us. Who knows how long they'll be gone from home, or what they'll have to do. They are ordinary people in truly extraordinary times.

I call my sister Erica when I realize that we're never going to make it to Shreveport. I tell her that I think we can make it to Vicksburg, about 100 miles west of Jackson, and ask if she can look for a motel for us.

I call her in fifteen minutes, and she tells me to call back every fifteen minutes after that. Vicksburg doesn't have many motels, and the few that are accepting pets are full or accept small pets only. Erica has pleaded with multiple motel managers to take Buddy along with Jack, but to no avail.

Rich proposes that we sneak 80-pound Buddy into one of the pet-friendly motel rooms.

"You know our luck, we'll get caught and end up sleeping in the car," I tell him.

Erica continues to search, and when I call her back she's giddy.

"Linda here in the office came up with this. But this will work!" She's so happy she's found a solution.

Rich leans toward the phone. "Yeah, put me in the dog crate in the car, and Lisa and the kids and the dogs in the beds, right?"

Erica laughs. "No, but listen this would work. Linda said find a pet boarding place for the dogs and get a regular motel room, since they do have rooms but not pet-friendly ones. So I have a room for you guys at a motel in Vicksburg and have two kennels at a vet's office there for Buddy and Jack!"

We continue south and listen to a caller on the radio report that the Wal-Mart in Hattiesburg, Mississippi has been broken into, and men with guns are taking over the city. Hattiesburg is over a hundred miles north of New Orleans. What in the world is going on in our country?

Entergy announces that it has brought in workers from eighteen states, and that customers along the Gulf Coast need to be patient and understanding, as power may not be fully restored for months.

Months! I guess we'll be in Houston for a while. A good, long while.

We are south enough now that we are back in "no cell service" land. Periodically, Samantha yells "cell tower" and repeatedly attempts to dial her phone, but there's still no service here.

We tune into NPR and hear that eighty-six ships are lined up in the river in the Port of New Orleans and no one knows when the port will reopen. New Orleans is the fifth largest port in the world, and the only deep water port in the United States served by six Class One railroads, which provide a transportation network to virtually anywhere in the country. There's speculation of the impact of the port being closed that include gas and oil shortages, delayed food delivery, and interruptions in receiving imported goods.

President Bush asks Congress for ten billion dollars in disaster relief.

It's dark when we pull into the vet's parking lot. Rich says he hasn't driven this much since he was twenty years old. We're relieved we made it, and scoot the dogs into their kennels in the boarding area of the vet's office. Buddy makes a heart-wrenching whine as we leave him. He's gotten used to, and likes, our near-constant attention. Jack, on the other hand, leaves us without looking back.

"Buddy looks sad," says John when we get back into the SUV.

"So sad," adds Sam.

"Oh no," I say, "We are not going back for the dogs and sleeping in the car with them. They'll be fine here. We'll be back here first thing in the morning."

We find a coffeehouse, get the Internet access code, and check email. Samantha's soccer coach sent a message to the Rage soccer team to let us know that they've evacuated to the Indian Reservation in Charenton, Louisiana. I remember now that the coach's wife is 1/12th or 1/16th or something Native American. Harold ends his email by saying that there is no soccer practice this week.

One of the girls' dads has replied to the message, saying that they've been in Lake Charles and are now on the way to Nashville. He signs his message, "Until we meet again Rage fans."

I start compiling a list of who is where, and jot down the information in my journal. For most people, it's a two-step process; first, a short-term evacuation destination that ends up being a pit-stop, and then a place where people will live for a while, maybe forever.

The Carbo family is in Memphis and planning to drive to Crestview, Florida. Our neighbors rode out Katrina in Wiggins, Mississippi and had an experience similar to ours, with no power and virtually no food, and have decided to go to California when it's safe to travel without fear of running out of gas. Chloe, who first went to Pineville, is now going to Houston. Molly and Allain, who were in school at Sacred Heart in New Orleans, first went to Houston, and are now going to Sacred Heart in Grand Coteau, Louisiana. Claire is one of the few people who went to Baton Rouge and is staying there. Almost everyone else is moving around.

An email from the kids' school asks us to reply to let them know where we are, and says that they are exploring setting up an extension school in Houston.

New Orleans, Louisiana is known as "NOLA," and the

city's newspaper, the *Times Picayune,* uses "nola.com" for its website. WWL is a local television station, and has WWL.com as its website. Both of these websites, as well as many others, are posting frequent news updates and have also become "lost and found" sites. Each day, the number of messages posted on the sites grows.

"Has anyone seen or heard from anyone living in the Lower Ninth Ward?"

"Skip Breaux and family, including Grandpa George, are in Baton Rouge and we are all okay!"

"News about Old Metairie would be very much appreciated. Have heard rumors it's flooded."

"Looking for the Comeaux family who live on Pratt Street."

"Liz and Don Campanello, our kids, and Buttercup and her puppies are on the way to Dallas—if any of y'all land there, look us up! We'll be at [address]."

"Does anyone know if Jesuit High School is going to reopen? Did it flood?"

"Need information about the condition of Lakeside Mall where I work."

"If someone is around, or can get to Greenwood Drive, please check on my cat at [address]."

"Just want to publicly thank [name of grocery store] for emailing us employees to tell us that our jobs are gone and that you wish us the best in our future endeavors. Thanks a lot."

"Has anyone heard from anyone at Memorial?" (Memorial is the uptown New Orleans hospital where forty-five bodies were later recovered amid allegations of euthanizing patients).

In the end, the nola.com website became a lifeline for those of us displaced from New Orleans. The website was described by *The New York Times* as a "release valve for the accumulating tales of misery from the city, providing news, crucial information and a missing persons forum," and had more than 17,000 posts within a week of Katrina.

We drive to the Vicksburg motel and on the way there, see that there are long lines waiting at the gas stations. We do need to fill up, so we'll need to factor this in before we leave in the morning.

We're all too tired now to eat, and "linner" seems to have sustained us. Rich and the kids burrow down in the covers and go to sleep.

I stay awake long enough to hear Anderson Cooper say, "Mayor Nagin has put out a desperate SOS. That is what he calls it, a desperate SOS. There are police barricading themselves on the roofs of buildings. There are snipers taking shots at MedEvac helicopters trying to rescue wounded people and evacuate the people of New Orleans. The mayor at one point has told people there are no more buses to evacuate them out. Just get to the highway and start walking out of the city. We have never seen anything like this in the United States of America."

DAY 6

Friday, September 2nd

I WAKE UP early, unable to sleep. There's a stack of *USA Today* newspapers in the lobby of the motel, and there's now a section of the paper called "Katrina's Aftermath." A photo under the headline "The looters, they're like cockroaches" shows four Louisiana Army National Guardsmen holding their assault rifles. I close the newspaper and turn my attention to the TV.

The news channels now are reporting mostly Katrina-related stories. CNN reports that the Federal Emergency Management Agency (FEMA) has ordered 25,000 body bags for the New Orleans area.

Even though it has been four days since Katrina hit, people are still stranded at the riverfront Convention Center. Many were picked up from elevated roadways or rooftops, and along with evacuees from the Superdome—estimated to be in the neighborhood of 20,000 people—were told that buses were on the way to bring them to safety. A woman holds her lethargic baby and appeals to the cameraman and viewers for water and food. The camera then cuts to two bodies covered by sheets near the side of the building.

Around 500 airboat pilots from Florida offer assistance, but FEMA refuses to authorize their entry into New Orleans. The airboat pilots stocked their boats with food, water, and medical supplies and were told by FEMA that without their permission, they would be subject to arrest and would not receive security and support services.

There's a report that people are continuing to be rescued from attics and rooftops, and at the bottom of the CNN screen, I see that a "renegade bus has arrived at the Astrodome." Apparently, a sixteen-year-old filled a school bus with people and drove them to the Houston shelter. The Pete Maravich Assembly Center on the LSU campus in Baton Rouge has 5,000 or more people now sheltering there.

New Orleans Mayor Ray Nagin appeals to federal and state officials and says, "Now get off your asses and let's do something. Let's fix the biggest Goddamn crisis in the history of this country."

Viewers who call in are clearly agitated as well. "Now tell me," says one, "If they can get all of those cameramen in there, why the hell is our government not able to get food and water in there?"

"What has happened to our country?" asks another. "It's third world conditions down there in New Orleans! Why can't anyone do something? How hard is it to drop pallets of water and food from a helicopter? We provide aid like this all around the world, but we can't provide it to our own citizens?"

A spokeswoman for the Red Cross says that the Department of Homeland Security "continues to request that the American Red Cross does not return to New Orleans," noting that access is controlled by the National Guard and local authorities. "We have been at the table every single day. We cannot get into New Orleans against their orders," she says.

Footage from the Gulf Coast is beginning to come in. Part of a huge oil rig is on the beach in Alabama, and no one knows where it came from.

The other major focus of the news is the looting, captured by the cameras for all of the world to see. The news stations let the cameras roll and viewers were left to draw their own conclusions if the looting occurred because of basic needs for food and water, or something else. I could understand the actions of the woman leaving a broken-in store with a loaf of bread and other food items, but when I saw Pottery Barn (*Pottery Barn!*) being ransacked and watched as people ran from the store carrying lamps, I couldn't quite believe it and certainly could not understand it. As hungry as we were in Brookhaven, it never occurred to me for a moment that I should break into the Crackle Barrel, a store, or someone's house—even for food.

These people on TV were oblivious to the fact that the cameras were capturing their every move, and they brazenly grabbed at whatever they fancied, destroying what little was left of the stores in the process. As I watch a group clear out a beer refrigerator, laughing all the way, I want to yell out at them, but keep quiet because Rich and the kids are still sleeping.

The Wal-Mart on Tchoupitoulas Street in New Orleans appears to be picked clean. The local newspaper, the *Times*

Picayune, reports that what began as a giveaway of essential items quickly erupted into a free-for-all looting extravaganza, with police losing control and civilians accusing police of stealing "all the best stuff."

There is no law and order in NOLA, and sympathy and compassion for the people of New Orleans are diminishing.

"I can understand looting for diapers and water if you're desperate, but to just go and take a TV from somebody's house? I mean, a *TV*? I just don't understand that. What is wrong with those people down in New Orleans?" asks a viewer who has called in to the TV station.

"Why do people insist on living there?" another viewer asks. "What do these people expect? They live in a low lying area and expect the rest of us to come to their rescue? There was a mandatory evacuation, they should have left, and now they're stuck there, and now they're complaining. And looting—oh my God, don't get me started on that."

However, what viewers weren't seeing were the behind-the-scenes communities that banded together. New Orleans has always been a mish-mash of people who chose to live together in a city that some have called "a hot mess." At the same time looting was shown over and over on TV, on the backstreets of NOLA and in the suburban neighborhoods, those remaining pulled out their grills, guitars, and beer and started cooking for whoever was in need of food. French Quarter restaurants emptied their freezers and cooked up what they had for whoever wanted it. Families in the Bywater and Marigny shared meals with one another, and music filled the streets. All over New Orleans, there were unpublicized accounts of neighbor helping neighbor.

Well-known chefs were also cooking up a storm. Chef

Paul Prudhomme cooked for free at a relief center for the military and residents staying in the French Quarter, and he and his team prepared 6,000 meals in ten days. Out in Metairie, Tommy Cvitanovich and his Drago's restaurant crew initially cooked whatever was on-hand, but as recovery workers streamed into the city, expanded operations and by mid-September, were serving over 1,500 free meals a day. In late October 2005, when the free meals ended, Cvitanovich estimates that 77,000 meals had been served.

We need to get gas, and ask the desk clerk at the motel if he knows which stations have gas. He tells us he remembers seeing a long line at a gas station nearby, and points in that direction. Just get on the feeder road and go up to the corner, he says.

There's a line of cars on the shoulder of the feeder road, all waiting to get into the gas station, and we take our place in line. After thirty minutes, I need to use the restroom and walk up to the station. What we're not able to see from our place in line is that only two of the pumps have gas, and there is a line of cars as long as our line on the street on the other side of the gas station. A paper sign on the pumps says "cash only, pay inside first" with "20 GAL max" scribbled below.

I walk back to our SUV, and we sit for another half an hour before reaching the pump, which now only has premium gas available. I peel three twenty-dollar bills from my wallet and although I'm dying for a nice, cold Diet Pepsi, I put it back in the refrigerated case when I think about possibly needing those two dollars in the future. I think about all of those times that I'd grab a Diet Pepsi, or let the kids get a candy bar or ice cream without giving it a second thought. So much I've taken for granted.

The cashier is chatting up the customer in front of me and asks him where he's headed.

"I honestly don't know," is the reply.

"What do you mean you don't know?" he probes.

"We're from New Orleans and we're still figuring that out."

At this point, I interject that we, too, are from New Orleans and we're in the same boat of not knowing for sure where we'll end up. The cashier looks astonished to learn this.

"You can't just roam around like nomads," he says. "You must have a destination in mind, don't you?"

The man tells the cashier that there are probably thousands of us nomads out there and no, we really don't know exactly where we're going.

The man is standing outside the store waiting for me, and tells me he finds it incredibly weird that the world outside of New Orleans is going on as usual, and here we are, caught up in this otherwise normal-appearing world when everything is anything but normal for us. We wish each other luck and wave good-bye.

Rich pulls out of the gas station and suddenly we're screaming, cars are honking, and brakes are slamming. We avoid a head-on collision by inches. The feeder road is a one way street, and Rich was momentarily confused by the line of cars on the shoulder waiting to get into the gas station. He thought he could take a left, but that only put us into one-way traffic, going the wrong way. Rich has to back up the SUV, and back into the gas station, in order to turn around.

The other driver is now out of his car, yelling "You fucking asshole, you almost fucking killed us!" Rich is mouthing "I'm sorry, I'm sorry," and I tell him to just focus on backing up without hitting anything. As Rich always does at awkward times like these, he gives the other driver a friendly little wave as he passes by in front of us, which provokes the other driver into slamming on his brakes to frantically flip us the bird with both of his hands.

As we head toward the vet's office to pick up Buddy and Jack, I tell Rich what I've seen on TV today. He says we should stop at a coffeehouse so he can sign up for locum tenens work. "I'll ask them to expedite my application," he says. "I'll also see if I can get temporary jobs close to Houston, but I'm willing to go anywhere to keep the cash flow going."

We find a coffeehouse with Wi-Fi, and the kids patiently wait as Rich types his application and I watch the TV. Carolyn Shanks, the CEO of Entergy, says that around a million people are without power along the Gulf Coast, and that the problem is the downed trees. Once trees are cleared, they can begin to restore power, first to evacuation shelters and hospitals, then water treatment plants, and then essential services, such as fire houses.

President Bush is now on the TV, smiling as he says, "Brownie, you're doing a heck of a job."

Our President is complimenting FEMA director Michael Brown. Two days after Katrina hit, Marty Bahamonde, one of the few FEMA employees in New Orleans, sent Brown an email message saying that the situation "is past critical" and informed him of the lack of food and water at the Superdome, and that some people were near death. Brown's entire response was "thanks for the update. Anything specific I need to do or tweak?"

Brown resigns ten days later, on September 12th. He'd taken over FEMA in 2003, and prior to joining the Bush administration, was the Stewards and Judges Commissioner for the International Arabian Horse Association for about ten years.

We get to the vet's office to retrieve Buddy and Jack, and the staff members tell us it's been crazy, with several dogs, cats, and a bird boarding there. They're also fielding calls for employment because they've been so busy and need additional help.

We head west on I-20 and begin to see signs for the Monroe, Louisiana evacuation shelter. We're passing by cities we've never been to. No matter which way we travel—north, south, east or west—we encounter a lot of traffic. Many of the cars contain evacuees, or are we refugees now? We see animal crates, suitcases, blankets and pillows in the cars we pass by.

Text messages start coming in again as we near Monroe. Cheryl still has not heard from her brother and is very worried. Rich receives a text message saying that East Jefferson Hospital has remained open, and the C-team is expected to report. We decide to work our way to north Houston, where George Bush Intercontinental Airport is located, so that Rich can hopefully fly out and get back to New Orleans, or rent a car and drive back.

We hear horns tooting and see people waving out of the cars in front of us. We look across the median and see at least twenty power company trucks followed by a dozen Army trucks going in the opposite direction. We join in and wave to the crews coming in to help.

Interstate 20 also has inconsistently flowing traffic, and we roll along at speeds varying from 15-20 mph to 60 mph. We eventually arrive at the Days Inn in Bossier City, the pet-friendly motel that Erica secured for us two days ago.

The dogs are wild from the long ride, even though we stopped several times to let them run around. John reaches in to get Jack from his crate.

Jack growls and bites John in the nose. It happens so fast that John drops the dog on the ground. John is bleeding and screaming that he hates the dog.

It's fairly dark by the SUV, so I take John over by the lights of the motel office. Rich and Samantha go looking for Jack, who has run off.

They find the runaway pup and return him to his crate in the back of the SUV. John calms down enough for us to examine him in the motel lobby. Our son has one set of tooth marks on the tip of his nose and another on his upper lip. He doesn't need stitches but his nose is swelling and turning red. The motel clerk brings us damp washcloths and a towel, and asks if we need anything else. He looks from Rich to John and back to Rich again. I've seen this puzzled look before, and quickly say that Rich has a black eye from Buddy jumping up into him, while thinking *he wasn't in a fight!*, and John was bitten in the nose by the other dog, *he was not beaten by his father!*

Rich, who has not particularly liked Jack ever since we got him, says, "I'm dropping that dog off at a Vietnamese restaurant," as we head to our room.

DAY 7

Saturday, September 3rd

THE MOTEL IS another evacuation camp, with tons of people milling around and lots of dogs and cats, plus a long orange snake in a clear acrylic box. The TV is on in the lobby, with a few people gathered around it. A reporter is interviewing a man on Canal Street who is holding a small plastic trash bag.

"Is that your food supply?" the reporter asks.

"No, it's most everything I own," the man replies.

The news reporter announces that the last of the 350 patients at Charity Hospital were evacuated yesterday afternoon. Those with medical problems were taken to the airport triage area, and patients with mental disorders were bused to a psychiatric facility in north Louisiana.

The next segment shows people in South Florida being asked what advice they have for the people along the Gulf Coast.

"It took years to recover from Hurricane Andrew," a man says, "and I'm not sure we're fully recovered yet. So my advice is that it's going to take a long time, much longer than you can ever imagine, until life is somewhat back to normal."

I'm remembering that Hurricane Andrew occurred in the summer of the year that Samantha was born, so that would be thirteen years ago. He's probably right about how long recovery is going take, as I remember back to 1995, and how we lived for months without walls in our house so that the studs could dry. We were still working on getting our house back together a year later. The scale of Katrina's wrath is much, much larger, so like the man said, recovery will take years.

We pack up once again and head west on I-20. The Days Inn sign by the road says, "May God be with you. Till we meet again, have a safe trip."

I call Erica, who answers with, "Hotline, how may I help you today?" She gets her assignment of finding us a hotel in north Houston that's pet-friendly, or a motel for us and a place to park the pets.

"Also, can you look into flights from Bush Intercontinental to New Orleans, but it's likely the airport isn't open, so maybe Baton Rouge? And investigate one-way rental cars from Bush airport to New Orleans, but I have no idea where a drop off spot would be. And maybe you can search and find out how to get into New Orleans, what roads are open? I know the Causeway is still closed, that was on CNN, and I saw that the twin spans of I-10 in the east are collapsed. So see if Rich can get in from the west?"

"Oh geez," says Erica. "Is that all? Anything else?"

"Well, while you're at it, maybe you can find us jobs, a place to live, and a school for the kids."

As we drive further west, my cell phone rings. The ring startles us all, as none of our phones has rung in several days. It's Cheryl, calling from San Antonio, and she tells us that she has heard her brother is all right, but has not actually spoken to him or heard from him directly. She was told by a neighbor who got back to Slidell that her house is still standing, has not flooded, and looks good except that the chimney is gone. She's enrolled Greg and Nathan at a school in San Antonio. Wayne, who works at the LSU Medical School in New Orleans, has heard that the school is relocating to Baton Rouge, and he may need to relocate there.

After we've driven for a while, we stop at a BBQ place in Alto, Texas for lunch. A sign in the bathroom says, "Spread seeds of kindness." The sign, along with mayhaw jelly and assorted jams, are sold in the gift shop. Women trawl the shelves and remark about the cute candles and knickknacks. One woman spots a garden flag with a big green frog and heads to the cash register. Aside from the food in this shop, there is not a single item that anyone would actually need sold here. Are these people oblivious to current events? How is it possible that life is going on as usual for everyone but us?

We walk the dogs, and I call Erica to see what she's come up with as far as accommodations go. She's booked us at a Best Western in Humble, near the airport, and has the dogs booked at Bed and Biscuit.

"Tell them to give Jack a bed but don't give him a biscuit," says John, still reeling from his injury.

"Vietnamese restaurant," mumbles Rich.

My journal is becoming filled with notes about directions. Maps and directions, that's all we had in 2005 to get from point to point. Bed and Biscuit is open until 6 p.m., and we need to take the FM 1960 exit, turn left, go one mile, look for a sign that says "Beckwith," take the small road next to it, make a left on Ramblewood, and look for the third building on the right.

We're riding in the car less than an hour when Samantha tells us she's bored.

"Look out the window," I tell her.

"There's nothing to look at. It all looks the same."

Samantha turns to John and says, "You look like a clown."

"No I don't," he says.

"Yes, you do. You have a clown nose."

"No I don't," he repeats as he strains to look at himself in the rearview mirror. Since last night, John's nose has grown to twice its normal size and is bright red.

"You look like Bozo with your orange hair and clown nose. Bozo, Bozo, Bozo," Samantha sing-songs.

"Samantha, you stop that RIGHT NOW. I've HAD ENOUGH!" says Rich. "If I hear another peep out of you, I'm going to….I'm going to…" Rich seems to be searching for what to say. Back home, when life was normal, he would say he was going to cut off TV watching, or banish her to her room, but here in the middle of Texas, he's at a loss for words.

"I'm going to do something you won't like," is all he can come up with.

We drive on, and Samantha is quiet. John is napping with his head propped against the window. With him sleeping, I can study his nose and see that it's a little less swollen than when he woke up this morning, but it sure is red.

We drop off the dogs at Bed and Biscuit, and I explain Rich's eye and John's nose injuries. Stay intact, Sam, I tell her. We don't need any more injuries in this family. The Bed and Biscuit owner gives us the "special Louisiana rate," which is touching and much appreciated.

The Best Western parking lot is filled with cars with Louisiana and Mississippi plates, and is yet another refugee camp. The desk clerk eyes us suspiciously, and I immediately explain the eye and nose situation. He laughs, and says that he didn't mean to look at us the way he did, but he's the general manager and they just can't have any trouble at the motel, with them being so full and all. He then tells us that four hundred chicken wings have been donated and are on their way, so stay in the lobby and enjoy!

Rich says he can't drive another inch today, so we walk to the Waffle House for dinner, and get a discount because we are from Louisiana. Hamburgers revive us, and we drive down to Rich's brother's townhouse in Jersey City. His son Alex and his family are staying there, along with Alex's mother-in-law. There's no room at this inn, nor do we want to impose on them.

We talk with the Louisiana expats about our mutual predicament, of not knowing where we'll be living next week or what we'll be doing. Like us, Alex is anxious to return to New Orleans to see what's left of his house and his kids' school, and see if he still has a job.

We drive back to Humble, and the kids settle down at the motel to watch TV. They're replaying President Bush's speech from earlier today. "One of our great cities is submerged," he says, "and the human costs are incalculable."

Rich and I go to the lobby of the motel to use the Wi-Fi to check emails. The clerk tells us the password is "giddy up." We're definitely in Texas now. Rich checks the status of his locum tenens applications and searches for ways to get back to New Orleans.

DAY 8

Sunday, September 4th

A LOCAL NEWS station reports that over 100,000 people from Louisiana are now in the greater Houston area, and Louisiana residents can get two weeks of food stamps, no questions asked.

I think about this influx of people from Louisiana. Who are all these people? It sounds like many are being sheltered at the Astrodome. If even half of us decide to live in Houston, will this help—or hinder—the economy and quality of life here? I have plenty of time to think about this as I wash our clothes in the motel's laundry room, and Rich takes the kids to the Waffle House for breakfast.

When we're back in our motel room, Rich's partner in his surgery practice calls, and Rich and Bobby talk at length about being able, or not able, to re-open their surgery practice in the medical office building next door to East Jefferson General Hospital. Bobby has heard that their building and the hospital had been surrounded by water for two days, and he and Rich are glad that their office is on the fourth floor. Bobby and his family are staying at the AmeriSuites in Atlanta, and I overhear Rich talking about how to get back to New Orleans.

Rich opens the laptop and before I quite realize what has just happened, he says he's booked an afternoon flight. He tells me he'll fly from Houston to Atlanta to Baton Rouge, and catch a ride into New Orleans with the other doctors who need to make their way back to cover the hospital and relieve the docs who are there now.

Over the past few days, we've received numerous invitations to stay with people in Houston. Several are from girls with whom Samantha has gone to summer camp in Wisconsin. One Birch Trail Camp family has asked us many times to come stay with them, and we now accept their kind offer.

We take Rich to the airport and make the hour-long drive into Houston. Sam moves her meager belongings into her camp friend's room, and John and I settle into the most wonderful guest room. The bed linens are so soft, the towels are fluffy, and the room is so comfortable that I feel like I've been teleported to the Four Seasons.

Carol and Ken grill delicious hamburgers for us, and I feel almost normal. They ask what our plans are, and I tell them we simply don't know. Carol says, "Stay as long as you need."

Rich calls to let me know he's made it to East Jefferson Hospital in Metairie. He's calling on some kind of secure working phone line at the hospital because his cell phone does not have service. He tells me that he and three other doctors were able to drive down from Baton Rouge to Kenner and come in on the old Airline Highway to reach the hospital.

Each had a medical pass, signed by the Sheriff, so they were allowed to proceed through all of the roadblocks staffed by soldiers.

"The only people on the road are military," he tells me. "The hospital has guards to keep people out who don't need to be here. I have an air mattress in the medical staff office that I can sleep on tonight, and I'm hoping I can go see how things look at our house in the morning. I rode in with Ed, the gastroenterologist, and he says he needs to check on his partner Howard's house. We're planning on checking out houses, if we can, tomorrow."

DAY 9

Monday, September 5th

IT'S LABOR DAY, so Samantha's camp friend Lauren does not have school, and she and Samantha sleep late. John is still snug in our bed. I tiptoe down the back stairs and find a note from Carol that says she's left the house, and breakfast is on the kitchen table. I tear up when I see the coffee, plate of bagels, and sliced melon all set out for us. I am so very touched by her thoughtfulness.

It's an unfamiliar feeling to sip coffee and eat a breakfast this good. My mind wanders to what we should do. I absolutely don't want to overstay our welcome here. We need to find a school for the kids, and the location of the school will influence where we live in Houston. I lived in Houston in the late 70s when I worked at MD Anderson Cancer Center, but Houston has tripled in size since then. I don't know where to begin.

Carol has left a note with instructions on connecting to the Internet, and I connect our laptop and read the dozens of emails in my inbox. In addition to offers to stay with people, there are offers to send us whatever we might need, and everyone wants to know how we are, where we are, and what our plans are. Sprinkled amid these offers are updates from friends and our kids' classmates' families. A number of kids already are enrolled in school, and there's no further word about a Houston extension school for our kids. I send a message to the school's email address asking about this, and wonder if I'll ever get a response.

I click through the various emails I've already read and make a list of schools that have enrolled kids from New Orleans. I start calling them, but because it's Labor Day, the phones are not answered.

I check a message thread for oncology nurses in New Orleans to see where my colleagues are, and find several updates. Suzanne wrote that from her hotel room in Dallas, she saw her mattress and bedding on CNN—out on the street in front of her condo in the Warehouse District. She recognized her stuff and her building, and wrote that some random guy was lying on her bed, smoking a cigarette. Several of us send sympathy messages to her, and a couple of nurses say they have extra bedding to give to her, they think. They're not sure yet; they'll have to see about this when they return home, but if they do, Suzanne can have it. Later, when Suzanne was able to get back to New Orleans, she found out, as we all suspected, that her condo had been totally cleaned out.

I also see several messages and posts from oncology nurses in north Louisiana as well as Houston asking if any of us know about the patients with cancer who have landed on their doorsteps. None had medical records, and most have little to no knowledge of their treatment regimens, and in some cases, even the type of cancer they have. The nurses ask that we send them any information we recall about these patients.

The kids are now awake, and I help them cut and toast the bagels. We spend the afternoon in the pool in the back yard, where I hear our kids laughing for the first time since we left New Orleans.

DAY 10

Tuesday, September 6th

JOHN WAKES UP at 7:30 a.m. and announces that he wants to go home. He's been tossing and turning all night and whimpering in his sleep. I can't tell if it's his nose that is bothering him, or if it's something else.

Rich calls my cell phone at eight, and when I tell him that we're thinking of coming home, he tells me to stay put, that New Orleans is no place for kids—or anyone—right now. He tells me that he and his gastroenterologist friend got to our house last night, but he couldn't call me afterward because the line to use the special phone at the hospital was too long.

To their amazement, they found that our house is still standing, did not flood, and even has electricity! I practically pass out hearing this news. This is better than I ever imagined.

We are on higher ground in River Ridge, plus we have a fire station at the end of our street. I'm thinking that's why our power has been restored so quickly.

Rich said the house stinks from the rotten food in the

refrigerator and freezer, and that we have a lot of trees down. There's no visible damage to the house except a couple of rooms with damp walls and bubbling paint, and the back of the garage has been crushed by trees. Another doctor's house has not fared as well.

Rich describes how he and Ed arrived at Howard's house in Metairie, near the lakefront, to find the front door opened. Ed reached under the seat of his car, pulled out a small wooden box, and extracted a handgun. "We might need this," he told Rich. They entered Howard's flooded house and were relieved to not find anyone there.

I tell Rich that John really, really wants to go home, and he asks how I plan to come in. There's a mandatory evacuation order that prevents people from re-entering the city until the major street clean-up is done. Many parts of New Orleans still have several feet of standing water.

Rich used his wallet medical pass to enter the city and his larger re-entry pass is in his SUV, which I'm driving now. John hears me talking to Rich and runs into the kitchen. In an instant, he is on his knees begging me to drive home. Mothers remember certain facial expressions on their children many years later, and John's sad little face is one I'll remember the rest of my life. I tell Rich we'll be home for dinner.

John is elated to be going home, and wraps a bagel in a paper towel for the road. Samantha storms off, saying that she wants to stay and find a school.

"We're going home because of stupid John and those stupid dogs!" she says as she starts to cry and attempts to leave the room. I pull her back and say that we're not going home for long, although I've toyed with the idea of home schooling and keeping our family together. I tell her we'll be back in Houston in no time.

She sits on the steps leading upstairs, crying hard. "I don't want to go! I want to go to school!" She may well be one of the few kids on the planet that actually *wants* to go to school. I can understand her yearning for normalcy. "We need to find a school! You saw the pictures on TV. We can't go back there—there's nothing there!"

I tell her that we need to go home to get her clothes so that she'll have something nice to wear when she starts school in Houston.

Samantha looks up, wipes her eyes, and says, "Let's go."

We drive up to Humble to Bed and Biscuit, and put the dogs in their crates for the ride home. John won't go near Jack, so I handle him with care, keeping him at arm's length and my head tilted way back. I'd rather he take out a piece of my chin than my nose.

We head east, first along FM 1960, and then take Highway 90 until we pick up I-10 near Beaumont. I decide to get gas at every station I see if we're below half a tank.

Just like every other excursion we've been on, the traffic zooms along the interstate and then slows or stops. We're either doing 60 mph or 20 mph. We pass by large pieces of equipment and double-wide trailers being hauled toward New Orleans. We stop once for a quick lunch and to let the dogs out, and curse the Baton Rouge traffic jam, which starts west of Port Allen, across the Mississippi River from Baton Rouge. Riding over the elevated bridge is painfully slow and enables me to see that there is nothing but stalled traffic everywhere. Even the back roads along the river behind LSU and Highland Road are stacked with cars.

I have Samantha text our neighbors who are staying in the Baton Rouge Marriott to find out where there is a gas station that's open. Lana writes back and says the Raceway on Bluebonnet has gas, so I eventually am able to take the exit and sure enough, the station is open and only three cars are in line. I buy the kids cold bottles of water when I pay for the gas and go outside to the pump.

A car pulls up to the adjacent pump and I see the driver and passenger high-fiving and smiling. The driver gets out and his face deflates when he sees the "cash only-NO EXCEPTIONS" sign. He bows his head, covers his face with his hands, and kicks the cement gas pump platform.

"Do you need some cash?" I ask him.

He looks up at me and back at his passenger. "Yeah, we only have credit cards. The ATMs are either not working because of the power being out, or are just out of money."

"Take this," I say as I hand him two twenties.

"Are you sure?" he asks tentatively.

"Yeah, no problem."

"Let me get your address so I can mail you a check," he says.

"No, really, don't worry about it. Maybe you can help somebody else out sometime."

He grabs my hands, says thank you a dozen times, and jaunts in to the station to pay for his gas.

We continue on to New Orleans and are directed off of I-10 to Airline Highway just south of Baton Rouge. We're waved through the checkpoint and do not need to present Rich's medical pass. We're in a line of utility and supply trucks going into New Orleans and breeze right through. We begin seeing fallen trees and a lot of debris that has been pushed to the sides of the road.

Traffic is bumper-to-bumper in La Place, twenty miles west of our house, and most of the traffic lights are out. The Winn Dixie parking lot is jammed with cars and there is a line of people waiting to get in. When two people come out of the store, two are allowed in. I had planned to stop here for groceries, but change my mind when a woman walking out of the store tells me that there's nothing much left in there.

We head on to River Ridge, and I have to turn around a couple of times until I find passable streets that connect to the street we live on. I heave a sigh of relief when we reach our house. We left Carol's house at eight-thirty this morning, fetched the dogs an hour later, got on the interstate, and it's now seven at night. A trip that usually takes six hours in normal conditions has taken us nearly eleven.

I pull into the end of our driveway and park behind my Tahoe. Our driveway has two trees down across it, and I see where Rich cleared a path across the grass so he could drive my Tahoe out. Rich has started a debris pile of downed tree limbs by the street and it's already four feet tall and at least thirty feet wide.

The kids run up to Rich, hugging him tightly. Especially John.

Although Rich has spent a good part of the afternoon cleaning out the refrigerator and freezer, the house still smells like a dead animal. The air conditioning appears to be working, and the house is fairly cool. There's a huge tree in our pool, and the water there is black.

There's not much in the pantry, but I find a couple of boxes of macaroni and cheese. I flick the gas cooktop on and nothing happens.

"I think the gas is out because we don't have any hot water, and the gas lights outside are out," Rich says.

Okay then, Plan B. I heat the water for the mac and cheese in the microwave, open two cans of sweet corn, and we sit down to a delicious dinner.

DAY 11

Wednesday, September 7th

RICH TELLS ME that Ray is covering at the hospital today, and tomorrow is Rich's day to cover. And Ray will be staying with us whenever he's not at the hospital, as we are the only people known to have electricity and water, the kind that comes out of the tap.

Rich opens the back door to let the dogs out. Both take off.

"Oh my God, Rich, why did you let them out? There's no fence back there anymore."

"I wasn't thinking," he says.

We step over the fallen tree right outside the back door that has miraculously missed our house by about six feet. We walk around the tree that has crushed the back of our garage. Although there's the big pine tree that has fallen directly into our pool, Buddy is in there swimming. He loves the water and loves to swim.

We call Buddy's name and he comes out of the pool. He's now a Black Lab with a Yellow Lab face. We stroke his fur and it's just thick muddy water, so we take him over to the garden hose to wash him off, and he becomes a yellow Lab again. I put him in the laundry room to dry off, and set off with Rich to look for Jack.

"Vietnamese restaurant," yells Rich as he searches for the dog in the azalea bushes by the house. There are multiple breaks in the fence on all the three sides of the yard, and we quickly determine that Jack is not in our back yard. He could be anywhere by now.

I scribble a note for the kids in case they wake up, and grab Jack's leash.

"Who's around in our neighborhood? Any signs of life around here?" I ask. According to news reports, there are people sprinkled around in most of the neighborhoods; people who either were unable to leave or decided not to. And both groups are likely to be armed.

"Haven't seen anybody at all," Rich says. "But I've mostly been at the hospital."

We walk down a nearby street to get to the property that abuts ours in back. Weirdly, there are no birds chirping, no squirrels scurrying around. No sign or sound of life anywhere.

Many in the area, including us, had turned our air conditioners off before we left, thinking that if we flooded, they might be saved if they weren't running. Without the usual sounds of air conditioners, traffic, and lawnmowers, the neighborhood is eerily quiet.

We walk in the middle of the street and call Jack's name. I add "come here little doggie" to hopefully alert anyone who might be watching us that we're unarmed and not a threat. We're not worried about our neighbors—we're worried about people who may be in our neighbor's houses. We've heard stories now of people squatting in houses, especially houses like ours that are structurally intact and didn't flood. One doctor at the hospital made his way to his house to find several people asleep in the beds upstairs. "And it wasn't Goldilocks," he said.

We walk up the driveway to the house that's directly behind ours, and I ring the doorbell anyway, just in case someone's inside. It occurs to me that this street may not have power, so I knock on the door and peek in the vertical glass panels on either side of the door.

A huge dog comes bounding toward me, barking loudly, and I spin back from the glass. I hear a second dog barking, and look down to see little Jack inside our neighbor's house.

"Hey Rich, you gotta see this."

Rich comes from the side yard and peers into the window.

"How in the hell did Jack get in there?" he asks.

"If they left their dog, I bet they left a door open in back."

"Maybe these people are in here," he says as he pounds on the door.

There's no response, so Rich tells me to stay put at the front door while he goes around back. He reasons that if the National Guard comes by, I'll be able to explain what we're doing. If both of us are found around back—or inside someone else's house—it will be a different story.

Through the glass at the front door, I see Rich in the house. He's soon beside me with Jack on his leash.

"The whole back of the house is destroyed so that's how Jack got in. I didn't see an opening big enough for their dog to go in and out. I was able to climb over a spot by the fireplace and got in. They left a big bag of dog food open in the kitchen, along with a five gallon pail of water, and I refilled it.

Their dog has enough food and water for now, and I'll come check on him in a day or two."

"Maybe we should take their dog to our house."

"I don't know, that dog wasn't all that friendly. You heard him barking. Plus Buddy is such a pansy that this dog might eat him alive. Jack obviously held his own against this dog. But then again, Jack has held his own against all of us."

The kids are awake when we return, and I find half of a box of Pop Tarts in the pantry for their breakfast. Rich and I scrub down the refrigerator once again in the hope of ridding it of its putrid smell.

Rich says he wants to drive us around New Orleans. He's already done "the misery tour" with his doctor friends, so he knows which streets are open and how to get around.

"I don't think it's a very good idea for the kids. I'll go, but they should stay home."

"Stay home and do what?"

"Pack up stuff to take back, watch a DVD, whatever. I just don't think that seeing the devastation would be helpful to them, and might even cause them problems."

"Our kids will be fine. They are well adjusted and it won't bother them."

"No, I think it might bother them."

"Then why did you drive back here?"

"Mainly so the kids, especially John, could be home for a couple of days. This house is an oasis to them. This is home. You didn't see John crying every night, and begging to come home. And Sam wanted to come get her stuff. I don't think either one wants to go on the misery tour."

Rich leaves the decision up to the kids. It's unclear if they decide to come along because they want to, or are afraid to stay home alone.

Rich easily passes through the National Guard checkpoint at the Clearview Parkway and Airline Highway intersection. The guards look a little puzzled to find two kids in the back seat but wave us on. We turn onto Veterans Boulevard and see the National Guard holding assault rifles in front of Clearview Mall. Every building along Veterans Boulevard has some degree of damage. The metal Storehouse roof is wrapped around the power lines, and a pink barbeque truck painted like a pig is lying on its side in a parking lot. A number of stores and businesses look ransacked. I see a lot of damage that was caused by Katrina, and a lot of damage that was not caused by the storm.

We pass Lakeside Mall, where additional National Guardsmen are positioned around the parking lot. We get as far as the 17th Street Canal, which was breached on August 29th, and get out of the car. The water on the street ahead is still almost as deep as the street signs. Airboats are launching from the street into the water, and National Guardsmen and Chicago police are patrolling the area. We see a canoe being rowed by people who somehow have made their way back to check on their property.

The scene is surreal. Although the water in the lake and the water in the neighborhood have finally equalized, I can't fathom how this water will be drained. I can't imagine the condition of these houses and their contents. They've been under water for ten days.

A flat rowboat pulls in with two men carrying plastic trash bags that jingle when they exit the boat. They look at the two women standing near me and shake their heads. One of the bags contains silver candlesticks and flatware, but they're corroded and there's consensus that they are not salvageable. There was nothing else that could be saved, the men explain. They describe the standing water downstairs, and the mold spreading on the walls, carpet, clothes, and bedding upstairs. The two women are crying now, as one of the men shows what he's filmed on a video camera.

"Let's go," I tell Rich.

We drive up Lake Avenue, parallel to the canal, and pass the old Peyton Place apartments where Rich lived in his single days. We park and walk up the canal levee. Prior voyeurs have left a ramshackle viewing stand consisting of shipping pallets and part of a wood walkway or deck that probably came from one of the nearby seafood restaurants.

From this perch, we can look over the top of the cement levee and see the levee breach on the opposite side of the canal. Part of the levee wall is tipped toward the Lakeview side. There's probably ten feet of water in the adjacent neighborhood.

A procession of helicopters drop sandbags into the gap and fly away. The sandbags look like tiny sugar packets when compared to the massive size of the breach.

We head back home and see a number of pickup trucks coming into New Orleans. None of the traffic lights work, and in many places, they're lying on the ground near the intersections. National Guardsmen or police direct traffic at major intersections, and we're on our own at the other intersections. The guys in the pickups don't know where traffic lights used to be, and buzz through the intersections. Rich nearly gets T-boned at West Napoleon and Clearview.

At the Clearview-Airline intersection, only a few cars are waved through at a time, and we sit and wait our turn. A man in a pickup truck is motioning me to lower my window.

"Do you have any trees down that you need cut up?" he asks. He tells me he's from Florida and is fully insured.

"No, we're good," I tell him.

This is the beginning of the yahoo invasion, when every Tom, Dick, and Harry with a chainsaw and a pickup truck make their way to Louisiana "to help"—or rather, cash in. Everyone seems to have trees down, so they go house to house looking for work.

Small signs, most handmade and some professionally done, have appeared at major intersections to let people know what's open. "Shell Station now open" says one. "Mr. Binky's Adult Superstore Now Open!" says another.

Two men are standing at our door when we get back to our house. They've noticed my Tahoe in the driveway and our downed trees, and say they can buzz up the trees for just $500 cash. And they can do the work *right now,* provided, of course, that we have the cash. The men are from Tennessee, and when I ask them where they're staying, they point to their truck. Motels and hotels are not yet open and most of the city still does not have power. People who live in New Orleans cannot get back to check on their property—we're supposed to have a phased-in return—yet these guys are getting in.

"Maybe they were really robbers!" says John. That actually crossed my mind when I saw the men standing at our door.

We work on our yard ourselves, and take off the plywood we had put on the front windows. We use it to block the gaps in our battered fence in the back yard. Every time I pass the pine tree in our pool, I wonder how we're going to get it out. Much of it's submerged in the water, so it must weigh a ton.

We're pulling branches to our growing pile by the street when another pickup slows down and stops. They'll clear our yard for $900 and they take credit cards, they tell us. How in the world do they take credit cards? They tell me they phone in the information to their office in Texas.

"Your cell phone works?" I ask. Apparently it doesn't work in New Orleans but works in Baton Rouge, which is an hour away and where they're staying. We decline their help and I point to our neighbors' houses, saying that they're all not home so there's no need to stop there. Like John, I hope these guys are in fact tree guys, and not burglars.

Rich and I press on with dragging branches to the street, and a third pickup truck stops. Rich drops his branch and puts his hand in his empty back pocket to signify "I'm armed." The driver and his teenage son stand on the street.

"May I come onto your property, sir?" the man asks.

"Sure," says Rich, keeping his hand behind him.

The man raises both arms to show he's not armed and his son does the same. Rich takes his hand out of his pocket and shakes the man's hand, and then the son's. The man is from Metairie, and it turns out that his wife works for one of the oncologists in town. He tells us he stayed during Katrina and is now looking for work, and says that he can clear the downed trees from our driveway for $300. He looks at the back yard and shakes his head. You're going to need a tree company for that, he says.

The man and his son finish clearing our driveway and yard just as Bobby, Rich's partner in his surgery practice, his wife Sharon, and their dog Tyson pull in. They've been in Atlanta for almost two weeks.

"We came straight here because we had to come in from the west," Bobby tells us. "How's the hospital look?"

"It's all right," says Rich. "Had water around it for a day or two but never closed. There are maybe thirty patients in there, and the hospital is providing basic services only. They have some of those medical cases from the Superdome and Convention Center, and they have a few of the people who stayed in Lakeview and nearly drowned or have big time medical problems. Joe was A-team and Ray and I have relieved him. Ray's at the hospital today, and I'm covering tomorrow. You can cover Friday. We have an air mattress in the medical staff office for all of us to sleep on. Ray's staying here when he's not at the hospital."

Sharon asks if they can stay the night. She's not sure if they have electricity at their house in Old Metairie, and they're pooped from their twelve-hour drive back, which normally takes eight. Of course you can stay, I tell her.

"How does our office look?" Bobby asks.

"It's good except that one of the windows in your office blew out, and there's some water in there. But no major damage."

"Have you heard from any of the girls in the office?"

"No, have you?"

"No."

"Cell phones still don't work, but there's a special phone at the hospital that works if you need a phone. And there's Internet at the hospital."

Bobby asks if Rich thinks he can get to his house to check on it in the morning.

"I don't know. There's still a lot of standing water over that way."

Unlike our dogs that don't seem to listen at all, Tyson sits up in the back seat when Bobby calls his name and follows Bobby into our house.

As Tyson saunters in, all eyes are on his large, swinging testicles. Boxer dogs have big balls, Rich helpfully tells our kids. The kids are mesmerized, and John asks if our dogs even have testicles.

Buddy and Jack appear at the door, and just as I'm about to say that Buddy is a teddy bear, but watch out for Jack, Jack takes a big bite out of Tyson's swinging package. Tyson winces and takes off for the kitchen with Jack in hot pursuit.

We all swing into action as Jack and Tyson growl and circle one another. Buddy sheepishly stands at the sidelines looking on. Rich puts my thick oven mitts on both of his hands and dives in to retrieve Jack from Tyson's underbelly. Bobby has Tyson by his collar, pulls him away, and deposits him in the guest room. "Bad dog!" says John as he shakes his finger at Jack.

"Vietnamese restaurant, no question about that," says Rich.

Sharon has brought us two bottles of wine and two MREs (single serving, military-issued meals ready to eat). One is chicken and noodles and the other is cheese manicotti. The meals heat on their own by bursting the bottom of the thick plastic pouches they're packed in. I pour the chicken and noodles onto a paper plate.

"Looks like throw-up," John announces. And actually, it does. The manicotti, on the other hand, looks pretty good. I also heat up some soup in the microwave, and attempt to make spaghetti using boiled water from the microwave and water heated in the oven. It comes out very hard and starchy, but it's edible, especially when doused in sauce. I tell Sharon that we have a gas cooktop but there's no gas, and that I'm going to add a one-burner electric hot plate to my hurricane prep list for next time. If there will ever be a next time—I'm not sure I want to stay in hurricane country.

Both of the MREs have crackers and tiny bottles of Tabasco sauce. The chicken and noodles MRE comes with Skittles candy, which John says is the reward for being able to eat the throw-up. John divides the Skittles equally among all of us at the table. The manicotti MRE has a piece of lemon poppy seed cake, which the kids refuse. Sharon and I devour it in a couple of bites, and push our Skittles allotment toward John and Samantha.

John gets in our king sized bed with us, so that Samantha can get in his twin bed, so that Ray can sleep in Samantha's double bed, and Bobby, Sharon, and Tyson can sleep in the guest room.

DAY 12

Thursday, September 8th

"I DON'T WANT to go back to Houston. I want to stay here with Dad," John wails. I tell him he needs to come with me, that New Orleans isn't quite ready to have kids back here, and that he needs to go to school.

"You're letting Buddy and Jack stay with Dad. They get to stay in New Orleans. Why can't I?"

"They're dogs, and they don't need to go to school," I tell him, although Jack could certainly benefit from being enrolled in obedience school.

Rich takes John aside to talk to him, and a few minutes later, John climbs into the back of my Tahoe and we set off for Houston.

The traffic was horrendous through Baton Rouge on our trip here, so I decide to avoid the state capital by going south to take Highway 90 over to Lafayette where it intersects with I-10. We have to stop a few times when John feels carsick, but each time he perks up and Samantha praises him for not puking.

After making quick stops for lunch and an early dinner, we enter the city limits of Houston around 9 p.m. Although Carol has given us an open invitation to stay at her house, it's late and I see a vacancy sign at a La Quinta, which the sign says is Spanish for high-speed Internet. Rooms for people from Louisiana are half-priced, the desk clerk says.

I connect our laptop to the Ethernet cord in the room. Several email messages have a link to "Wake Me Up When September Ends," a song recorded by the band Green Day. The song was originally released in June, and re-recorded in early September with Katrina news sound bites added. Although the basis for the song is the death of lead singer Billie Joe Armstrong's father, who died when Armstrong was a child, the song has become a tribute song when the band dedicated this version to Hurricane Katrina survivors. The lyrics resonate with me and I listen to the song three times in row.

DAY 13

Friday, September 9th

JOHN IS ONCE again thrilled to see a waffle maker in the breakfast room and proclaims that it's his second waffle in his whole entire life that is "real" and has not come out of a toaster. We go back to our room where I tell the kids to start reading one of the books they've brought from home. Their school calls it "free reading," which means reading something that is not required to be read.

I use our computer to look for apartments with a short-term lease. I call each complex and confirm that they have apartments available, but I'm told I should come in as soon as possible because "those Louisiana people are coming in all the time now." I make a list of three places to look at. When I check my email, there is no further word on the kids' school starting an extension school in Houston, so I jot down the names of schools that New Orleans kids have enrolled in. I call each one, only to be told that there are no more openings.

Samantha's camp friend Lauren goes to Spring Branch Middle School, which would be perfect for our kids since

John is in sixth grade and Samantha is in eighth grade, and both kids could go to school there. However, in order to go to the school, you must live in the school's geographic zone. The zone is all residential—no apartments.

We pack up the Tahoe and look at the first of three apartments. It's fine, so I ask about the school zone. We head to Grady Middle School so I can enroll the kids there, but there are no spots available in the eighth grade.

We head to the second apartment I found online. Before looking at it, I ask what school zone it's in. Grady. Ugh.

We stop at Amy's Ice Cream, mainly because they have Internet access there. The tip jar has a sign that says that all of the money in the jar is going to Katrina victims.

I use the laptop to search Houston schools and learn that over 5,000 students have already enrolled in public and private schools in Houston. *People* magazine calls them Generation K. Over 200,000 refugees are estimated to now reside in Houston, and it will be three to six months before Gulf Coast residents can expect to return home because of the mass destruction and power outages.

Power outages at the Aquarium of the Americas on the Mississippi riverfront in New Orleans have left many fish and aquatic creatures dead. The staff there were ordered to evacuate, and exterminated the piranhas before they left in order to prevent them from getting loose and reproducing in the river. Prior to leaving, the staff frantically arranged to have the penguins and otters flown to the Monterey Bay Aquarium in California. The privately chartered flight was financed mostly by actress and animal lover Betty White. For two of the penguins, Buck and Emma, it was a homecoming of sorts because they were originally on exhibit at the Monterey Bay Aquarium before being sent east to New Orleans.

Lauren's mom Carol finds out that I may be able to enroll our kids at the school her daughter attends if we don't have an address and have someone in the school zone vouch for us. Carol does this for us, and I write "we're moving around" where it says "address" on the enrollment forms.

Samantha, John, and I approach the counter in the school office when our names are called. There are two other families, presumably from somewhere on the Gulf Coast, sitting in the little school desks in the hallway with us, filling out paperwork.

"Do you have their birth certificates?" I'm asked.

"No, they're in our bank box. We left on a Sunday morning."

"Do you have any school records with you?"

"No."

"Will you be able to get them?"

"I don't think so because their school has seven feet of water in it, and I saw in an email that the computer back-up place also flooded, so all records were destroyed."

"Do you have their immunization records?"

"No."

"Are your kids up to date on their immunizations?"

"Yes."

"Do either of your kids have special needs, like ADD or ADHD?"

"No."

"Okay, then, bring them in on Monday morning so we

can get them tested and figure out which classes they need to be in. Have a nice weekend!"

Rich and I are eternally grateful to Carol, our guardian angel, who has gone to bat for us. The kids now have a school.

Samantha checks her email while I call Suzanne, who according to the email she sent, now has a cell phone with a 713 (Houston) area code. Her son Colin is one of John's best friends.

Suzanne has found an apartment and asks if I might be interested in an apartment in the same complex. She booked two apartments, thinking that her mother-in-law would want the other, but her mother-in-law has decided to live in Dallas. It would be wonderful for John to have a friend nearby, so I take the apartment sight unseen.

The two-bedroom apartment is on the second floor, and Suzanne's apartment is just across the parking lot. We're on the end of the building, next to the brick barricade that hides the dumpsters. An adjacent fence divides the complex from the shopping center next door.

We unpack my Tahoe and bring in two airbeds, bedding, and pots and pans that we've brought from our New Orleans house. The larger of the two bedrooms has a walk-in closet, and John decides the closet will be his room.

The kids go off to explore the apartment complex. They're back in no time at all.

"How's the pool look?" I ask.

"It doesn't have any water in it," they reply.

Samantha turns on the laptop and connects to the Internet. All of the available networks are unsecured and named things like "CP" or "starfish," and somehow she's connected even though we don't yet have, but plan to get, an Internet provider. Sam starts IM'ing her friends.

We learn that most have started school. The Noble twins are in Virginia. Ian is enrolled at River Oaks in Houston. Another Ian is going to fly to Connecticut to enroll at the Rectory. Our neighbor Taylor is now in Vicksburg, where her mother has been sent to work.

Rich calls to ask about the apartment and school situation. He's done nothing more than give tetanus shots at the hospital for the past two days.

John sits by the window and watches for Colin to come home from school. He's ecstatic when he sees Colin get out of the car and bolts out the door.

DAY 14

Saturday, September 10th

AFTER A NIGHT spent sleeping crosswise on the two air mattresses pushed together, the kids and I go shopping for food and household supplies at Target. On the way back, we stop by a furniture rental place to find out how much a couch, a mattress set, and a dining table and chairs would be. The rental price seems high, so I pick up a copy of the *Houston Chronicle* and look for used furniture. Buying a used mattress creeps me out, so I look at ads for new furniture. There are several offering deep discounts for "Katrina victims."

John stays with Colin while Samantha and I head out to find furniture. We get a mattress set for my room, a couch, and a small square dining table and four chairs. I also get a plastic folding table for my desktop computer that we brought back with us from New Orleans.

John and Samantha both have air mattresses to sleep on, and I have a bed. We have air conditioning, running water, food in the fridge, and the kids have a school to go to. Life is good.

DAY 15

Sunday, September 11th

IT'S THE FOUR year anniversary of 9-11. I unroll the American flag that I bought at Target and place it in the flag bracket outside our front door. I had hesitated for a moment, wondering if it was something we could afford, and then put it in our cart.

DAY 16

Monday, September 12th

IT'S BEEN SEVENTEEN days since our kids were in school, and today is officially the start of a new school year for them. The 1,200 kids at Spring Branch Middle School have been in school for almost a month. John barely eats any breakfast, and Samantha spends an inordinate amount of time doing her hair.

It's pep talk time in the car as I drive the kids to their new school.

"You're not going to be the only new kids at this school," I tell them. "You'll probably see those other kids we saw Friday. When I was on my computer this morning, MSNBC said that 130,000 kids have been displaced because of Katrina. So you're not alone."

They're both looking down and visibly nervous as we enter the school's office. Sam and John are whisked away for testing, and I'm told they'll meet with their counselors and start classes today. I can pick them up at 3:20 p.m.

I go back to the apartment and Suzanne comes over.

She's heard that her house has flooded, but only the bottom floor playroom was affected. Her mother-in-law's house in uptown New Orleans has flooded, and she'll be coordinating the repairs there. We share what we've heard about mutual friends and where they are now, and wonder if the kids' school will ever reopen.

I tell Suzanne that Samantha and John are now enrolled at Spring Branch Middle School. I'm worried about how well they'll adjust since there are four hundred kids in each grade. Our kids and Colin and his younger brother all had attended a school in New Orleans with fifty to sixty in each grade. Suzanne's boys are going to a small private school in Houston, but even so, are having a challenging time adapting to a new school environment, along with everything else going on.

Samantha and John are very quiet on the ride home from school.

"So, how'd it go?" I ask.

"Okay," says Samantha. John remains silent.

"John, how was school?" I ask.

"Okay," he says.

After a few minutes of silence, Samantha asks John why he wasn't at lunch.

"I was there," he says.

"I didn't see you. I looked around for you but didn't see you."

"I was toward the back, close to where the food line is," he tells her.

"I walked all around there with Allison. I made her walk with me to look for you."

They talk back and forth, and it becomes clear that Samantha was thinking she was having lunch with the entire school, when in fact she was eating with only the kids in her grade.

On the way into the apartment, Sam and John hand me a bunch of papers that I sort through at our tiny dining table. The first thing is the "What You Should Know About Joining a Gang" brochure. Next are the school's dress code, a flyer for the football game on Friday, and their ID cards from the National Center for Missing and Exploited Children. At the bottom are copies of their school schedules.

"What's IPC?" I ask Samantha, who is already IM'ing her friends to compare new school stories.

"Intermediate something or another," she says. "It's a hard class."

John asks if he can go over to Colin's and scoots out the door. We don't have cable, and don't even have a TV, so I get on the computer and go to the New Orleans news sites as well as CNN and MSNBC. I see a video clip of House Majority Leader Tom DeLay visiting the Reliant Center, which is now a refugee center next to the Astrodome. He goes up to a group of New Orleans kids and says, "Now tell me the truth, boys, isn't this kind of fun?" The boys nod yes but looked perplexed.

"Tom, Tom, Tom," I say out loud to the computer screen, as if he can hear me. "Fun? *Fun?* Does it look like it's fun in there?" While I'm all for making the best of a bad situation, DeLay's comments don't sit well with me at all.

Officials in New Orleans announced the first "look and

leave" opportunity, and footage of cars parked along Airline Highway on the outskirts of New Orleans is shown. Dozens of people plan to wait there overnight so that they'll be among the first to return to their homes tomorrow. Those interviewed say they don't know what to expect when they get home.

DAY 17

Tuesday, September 13th

JOHN WAKES UP and says he has a stomachache and can't go to school. Samantha falls down the stairs when she goes outside to see if she needs a sweater. The kitchen sink doesn't drain, and the towel bar in the bathroom has fallen off.

I tell John he is going to school, and to go to the school nurse if he still feels sick, and then wonder if the school even has a school nurse.

John extracts his folded schedule from his pants pocket and lays it out on the table. He grabs a pen from my makeshift desk and crudely draws a map on the back as his eyebrows furrow in concentration. He tells me that he went into the wrong classroom yesterday, got there late, and the teacher blurted out, "Oh great, another one" as he walked in. As he's talking, I can tell he was mortified. "And then when the teacher saw my paper and saw I was in the wrong class, she practically pushed me out the door," he says.

When I drop the kids off at school, I see John pat his

front pocket to make sure his schedule and map are still in there.

I call my parents to update them. "You can talk to a man on the moon, but you can't talk to someone in New Orleans! We have been trying to call you I don't know how many times!" my father says. "And look at that mess down there. Still! Where are all the people going to go?"

I tell them that many are here in Houston. He asks how long we'll be in Houston, but I don't know. He asks about Rich and his work. I tell him that Rich isn't doing much at the hospital and that it's still open only for basic services. His medical office building remains closed.

"I keep going to the local news and message threads on the computer," I tell him. "It sounds like people don't want to go back to New Orleans if there are no schools, and no grocery stores, and no jobs. And the schools and grocery stores and businesses are saying they won't reopen unless people come back."

"What's Richard going to do?" he asks.

"I don't know," I tell him.

A few minutes later my cell phone rings, and it's my friend Becca calling from Oregon.

"Oh my God, Lisa, I have been trying to call you for days!"

I tell her about our evacuation to Brookhaven, and how we're now in Houston. She tells me I should write a book.

"Bec, this is like childbirth, it's something I'd rather forget," I tell her.

DAY 19

Thursday, September 15th

MY CELL PHONE rings and I don't recognize the number. It's the daughter of a friend of mine. My friend died a couple of years ago, and I've kept in touch with her daughters, mostly through cards sent at Christmastime. She tells me that she and her sister are all right but haven't heard from her sister's husband since he left his house to check on neighbors on the day after Katrina. The neighborhood had flooded, and the two sisters walked to dry ground, where they were picked up by an Army Hummer and taken to the I-10 cloverleaf at Causeway Boulevard. From there, they were bused to the airport and told to get in a line. She and her sister stuck together and boarded a plane. Only when they were onboard were they told that they were going to a relief shelter in Little Rock. She asks how our family is doing.

When I tell her we're in Houston, she asks for a big favor, which in retrospect wasn't big at all.

I don't want to put off what I've been asked to do, so I go next door to Randalls Food Market for a thick black marker and a piece of white poster board. I pencil out the message for my sign, go over it with the marker, and head to the Astrodome.

Although I've seen footage of this evacuation shelter, seeing it firsthand is at first overwhelming. In order to even enter, I'm asked why I'm here and my purse is searched. Upon seeing row after row after row of cots and bedding, I wonder if I'll be able to walk these aisles and make it to carpool on time.

Most of the people are sitting in their spots, and each family or group is identifiable by the closeness of their cots relative to the next group of cots. I can't fathom sleeping in this place night after night.

I'm not quite sure how to do this, but see a number of other people, who like me, have come here with signs. We hold our "Have you seen [name]" or "Looking for [name]" signs in front of us as we walk, usually at chest height, but sometimes over our heads to stretch out our bent elbows. Fortunately, people look up as I walk by and some shake their heads no.

I walk and walk and walk and walk. Up one row, down another.

I walk over to the Reliant Center, an exhibition hall that has now become an evacuation shelter and has thousands of people staying there. It opened when the Astrodome reached its capacity of 15,000 evacuees.

I walk up and down the rows of cots at the Reliant Center, and recognize some of the sign-holders from the other building. I cross paths with a woman who tells me that there are several other community shelters open in Houston, with about 4,000 people in them. She wonders if she'll ever find her relatives.

"Hey lady," yells a guy at the end of a row, "you mean the dude who works at Acme Oyster House?"

"I'm not sure," I tell him as I fish my cell phone from my purse.

I make a quick call. Wrong guy.

I walk the Reliant Park shelter for an hour and a half. On the way out, I call my friend's daughter to say that it doesn't look like her brother-in-law is here, and tell her I've posted a message on the already-swamped message board.

Louis Armstrong New Orleans International Airport has reopened for commercial flights, with flights to Atlanta on Delta Airlines, and flights to Memphis on Northwest. For the past three weeks, the airport allowed only military and humanitarian flights.

President Bush is on TV again, and I watch the live video on my computer. This time he's in New Orleans, standing in front of St. Louis Cathedral in Jackson Square. "There is no way to imagine America without New Orleans. This great city will rise again," he says.

DAY 20

Friday, September 16th

MY JOURNAL ENTRY for the day consists of three words: we have ants. Ants have invaded our apartment in both the kitchen and bathroom, and climb like little armies up the corners of the cabinets. We have no food out, so I don't understand how this is happening. It's been raining a lot, maybe that's it. I walk next door to Randalls and buy cans of ant spray. I fumigate the rooms, and watch the ants move spastically and then no longer move at all.

DAY 21

Saturday, September 17th

JOHN HAS GONE over to Colin's to play, and Samantha wants to go out for lunch. Rich and I have been keeping our money worries from the kids, and I've been watching every penny. Although Rich's medical office building remains closed, he received an email informing him that the September rent was overdue. Patients at the hospital are mainly construction workers and debris-hauling crews without health insurance, so there is little to no income from this work. Our expenses are higher than we ever could have imagined, and we now have two of everything: two homes, two electric bills, two water bills, and two natural gas bills.

I take Sam to La Madeleine where we each have a cup of soup; $3.99 x 2 plus tax. We eat three pieces of bread loaded with butter and drink the water from the tap. Samantha is surprised that I don't have a Diet Pepsi, and I tell her I'm trying to cut down on caffeine, when in fact, I haven't had a Diet Pepsi since Katrina. They're just too expensive now.

Samantha reveals that she used to think that being the

new kid at school was a good thing, and that being new made you the center of attention, at least for a little while anyway. She's feeling like she's an outcast, especially when she hears teachers talking about "the Louisiana kids." She also tells me that John is being bullied at school.

"By who?" I ask as I feel my intestines tightening.

"The kid with the mustache."

"Whaddya mean, the kid with the mustache? John's only eleven!" My voice is rising and the people at the next table look over toward us.

"It's that kid in his grade who got held back four or five times."

I interrogate John when we get back to the apartment. He plays down how he's been treated, but it's clear that Mustache Kid is no friend of John's. I think I'm more upset about it than he is.

Suzanne calls and asks if Colin, his younger brother Nicholas, and their dog Apache can spend the night. She and Gregory want to go back to New Orleans to check on things. She also has John and Colin's classmate William for the weekend, so he'll be staying with us as well. William's dad has gone to Morgan City, where he is now assigned to work, to find housing.

The four boys and Apache get the living room area as their bedroom and are giggling far into the night. I think about John being in school with Colin and William since they were five, and how difficult it has to be for a shy, quiet kid like John to go from a school with fifty kids in a grade to a school with four hundred in each grade. I'm grateful John has some of his New Orleans friends here.

DAY 22

Sunday, September 18th

THE FIVE KIDS eat a ton of pancakes, and since I don't have any dog food, Apache has pancakes as well. Samantha alternates IM'ing with getting her homework done, and says the IPC course is definitely the hardest class she's ever taken. She's also taking what used to be called Home Economics, but is now Skills for Daily Living or something like that. Samantha is in a group of four that have the harvest gold stove, and she's happy that one of the four in the group has detention, so that means more food for the other three.

The death toll is now 883 in Louisiana, 219 in Mississippi, and 18 in Florida, Georgia, and Alabama. In St. Bernard Parish, just southeast of New Orleans, it's determined that only five of over 25,000 homes did not flood. Katrina's eye had passed over the eastern portion of the parish and sent a 25-foot storm surge into the "MR GO" river outlet, which in turn destroyed the levees there.

DAY 23

Monday, September 19th

THE NURSING EDUCATION lectures I had scheduled for September were either rescheduled or provided by other nurses I work with. I spend most of the day changing my airline tickets for upcoming lectures. Although the airlines that I have tickets for have cancelled all flights into and out of New Orleans, all of these carriers, except for American, refuse to refund my money and insist on charging a change fee to rebook my tickets out of Houston.

I write in my journal as I am on perpetual hold. Nineteen minutes waiting to talk to US Airways, a 35-minute wait to talk to the now defunct America West, and a 45-minute wait to talk to United. I receive a refund of $301.80 from American in less than four minutes, no problem, no questions asked.

Cheryl calls from San Antonio. We talk for over an hour about our money worries, worries about our kids and how they're adjusting to their new schools, and being separated from our husbands. Wayne has gone back to New Orleans to attempt to retrieve cell samples and research documents from his office at the medical school. Cheryl tells me that just when you think you can't possibly cry anymore, the tears come easily. I know what she means.

I switch on the computer and scan the Houston and New Orleans news. The New Orleans Saints football team plays their first game of the season tonight, against the New York Giants. Although it's a home game, it's being played at Giants Stadium. The Saints have been in San Jose, California, where they stayed for a few days after flying there for a preseason game against the Oakland Raiders, and they're moving to practice facilities in San Antonio where owner Tom Benson started his car dealership empire. For the rest of the season, home games are going to be split between LSU's Tiger Stadium in Baton Rouge and the Alamodome in San Antonio.

The National Weather Service is tracking Tropical Storm Rita, which is anticipated to make landfall around the Houston area on Saturday.

I snap off the computer, grab my purse, and head to the grocery store to get a case of water and food while there's still some in the store.

DAY 24

Tuesday, September 20th

ON THE WAY to school, I notice for the first time that our kids are talking about other kids in the past tense. "Mallory was a defender on our soccer team," says Sam as she gives me updates on her New Orleans friends.

I go to my computer, as I do every day now, but today I mark the National Hurricane Center website as a favorite. It's unbelievable that I'm having to concern myself with yet another hurricane this year. Tropical Storm Rita is now a category 2 hurricane, and the Center adds that they may run out of names for hurricanes this year.

I'm getting edgy about this hurricane headed for Houston and decide to go walk around a mall. A hair salon has a sign that says 50% off for people with a Louisiana driver's license. That would be me. I timidly ask how much a haircut would be with the discount. Ten dollars, I'm told. I've never really thought twice about having my hair cut before, but now think about the ten dollars plus tip and decide to walk around the mall.

I look at my reflection in the glass of the stores as I walk by them. My hair is incredibly shaggy, and I consider cutting it myself, but then remember when I did that in seventh grade and how I sobbed for weeks afterward.

I sweep some coral blush across my cheeks and try out some lipstick at a department store counter. When I look in the mirror, I hardly recognize myself. Despite the makeup, I have dark circles under both eyes and look pale and gaunt. I look like I have some disease eroding my body. Maybe a haircut will help, especially since I'll be back to work in two weeks.

I go back to the hair salon, and the receptionist asks how we fared in Katrina. I'm used to giving the condensed version now. We evacuated, our house is fine, we are ever so grateful to the people in Houston, and we're not sure how long we'll be here.

My stylist comes to the reception area and tells me that I'm her twelfth Louisiana haircut this week. She says that people have actually been shaking in her chair. She fiddles with my part and its dark roots, looks up at the clock, and tells me that she's going to perk up my highlights free of charge. "It's the least I can do," she tells me.

The kids tell me I look great when I pick them up from school. And I feel a lot better too. It's amazing what a haircut, and an act of kindness, can do.

Samantha tells me that one of her new friends has asked her soccer coach if Samantha could join the team, even though the season already has started, and the coach said yes! Samantha is excited about playing soccer again, but her face quickly deflates.

"I don't have any cleats. They're back in New Orleans,"

she says. I tell her that perhaps she can practice in her Nikes, and Dad can bring her cleats when he comes over next Thursday to be with them while I fly to Chicago to work.

There is a ton of traffic on the roads, and the clogged entrances to grocery stores are causing much of the back-up. Houstonians are stocking up for the weekend ahead.

"Sam, what did you draw for the counselor today?" asks John. Counselor? My ears perk up.

"Brookhaven," she says. "What did you draw?"

"The water in New Orleans. The dead dog we saw floating. Those people crying in the boats."

I can't stand it. "What are you guys talking about?"

They tell me that the Louisiana kids had to go to the counselor again (again?!) to talk about their feelings about Hurricane Rita. Because no one wanted to talk, they were instructed to draw a picture of their memories of Katrina.

"So, Sam, what did you draw for Brookhaven?" I ask.

"Being in the bathroom with the motel flooding, and the windows blowing out."

I can only imagine the face of the counselor when she saw those drawings.

DAY 25

Wednesday, September 21st

THE AIR IS less humid today, and it's breezy—telltale signs that Rita is on her way. Here we go again.

Rita is now a category 4 hurricane with winds of 135 mph. Rita is still headed west, toward Houston. A mandatory evacuation has been ordered for Galveston. People in the New Orleans area are encouraged to evacuate because of concern that the storm surge could once again inundate the city with water. Standing water remains in some parts of New Orleans, despite the fact that it's been nearly a month since Hurricane Katrina.

The Louisiana refugees at the Houston Astrodome and adjacent Reliant Center are being moved, with many being sent north to the Dallas area. The few refugees still in the Superdome and Convention Center in New Orleans are in the process of being evacuated.

Erica calls and says, "Jim Cantore is in Houston. So you know it's gonna be bad there!"

I tell her our plan is to go home since it will likely be

several days before school resumes in Houston, plus our house is not in the storm surge danger zone in New Orleans. I talk about the predicted wind speeds, and when I casually say it's a "cat 4" hurricane, Erica says I sound just like Jim Cantore and that I've been watching The Weather Channel far too long.

Suzanne calls and tells me they're flying to Long Boat Key in Florida today, and taking their dog Apache with them. "We should have gone there in the first place, before Katrina," she says.

I look up flights to Baton Rouge and learn that they're all full or already cancelled. I shudder at the thought of evacuating again by car, but realize that we'll need to pack up and go.

I drive around for about half an hour until I find a gas station with gas, and fill up my Tahoe. I also make a stop at Randalls on the way home, and buy an additional case of water bottles and enough non-perishable food to last us several days.

When I pick up the kids in the afternoon, they tell me that school is closed for the next two days. I tell them that we're heading home to New Orleans very early in the morning. They can sleep the entire way if they want.

My cousin Virginia sends me an email inviting us to her ranch in Los Lunas in New Mexico. She says that gas is already in short supply there, but our kids can ride her horses to school.

John starts his homework, which consists of defining the word "evacuation" and writing one to two pages about his upcoming evacuation experiences.

"Hey Mom," he calls, as he sits at my computer. "Did

you know that there are two definitions for evacuation? The first one is 'the action of evacuating a person or a place' and the second one is 'the action of emptying the bowels.' Do you think my teacher wants me to write about the first definition or the second?" he asks with a laugh.

"They're pretty much the same thing," yells Samantha from the couch.

DAY 26

Thursday, September 22nd

JOHN AND SAM are groggy as I lead them to my Tahoe in the darkness. It's 4:25 a.m. when I pull out of our parking space. The kids are in the back seat, bundled in blankets and pillows. The first half hour of driving out of Houston is a breeze.

The traffic going east comes to a crawl, and I see a group of people pushing a car on the side of the interstate. There's little to no traffic coming in to Houston. Everyone is headed out of town.

We plod on, the sun comes up, and the kids wake up at 8:30 a.m. I've had the radio as my company, and hear that 2.5 to 3.7 million people are in the process of evacuating, making it the largest evacuation in United States history.

Rich's cousin's wife Suzy, who had invited us to their place north of Houston, calls me.

"I can't believe I got through," is the first thing she says and we talk a bit about her being able to call my NOLA 504 area code, and how she's unable to call cell phones in the 713

(Houston) area code. I tell her I can't believe we're evacuating again.

"Rita was tracking to the west, but now it's turning north a little, that's the latest," she says, and she again invites us up to her place. I tell her that I'm inching—literally—my way toward Beaumont and that our plan is to continue on home, and thank her for calling again to invite us to her house.

The traffic is so slow-going that when I see a sign for Port Arthur via Highway 73, I look at my trusty Rand McNally *Atlas* and see that I can take Highway 73 to Port Arthur and follow it up to Bridge City and into Orange, where it connects with I-10. We would bypass Beaumont and hopefully bypass some of this traffic.

I take the exit and pull into Shipley's Donuts at 9:30 a.m. We're amazed it's open because they're in the process of boarding the place up. We've gone 89 miles in 5 hours and 49 minutes, so I make the kids do the math since they're out of school yet again. They scribble the long division in their school notebooks and tell me we've averaged 15.3 miles per hour. John says he can ride his bike faster than that.

"It looks like it's turning east," says the woman behind the cash register. She pulls two little cartons of chocolate milk from the refrigerator case, puts them on the counter next to our donut box, and nods toward the kids. "More than likely gonna go bad anyway, so take these."

We use the restroom, and eat our donuts in the car because I'm anxious to get on the road again. The sun is blazing, so I have the air conditioning blasting as we leave Port Arthur.

We're moseying along and following the signs for Bridge City. As its name implies, there's a bridge that goes over the Neches River that we need to cross. We're almost to the bridge and my heart sinks. State Police cars are blocking its entrance; the bridge is closed because of the high winds.

The line of cars ahead of us is turning around and we wait our turn. I now have three-quarters of a tank of gas, it is 99 degrees outside the car, and my engine is beginning to overheat.

We backtrack toward Port Arthur, and I see from the map that I'll need to head northwest to get to Beaumont and I-10. It's very slow going now, as many people apparently decided to take the same "short-cut."

At 11 a.m., we've gone 103.5 miles. In six hours.

Suzy calls again and asks where we are. The pause on her end of the line tells me that she's mentally calculating our progress. "You said Port Arthur?" she asks. Yes, I tell her.

"Wow, I thought you'd be farther along than that. But from what I'm seeing on TV, every road is gridlocked." I tell her that I can certainly confirm that and let her know how much I appreciate her calls.

I stop in a deserted church parking lot so that we all can pee in the bushes around the building, and I turn off the Tahoe for a few minutes so that the engine can cool down. We sit in the shadow of the church's entrance doors for about half an hour and get back on the road.

I hear on the radio that Hurricane Rita's path has taken a more northerly route now, and is headed for the Port Arthur, Texas to Cameron, Louisiana area. Which is right where we are.

Dear God, dear God, dear God, please get us out of here.

We continue on at a snail's pace. We're just a few miles from the Gulf of Mexico.

This is a bad, bad, bad situation we got ourselves into.

I wonder if we stayed on I-10, where would we be by now? Would we have been able to get home to New Orleans? Or would we still be sitting right there on I-10 an hour east of Houston? And there are so many people sitting on I-10 and sitting here around me. Where are we all going to go?

At 11:57 a.m., something or another has halted the traffic. We sit idle for 54 minutes.

It is 105 degrees outside. I've turned my Tahoe off, hoping to cool the engine some. But it's only roasted us.

I am hot, I am tired, and I feel like crying out of sheer frustration. The kids are sweaty and worn out. They're very quiet because they know Mom's upset and about to have a nervous breakdown.

We creep along and I have the kids do the math. What's 2.3 miles in 24 minutes, I ask them.

"Five point seven five miles an hour," calculates John. "I definitely can ride my bike faster than this. Actually, I think I can walk faster."

Suzy calls again and it's like a crisis hotline call, only in reverse. I am so grateful to hear her voice; how did she know to call right at a time when I'm on the brink of losing it? Her voice is comforting and she asks where we are. When I tell her we're still near Port Arthur, she says that's where we were three hours ago. Yes, that's correct I tell her. This evacuation is as slow as Katrina's. She tells me to get out of there because Rita is now headed straight for Port Arthur.

At 2:07 p.m., as tears run down my face and I frantically wipe them away so the kids don't see them, I see the sign for the interstate and it's only 3¼ miles away! My spirits bound. The Tahoe's engine temperature is now 240 degrees.

At 3:30 p.m. on the nose, I'm at the entrance ramps for I-10. The traffic going east is not moving at all. There is very little traffic heading west, back to Houston. I have half a tank of gas and my engine temp stays at 260 degrees, which is the highest number on the dial.

We'll never make it to New Orleans, and since Rita is shifting toward the east, away from Houston, going west makes sense. It has been a nerve-wracking day, so when I'm faced with the choice to go east or west, I pick west.

Almost everyone's going east. The traffic back-up on I-10 is just horrendous. As I keep driving, I notice that there's a surprising number of cars and trucks headed toward Houston with us, and I see others join us when we reach some grassy areas and cars cross over to leave the exodus and join the defeated.

Once again, cell phones are not working well. Samantha is able to text some of her friends and discovers that many are stuck in their cars on I-10, fairly close to Houston.

I'm anxious to get back to our apartment, crack open the Tanqueray, and go to sleep. It feels great to see sixty on the speedometer. My head really hurts. It may be the heat, or it may be the four donuts I ate earlier in the day. In any event, I squint at the road ahead and it registers that a car is coming toward me in my lane. And coming fast. I glance to the passenger side mirror, and grateful that no one is in that lane, swerve over just in time to avoid a head-on collision.

I have to pull off the interstate to catch my breath and let my pounding heart slow down. I sit with my head down between my knees for a few minutes. The kids are frightened and worried by this. I don't think they realize how close that was.

I look up and see that the trend of driving on the wrong side of the interstate has started. There is no contraflow here. These people have chosen to get on the other side of I-10 to beat the traffic. Don't they realize that there are people like us on this side of the road?

I now drive in the far right lane and hug the shoulder. I can't believe it, but there are cars heading toward us—in both lanes! It's simply chaos here. Has everyone lost their sanity in their anxiousness to get out of town? Where are the State Police?

I soon see where the police are, at about the same time that I realize that there is no one coming toward us on our side of the interstate. We pass a horrible head-on collision and by the looks of it, both cars were going fast.

I have to slow down to pass by it, and attempt to get the kids to look out the window on the other side of the car. I see them staring at the mangled cars instead.

We get back to our apartment at 5:30 p.m., and I burst into tears when I finally put the Tahoe in park and shut it off. The gas level is just above the big "E," yet we've somehow made it back here.

I make myself a gigantic gin and tonic, and try texting Rich to let him know we're back in Houston. He calls from the hospital around 6 p.m., and says that the water is already rising in New Orleans, and that at least six inches of rain and winds of 40-50 mph are expected. He says he's relieved that we haven't been able to make our way there and tells me what I already know, that Rita has taken a more northerly turn and is headed for southwestern Louisiana.

Belief.net is marked as a favorite on my computer, and

I've gotten in the habit of reading its "daily inspiration" every day, usually when I first get up in the morning. We left so early that I didn't have a chance to read it this morning and I read it now. Today's inspiration is: "The really happy man is one who can enjoy the scenery on a detour."

"You have got to be kidding me," I say aloud as I click off the site and try to erase Port Arthur from my memory.

I watch news updates and see the enormous traffic jams out of Houston in all directions. The reporter adds that the people going east are unknowingly heading into the path of the hurricane. The news headlines on the online sites are "Rita Makes the Big Easy Queasy" and "Uneasy in the Big Easy."

I see a clip of Louisiana Governor Blanco encouraging people to evacuate the New Orleans area, and she adds, "For those of you who refuse to leave, put your social security number on your arm in indelible ink."

DAY 27

Friday, September 23rd

BANG, BANG, BANG. I wake up and look out the window to see the door to the dumpster enclosure flinging open and then slamming closed, and then opening again with each gust of wind. I go downstairs to close the latch and encounter our downstairs neighbors at the doorway. They're hearing the same thing. As his wife and I push against the door to hold it closed, Downstairs Guy secures the latch. He then moves two cement blocks, presumably used to hold the doors open for the garbage truck, against the doors and we all go back inside. I tell them to come up if we start to flood, and they tell me to come down if the roof blows off.

I've frozen several plastic bottles of water to use as ice to keep food cold, and then to drink as they thaw. The bathtub, kitchen sink, two plastic trash cans, and a plastic mopping pail are filled with water. I've moved Samantha's air mattress from her room into mine, and put it between the bed and the closet, away from the window. I nailed two blankets over the bedroom window and hope they're strong enough to catch the glass if the windows blow out.

Rich calls my cell phone. It's been a month since Katrina and we have the reverse Katrina situation; calls to and from 504 (New Orleans area code) are able to go through, but calls to and from Houston area codes don't. Rich says that patched levees in New Orleans have just broken and the Ninth Ward is again under water.

Samantha thinks she left her calculator in the car, and I head downstairs to look for it. Missy from the building across the way is walking her dog. The wind is blowing hard and we sweep our hair from our faces as we talk. She tells me that she and her family tried to head west in three cars, but turned around and came back when they couldn't take it any longer. She said she peed in the car into a dog bowl. There was nowhere to go. "Not a bush anywhere, not a tumbleweed, nothing!" she tells me.

I find Sam's calculator on the floor of the back seat. The trees are now swaying and branches are beginning to crack, pop, and hit the ground with a thud. And it's getting darker, which means that rain will soon start to fall.

We still have electricity, so I scramble all of the eggs left in the carton. The kids silently stare out the windows as we eat.

Amazingly, we still have Internet access, so I catch up on the news. An evacuation bus from a Bellaire nursing home is on fire on I-45, and twenty-four people are on the bus.

I read horror stories of people stuck on the road; one is "Escaping the Escape," and a photo shows vehicles stuck at the side of the interstate. The reporter writes that it's an irony for Houstonians to run out of gas since they're at the epicenter of the gas and oil industry.

Another photo is captioned "A shocking sight from on high," and shows people gasping during a flight into Houston when they saw the gridlock below.

There are reports of traveling only 60 miles in fifteen hours. On his blog, Chris Draffkorn writes, "Texas has gone nuts. Never have I seen so many cars on the road all at once. The roads are now a parking lot of overheated cars."

We still have power in the afternoon, although it's very dark outside, the wind is howling, and rain is pelting the windows. We're all wearing multiple layers of clothing, and the kids are wrapped in blankets as they watch *Donny Darko* on the DVD player. You'll thank me later, I tell them, when the air conditioning goes out and it starts to heat up in here.

When the DVD finishes, the kids work on their homework and I watch the news on my computer. There are reports of people dumping their pets at gas stations, including some that died en route. John hears this and asks me to turn off the news.

I go to our kids' New Orleans school's website and learn that families have scattered all over the United States from San Francisco to Boston. Several families are in Florida, presumably at their beach houses. A couple of the teachers have set up what is essentially a one-room schoolhouse in Houston. It's too little, too late for our kids.

Rita has weakened to a category 3 hurricane with 130 mph surface winds. Landfall is predicted between Sabine Pass, Texas and Johnson Bayou, Louisiana. The Houston area is told to expect at least two days of torrential rainfall and wind gusts of 75 mph, starting tonight.

DAY 28

Saturday, September 24th

AT 2:05 A.M., I hear a loud bang followed by silence. The glow of the bedside clock radio is gone, and the air conditioning units are no longer humming. The entire apartment complex is shrouded in darkness.

It is 62 degrees in the apartment. I crawl back under the covers and lie there awake until 7:30 a.m. and a sliver of light appears.

The kids wake up at 8 a.m., and John tells me to call Entergy to restore the power. Yeah right.

By 9 a.m., both kids say they're bored.

Across the apartment complex, each unit has a little balcony. People in those units go out on their balconies every now and then, look around, and go back inside.

We play cards for a while, then Hangman, and then tic-tac-toe. The kids work on their homework. Across the way, the tenants are now sitting outside on their balconies in varying stages of undress.

At 3 p.m., the rain stops and the sun starts shining.

Time for a walk. We don our rubber flip flops and head outside. Before I let the kids out of the door, I look around for downed wires, but don't see any. The wind is still brisk.

We find a family like ours, walking around aimlessly to kill time. They're from Lakeview, one of the most flooded areas of New Orleans, and tell us that they too had tried evacuating but turned back when they encountered gridlock for hours. They look resigned to these hurricanes, worn out, defeated. We probably look the same to them. They have two kids that look a few years younger than ours, and we share our "here we go again" stories of stocking up on water and food. It starts to rain again, and we jog toward our apartments.

Time passes agonizingly slowly. It's now hotter inside our apartment than outside, and it's about 90 degrees outside.

"Can I have another treat?" John asks. I look at my watch; it's 6:30 p.m. and he last had a "treat" at 5 p.m. Sure, go ahead, I tell him.

John whips open the freezer door, grabs a frozen water bottle, and quickly closes the door. I had yelled at the kids at lunchtime, when they opened the refrigerator door and were just standing there with the door wide open as they were deciding what to eat or drink.

John takes his water bottle and rubs it around his face, neck, and bare chest. He's down to just his shorts; Sam and I are identically dressed in shorts and a sports bra. John passes the bottle to Samantha and then on to me. I wish we had a battery operated fan.

DAY 29

Sunday, September 25th

WE ARE SO hot when we awaken that I take the kids to my Tahoe and we sit there for half an hour with the air conditioning blowing on us. At this point, I'll gladly walk somewhere for gas if we run out.

According to news reports on the radio, Houston has dodged a bullet and is bracing for the return of the three million people that evacuated. It's the second day of flooding in parts of New Orleans. In a Reuters report, Trevor Cormier in Port Arthur said he "scared himself to sleep." Virtually every building in Port Arthur is damaged, and I wonder how the Shipley Donut store fared.

An estimated 100,000 evacuees are staying in 1,042 shelters in 26 states and Washington, DC. The 7,000 already sheltered in Houston for Katrina were moved to north Texas, Arkansas and Tennessee to keep them safe from Rita.

Samantha has been texting her friends, and Allison and her family invite us to their house for the night. When Samantha says the magic words, "They have a generator," John runs for his toothbrush and is ready to go.

We're on empty when I start the car. Please God, please God, please God let there be enough gas to get over to the Rudys' house.

We are stinky and sweaty guests when we arrive, and I shiver when we walk in the door. Both of our kids have flushed faces, and when I look in the bathroom mirror, I see that I, too, have the face of someone who's been in 90-plus degree heat far too long.

The three of us take showers, and even though it's only eight at night, we head to bed, finally able to sleep in comfort.

DAY 30

Monday, September 26th

SCHOOL IS CLOSED again today since so many people need to return to Houston, and it's hot and humid. The high is going to be 99 degrees, and a heat advisory has been issued.

Cable is still out at the Rudys' house so Russell, his wife Cathy, and I listen to a radio. About 200,000 households in Houston are without power. I am ever so grateful to the Rudy family for their hospitality; it's been the best sleepover ever.

Not wanting to impose on the Rudys' and curious to see if our power has been restored, we decide to head back to our apartment. Russell has cans of gas, and pours five gallons into my tank. It's a gesture of kindness that makes me tear up even today when I think back on those days.

Power is on at the apartment, and it is ice cold inside because I'd left the thermostat on sixty. We have no damage at all, and when I take down the blankets on the bedroom window, I see Randalls Food Market employees pushing shopping carts filled with decaying food toward a dumpster. Out with the old, and in with the new.

The store's blinking sign now says, "We have milk!" so the kids and I walk over there. Employees in their little red vests are in the process of restocking the shelves, but many sections of the store are still decimated.

We get some milk and a package of partially melted chocolate chip cookie dough. We make the cookies when we get back to the apartment and have them for lunch.

President Bush announces that he's pleased with the Hurricane Rita response. Many of Samantha's friends are still on the road, creeping back toward Houston. It's a painfully slow process, and many are wondering why a reverse contraflow has not been initiated to assist people in returning.

Because Hurricane Rita did not cause much, if any, damage in Houston or New Orleans, media coverage quickly dropped off, and the people in its path in southwestern Louisiana were quickly forgotten about by the general public. Few people realize that Rita maintained category 5 hurricane intensity for eighteen hours before weakening into a category 4. As it weakened, it curved northward toward a ridge of high pressure and a larger eyewall formed, which expanded Rita's huge wind field. Rita further weakened into a category 3 hurricane just prior to making landfall on the morning of September 24th in southwestern Louisiana, just south of Port Arthur and very near the Texas-Louisiana border. In Cameron Parish, the storm surge was estimated to be fifteen feet high, and homes and businesses in small communities along the coastline were essentially washed away or completely destroyed.

High winds and flooding from the storm surge along Rita's northward path caused extensive damage in Calcasieu

Parish. In Lake Charles, an eight-foot-tall storm surge traveled up the ship channel from the coast. The city experienced severe flooding, with reports of water rising six to eight feet in some areas.

Residents of southwestern Louisiana were told to expect long delays in restoring essential services, such as electricity, phone, and cellular service. With New Orleans and other parts of the Gulf Coast still under repair, there simply were not enough utility repair crews to go around. The people in communities hit by Rita were essentially left on their own to repair and rebuild.

I receive a call from a nurse whose family had a get-away place in Holly Beach, which is known as the "Cajun Riviera." Their fishing camp is completely gone, and it took her family a while to figure out exactly where it had been. She also mentions that while traveling around the area in the first few days post-Rita, she never saw a Red Cross truck or a TV crew. But what she did see was the spirit of southwestern Louisiana hard at work cleaning up and not waiting around for someone to come help them. Self-sufficient, strong-willed communities banded together and began the long journey of recovery.

Other news being reported is that New Orleans is virtually childless because of a lack of schools and housing, compounded by the risk of contamination from gas, oil, and chemicals that have saturated buildings and the ground. Families are staying away.

Workers continue to make their way to New Orleans, and Rich tells me that he's fairly busy taking care of chainsaw injuries and guys who have fallen off of roofs. People have also been injured in car wrecks caused by the traffic lights still being out.

Rich and I start our State Farm list. At first it doesn't seem like we've had much damage to our house, but the list grows and grows: the wet walls in Samantha's room, the soggy ceiling and walls in our bathroom and closet, the mold on the ceiling of the sunroom, the crushed aluminum patio cover, the back of the garage that still has the fallen tree on it, our swimming pool that still has the big pine tree in it, and the destroyed fence in front and back.

DAY 31

Tuesday, September 27th

NO SCHOOL AGAIN today. It will be nothing short of a miracle if our kids make it through this school year. I use the computer to search the Louisiana and Texas Departments of Education to determine how many days of school can be missed, but don't find a definitive answer.

The heat index is 110, and Sam has her first soccer practice in the afternoon. Coach Ross welcomes her, and she knows a few of the girls on the team, so she soon feels at home. John and I sit in our folding chairs on the sidelines as the girls' families introduce themselves. I'm starting to think that our lives now have some semblance of normalcy.

DAY 32

Wednesday, September 28th

JOHN IS ROOTING around for the paper that has his school schedule on the front and his hand-drawn map on the back. He's already forgotten where he needs to go. I drop off the kids at school and read news updates when I return to the apartment.

Jonathan Weisman with the *Washington Post* is reporting on what he calls "the FEMA cruise ship fiasco." FEMA contracted with Carnival Cruise Lines to cancel the vacations of 100,000 people in order to provide 10,000 beds on cruise ships for aid workers and returning residents. Hasty negotiations led to a $236 million agreement, and Weisman calculated that the government is paying $1,275 per person per week. He compares this to an ad for $599 week-long cruises, and points out that the $599 includes entertainment, plus the ship is moving.

MSNBC.com reports that it's still a long road ahead for New Orleans. Only 17% of the city has power. Five thousand soldiers and 4,000 National Guardsmen are still in the city.

An investigation has begun to determine why 250 police officers in a force of 1,750 left their posts and fled the city. Some allegedly left in hijacked or stolen vehicles. Health concerns are emerging amid reports of gas leaks, mold, rodent infestation, and toxic sludge.

I pick up Samantha and John from school and find a thousand dollar money order from my mom and dad in our mailbox. My parents, the retired dairy farmers, are giving money to the wife of a surgeon. It's for the kids, my mother writes. So they can eat some meat. Apparently she's heard of the parade of pasta and rice dishes our kids have been eating. She also wants me to get a little TV and cable so that Sam can watch her favorite show, *The O.C.*, and hopes it's enough so that I can take the kids out to eat every now and then.

As John starts his homework at the dining room table, he casually mentions that he missed two classes today, one to have his eyes checked and the other to talk to the psychiatrist. Psychiatrist?!

Yes, he says, the shrink guy. Not the counselor. He describes how he and the other four sixth grade kids from Louisiana had to go to "some office" and "talk about their feelings."

Samantha is lying on her stomach in the living room area doing her homework. She rolls over to her side and says that she, too, had to talk to the shrink and asks if I scheduled her to talk to him. Wasn't me, I told them.

I ask the kids where they want to go for dinner. They look very surprised and suspicious that I'm asking this. No, it's not a bribe. John asks if I'm kidding. I tell them that after our Rita evacuation and a day with the shrink, they deserve a nice dinner and that Grandma and Grandpa are treating.

After a long discussion about where to go, the kids say they want to eat at Macaroni Grill. Both of them order pasta for dinner.

DAY 33

Thursday, September 29th

MY FRIEND LIESEL calls and tells me that her house in mid-city, as well as the house next door that she and her husband own and rent out, flooded in Katrina and subsequently were looted. She's staying with her husband's aunt in Lafayette and looking for houses north of Lake Pontchartrain in places that never ever flood. I tell Liesel that our home is her home, and invite her to stay at our house when she's in New Orleans.

Liesel and her husband Paul stay at our house for a few days while they remove the wet sheetrock from their two houses. Rich is the innkeeper and has Ray, Bobby and Sharon, and two of Sharon's friends staying at our house. Plus the three dogs. And now Paul and Liesel.

The headline in the *Houston Chronicle* is "Lessons Come at a High Cost: 107 Lives." In addition to the twenty-four Bellaire nursing home residents who died when their chartered bus caught fire, casualties of Hurricane Rita include a two-year-old crushed beneath the wheels of a pickup, a fatal crash that occurred when the driver fell asleep after 26 hours in traffic, a 92-year-old who died in the gridlock, and a man and his two children who were thrown from their overturning car.

"Getting out should not be a disaster in itself," notes Houston Mayor Bill White.

I head to Bush Intercontinental Airport for my flight to Chicago, where I'll be doing several nursing education programs over the next two days. Limited flights between New Orleans and Houston have recently resumed, and Rich flies in to Houston around 1 p.m. to see the kids and be with them while I'm gone.

Rich and I sit in a coffee shop just outside of the airport security area and talk for about an hour. He tells me that the Shimmy Shack near our house has reopened and that it's the only restaurant open for miles around. There are two things on the menu, hamburgers and cheeseburgers, and there is a full bar that operates on the honor system because they lack staff. Rich said he and Ray went there for dinner, made their own drinks at the bar, and then told the solo server what they were drinking so he could add it to their bill. He also said that people have to share tables so that everyone can have a seat, and he and Ray shared a table with two National Guardsmen and their assault rifles.

"Have you heard from the girls in your office?" I ask.

"Yeah, as soon as Bobby and I texted them about where to send their paychecks, they all texted right back."

He's had long conversations with Bobby about keeping the staff on the payroll and continuing the employees' health insurance and benefits. Rich and Bobby estimate that the direct deposit checks from Blue Cross and other companies will cover payroll for just a couple of months. There's still no mail delivery anywhere in New Orleans.

"We can make payroll and pay the office rent because the insurance checks are payments for the work we did in July and August," says Rich. "We haven't worked at all in September and what work we've done is mostly no-pay patients. So going forward, we won't have any money coming in."

I show Rich my checkbook with the Houston rent and utilities expenses, and tell him about the money my parents sent, which I've stashed in a coffee cup in the cupboard. I ask him to go TV shopping with the kids.

Rich's applications with the locum tenens agencies are still being reviewed, and he tells me that he and Bobby heard that the LSU Hospital up in Bogalusa, about two hours north of New Orleans, is looking for a surgeon. As the population scattered northward, the hospital's patient population swelled.

"Bobby and I are going to go up there when I get back and talk to them. It could be the answer to our prayers."

It's time for me to go through security and fly to Chicago, so I hand Rich the keys to my Tahoe and give him a page pulled from my journal where I've drawn a map showing where the Tahoe is parked in the airport garage. It takes Rich half an hour to find it.

DAY 35

Saturday, October 1st

THE OFFICIAL KATRINA death toll along the Gulf Coast is now 1,163. Electricity has been restored to 28% of the homes in New Orleans. The Ninth Ward, which re-flooded from Rita, is now almost dry. MSNBC.com is reporting that pumping water out of Lakeview is nearly complete, and residents may be able to return there by midweek.

Some of the schools in Jefferson Parish, west of Orleans Parish in which New Orleans is located, are scheduled to reopen on Monday. Only 60% of children in school prior to Katrina are believed to be enrolled in school now. Many people are still moving around, and many more have applied for FEMA trailers, which for the most part will be placed in FEMA trailer parks around Louisiana and Mississippi.

Our kids' New Orleans school posts its tuition refund policy. No refund at all for those of us who have paid tuition for the year. There is no sacrifice on the part of the faculty and staff; they will essentially receive a five-month-long paid leave, maybe longer.

I envision that our savings will soon be eaten away. I was counting on a tuition refund, even partial. Doesn't the school have insurance? Haven't they, like the rest of us, been saving for the proverbial rainy day? If there's nobody at the school, where is the money going that would have been spent on food and electricity? And why didn't they promptly set up an extension school in Houston, or somewhere else, so there would be continuity in the education of our children? I'm so angry at the school that I pound my fists into my thighs and then realize how much it hurts.

The tuition we paid is gone, Rich has no income for a few months, he's keeping his staff on the payroll, he's continuing to pay everyone's health insurance premiums and retirement contributions, we have to pay the September estimated taxes by the 31st, and our homeowner's insurance adjuster surely will find lots of exclusions for the repair work needed at our house. How much more stress can we take?

DAY 37

Monday, October 3rd

I FLY BACK to Houston on Sunday night, and take Rich to the airport on Monday morning after we drop off the kids at school. On the way back to the apartment, I realize that my back and butt are roasting. At the traffic lights, I push the heated seat buttons repeatedly, thinking I inadvertently turned them on. Still nothing. They won't go off no matter what I do.

My shirt is soaked through with sweat as I search Chevy dealers on the computer. I talk to a service technician who tells me that it's got to be the wiring since it's unlikely that both the seat and back heating buttons would break at the same time. I ask if I can do something myself, like disconnect the wire or pull out a fuse since I absolutely cannot afford car repairs, and he says no, not unless you know what you're doing.

The kids ask why I'm sitting on a big comforter when I pick them up from school. They think it's hilarious that my heated seat won't turn off and it's 84 degrees outside.

New Orleans Mayor Ray Nagin is on the nightly network news. We now have a small TV perched on the box it came in, and the mayor says that the city of New Orleans is in the process of laying off 3,000 employees. "The problem is, we have no revenue stream," he says. I think about what this means. Without funding, essential city services, such as fire and police protection, will likely be reduced. I start to seriously think about living somewhere other than New Orleans.

Former President Clinton is shown meeting with refugees staying at the shelter in Baton Rouge. He's helped raise $100 million and people are wondering where the money will go, and who will distribute it.

A military official comes on and says that door-to-door sweeps for corpses are being suspended.

It's officially the first day of resumed classes in some schools, mostly in Jefferson Parish. Peter Whoriskey reports in the *Washington Post* that despite some schools reopening, "it still looks like a ghost town."

In East Palo Alto, California, $1,500 in small bills and change collected by school students for hurricane relief is stolen. Wells Fargo replenishes the money and adds $11,000.

DAY 39

Wednesday, October 5th

TODAY IS THE first day of the next phase of allowing residents to return to New Orleans. Everyone except those who live in the Lower Ninth Ward, the hardest hit area, are now allowed to return.

The big news story on my computer is "Hurricane Stan's Death Toll Rises." Hurricane Stan? I read on and learn that at least sixty-five people have died in Central America as a result of Hurricane Stan, a hurricane I heard nothing about until today. I'm now on the other side of a natural disaster, passively reading about it. How sad that these people have died.

In other news, Amtrak trains to and from New Orleans will resume service on October 9th and the New Orleans Wal-Mart will reopen on October 10th.

The website nola.com is reporting that the twenty-story Art Deco Charity Hospital, which opened at its present site in 1939 and was once the nation's second largest hospital with 2,700 beds, has sustained over $340 million in damage and remains closed. The hospital and its clinics had provided care to half a million patients per year.

Without the Charity Hospital system fully functional, medical care in New Orleans has shifted to other hospitals. Injured construction workers are going to East Jefferson General Hospital on the East Bank, where Rich works, and West Jefferson Medical Center on the West Bank of New Orleans. Pregnant women are now going to Touro Infirmary, instead of Charity Hospital or its affiliated University Hospital.

University Hospital was previously known as Hôtel-Dieu (French for House of God) and was operated by the Daughters of Charity until it was purchased by the LSU system in 1991 and converted into a teaching hospital for the adjacent medical and nursing schools. I was teaching in the LSU School of Nursing at that time, and witnessed the transition firsthand. The crucifixes were stripped from the walls of the patients' rooms, the nuns and many long-term Hôtel-Dieu employees left, and the state employees moved in.

Like its sister hospital, Charity or "Big Charity" as it became known, the 575-bed University Hospital sustained severe flood damage during Hurricane Katrina and its patients were evacuated by boat and helicopter after the storm. The hospital had its cafeteria, which prepared food for the staff as well as the patients, in its below-ground basement. The pharmacy, a key area of hospital operations, also was in the basement. Anything below ground is an oddity in New Orleans because many parts of the city are below sea level, and the city's low elevation is the reason that people in New Orleans are buried above ground. Many times as I rode the elevator down to the basement, I would think how stupid is this, and stupid it was as the staff learned in August 2005. Nurse friends of mine who stayed at the hospital during Katrina resorted to scouring their lockers for food for their patients, and one remembers dividing a box of saltine crackers among twenty patients and family members while going hungry herself.

In addition to the structural damage sustained by University Hospital during Katrina, flooding submerged the emergency generators, which ironically were located on the first floor. Like other buildings in New Orleans, the hospital's sewage system also failed, and it was estimated that the hospital had $105 million in damage. University Hospital was eventually renovated and reopened 85 of its beds on November 20, 2006.

"Rummel T" on the higher ground of Metairie has opened. The Archbishop Rummel Transition School is a temporary school for displaced Catholic high school students. Previously an all-boys' school, an estimated 1,300 girls and boys are enrolled at the school, wearing the uniforms of fourteen different schools. Platoon scheduling has traditional Rummel students in school from 6:30 a.m. to 12:30 p.m., and transition students attending from 1:30 p.m. to 6 p.m.

According to the Red Cross, 27,977 people still are residing in 244 shelters. It's been 5½ weeks since Katrina.

What's being called "FEMA City" is being built in Baker, Louisiana, north of Baton Rouge and 92 miles northwest of New Orleans. The site has 500 travel trailers, and the goal is to place 3,000 trailers there in the next fourteen days.

The United States Postal Service initially stockpiled mail destined for New Orleans in Houston, and moved it to Dallas just prior to Hurricane Rita. Bags and bags of mail are now sitting in Baton Rouge. Mail service has not resumed in New Orleans, and it is unknown when it will resume.

DAY 40

Thursday, October 6th

I'M STARTING TO get mail at our new address in Houston, and receive a check for $500 from Regina, an oncology nurse in Denver, and her husband who ask that I distribute it directly to people in need.

"Tom-Kat to Have a Kitten" is the big news today. Katie Holmes' pregnancy supersedes news about recovery along the Gulf Coast. I'm starting to notice that national attention on our little corner of the world is beginning to fade.

In Mississippi, half a million dollars in casino revenue has been lost, 15,000 casino workers have been laid off, and Governor Haley Barber has signed a bill to help the casinos rebuild. At the same time, there is a real estate boom in Mississippi, and even damaged houses are going for top dollar because housing is in such short supply.

Samantha and John do not have school tomorrow because of a teacher in-service day, and I've used my airline credits to book flights home. It's after dark as we circle and approach the runway in New Orleans. Off to the right I can see a large swath of blackness in the Gentilly, Lakeview, and Ninth Ward areas of the city. A huge area of our city remains pitch black.

DAY 41

Friday, October 7th

BUDDY IS SO happy to see us that he keeps jumping up on each of us and embraces us with his long front legs. We look like we're dancing with him. Samantha goes to give Jack a little pat on the head but backs away when he growls. John avoids the mutt altogether.

We continue to clear the debris from the front lawn, and attempt to remove the battered fence in front. It's a warm day and a stench is in the air.

"What is that smell?" I ask Rich.

"It's coming from there," says Rich, pointing to our neighbor's yard. "I went over to ask about it because I thought maybe an animal had died or something. They said they buried their rotten food back there after they got back last week."

"Smells like they didn't bury it deep enough."

Rich tells me that people are being told to either bury rotten food or bring it to a drop-off point. There are rotten food dumpsters at Clearview Shopping Center, and the streets around the shopping center reek. Most people are not attempting to clean, or clean out, their refrigerators and instead leave everything inside, tape them closed with duct tape, write a warning message about their contents, and kick them to the curb.

We share stories we've heard about people's experiences with their refrigerators upon their return to New Orleans. Just opening the door was enough to send some running from the room gagging, and a few admit to vomiting on the spot. Everyone has an "opening the refrigerator" story, and what I realize when I hear these stories is that nobody is exaggerating.

Katrina debris has been divided into categories so that it can be sorted and disposed of properly. Putrescibles, or rotten and spoiled food, is a new category that has been added to the categories of vegetative debris (tree branches), white goods (appliances), electronic waste (computers, TVs, etc.), and automotive waste, which not only includes tens of thousands of cars and trucks but also batteries, tires, and motor oil.

We take another "misery tour" of New Orleans. The previously flooded Lakeview and Gentilly areas are now drivable, and everything there is covered in dried mud. The water line on the houses is eight feet or higher in many places. A few houses have holes in the roof where hatchets were used to escape the rising water. All of the houses have the creepy "X" spray-painted with the date the house was searched, the affiliation of the search team, and the number of dead inside.

The West End Boulevard "dump pile" is easily three to four stories high and half a mile long. Household debris, including furniture, mattresses, and clothing, is being bulldozed into an ever-growing mountain. Further down the street, we see flooded cars stacked one on top of another, compressed and waiting for transport to their next, and final, destination.

Our debris pile has been picked up by the "claw," a dump truck with an extension arm that is able to hoist the tree debris into the back of the truck. "Claw trucks," as we call them, roam the city in search of piles to retrieve, and head to one of the landfills.

Our garbage is now being picked up once a week, but recycling has not resumed. I'm not able to find a recycling drop-off center in the area, so we—and everyone else—toss everything into our trash.

Liesel and Paul, who have been periodically staying at our house, present me with a bottle of some kind of wine that was submerged in the water in their house for at least three weeks. We wonder if it's safe to drink and pop the cork. The label has disintegrated and we discover it's some kind of white wine that tastes just fine. We sit in the backyard jungle while Buddy takes a swim in the murky water of the pool. Rich tells me that Buddy has been swimming a lot, and shows me how he's left the end of the garden hose by the steps of the pool so Buddy can be hosed off.

Paul has been referring to Rich as the "Branch Manager." The joke started when he saw Rich hauling a tree limb to the street and it's stuck. Paul then tells me that Rich has been bringing pieces of the destroyed back fence to the street, so he spends a lot of time at board meetings, ha ha.

I notice that our house is immaculately clean. Sharon and her two friends have kept the place spotless, and when I throw some towels into the washer, I notice an array of laundry products. Looks like everyone wants to replace what they have used, and I now have enough laundry detergent for months to come.

Two countertop microwave ovens have appeared in our kitchen. I'm not sure who they belong to, and find out that they're for cooking and heating water since we still do not have natural gas service and we have a gas cook-top and gas hot water heaters. I'm hoping that gas service will be restored fairly soon and rule out buying an electric hot water heater. Not only is it something we can't afford right now, I also doubt I could find someone to install it.

The kids and I quickly get the hang of heating water for bathing. We fill three large Pyrex bowls with water and heat them in the two countertop microwaves and the one mounted above the gas cooktop. The kids fill both sides of my double sink with cold water to the half way point, and I pour two bowls of the hot water into one side, which becomes the "washing" side. The third bowl of water is poured into the other side, which is our "rinsing" side.

The system is surprisingly efficient, although I wish we had electric kettles, like they do in Europe, to speed up the process. We also found that leaving the dark green garden hose out in the sun heats up the water within it, and we've used the hose to rinse our hair after shampooing.

DAY 42

Saturday, October 8th

OUT OF HABIT, I open the door to Samantha's room to check on her, and see Ray slumbering in her pink flowery sheets. Oops, forgot she's sleeping downstairs on the living room couch.

Rich and Bobby have been hired by the 74-bed LSU Bogalusa Medical Center, and decide that each will work in Bogalusa for a week at a time. While one is working up there, the other will work at their Metairie office. Both will need to live close-by since they're general surgeons and must be able to get to the hospital quickly.

Bogalusa is 70 miles north of New Orleans, near the Mississippi state line. The small city of 12,000 was founded when the Great Southern Lumber Company opened its mill in 1906, and it is called the "Magic City" because it was built in under a year to provide housing for the saw mill workers. The saw mill closed in 1938 but was replaced by a paper mill and a chemical plant.

Bogalusa is well-known in the medical community

because of the Bogalusa Heart Study. The longitudinal study began in 1972 to identify cardiovascular risk factors in children and follow these children into adulthood. Bogalusa was chosen as the study site because about half of its population is white and half is black. The study was the first to document that heart disease begins in childhood.

The Bogalusa area received winds of 125 mph during Hurricane Katrina, and many homes and businesses were damaged or destroyed. Some areas were without power for over a month.

Rich and I ride across the 24-mile Causeway Bridge to reach the Northshore. The twin span bridges on I-10 east of New Orleans, which we used to evacuate, sustained a lot of damage and have not yet reopened. Consequently, there is a lot of traffic, including tractor trailers, on the Causeway. As each big truck passes us on the narrow lanes, I hold my breath and close my eyes.

We make it across the Causeway and take Highway 21, which has signs saying "scenic byway," but there's mostly devastation on both sides of the highway. We pass a place where it looks like a tornado made its path. Nothing remains standing in this area.

We pass by a cute little horse farm with a small Acadian-style house. "That's what I'm looking for," I tell Rich. "A place like that would be great for the kids. On the week that you're up here, we could come up on Friday afternoon and leave on Monday morning when you leave to go work in Metairie. It would be nice to spend the weekends up here."

"I think we should look at rentals, if they have any up in Bogalusa," says Rich. "I just took out a line of credit on our house so we can pay for the house repairs and cover our bills. We can't afford another mortgage."

"I agree, but you've seen what rents are going for up here. They're getting top dollar from all of the people who are coming in and need short-term housing. I almost think we can buy something and have the payments end up the same as, or maybe even less than, renting."

We continue the drive up to Highway 40 and take the 1075 shortcut into Bogalusa. Rich takes me around the hospital and introduces me to Regina, the Nursing Director and interim CEO. We tour his new office, which already has a paper "General Surgery" sign stuck to the front door.

Rich's office was built sometime in the '60s and has lime green cinderblock walls, orange plastic chairs, a gold sunburst clock on the wall, and big light balls hanging down from the vaulted ceiling. The office has three exam rooms and there's a small room with a desk in the back.

From the hospital parking lot, I see plumes of white smoke billowing from the paper mill and tell Rich it smells like fire ant powder everywhere. "Tastes like chicken," he replies.

Rich and I drive around Bogalusa to kill time before we meet up with a real estate agent to look at property for sale or rent in the area. We pass a one-story apartment complex near the hospital, and Rich pulls in. "This would be perfect," he says and heads to the door marked "Office."

He's soon back in the car. "That was quick," I tell him.

"I walked in and asked if units were available, and the guy said yes. I asked about the rent, which is pretty cheap. Utilities are included too. I was ready to sign a lease when the guy asked who the apartment was for. When I said it's for me, he started laughing and said I can't live here."

"Why not?" I ask.

"Apparently, I'm too young. This place is for seniors on fixed-incomes."

We drive to the realtor's office, and are driven around Bogalusa to find a place to rent or buy. The pickings are slim.

We pass by a pretty pink house on Atlanta Street with a "for sale" sign in front. As I begin to tell the realtor that the house looks nice, she interrupts me.

"No, no, no. Not the pink house. I'm taking you to that bluish house up there."

"Can we look at that pink house?" I ask as we drive past it.

"That just sold yesterday. Some doctor from New Orleans who's going to be working up here bought it."

Rich turns to look at me in the back seat. "I wonder if it was Bobby. He hasn't mentioned anything, but we haven't really seen each other either."

Rich texts Bobby and learns that Bobby did indeed buy the house. Rich and I can stay there anytime.

Rich and I look at the few available houses, but all require extensive repairs, and there are no apartments or houses to rent anywhere in the half-hour radius around the hospital. The two motels on the outskirts of town, as well as the few motels in the area, are filled with utility repair crews from other states. We are tired and defeated as we make our way back to New Orleans.

"I can stay at the hospital. They'll give me a room if I'm on call. And we can stay at Bobby's after he moves into his house if we need to," says Rich.

"That will get old. You'll be at the hospital around-the-clock for a week at a time," I tell him.

We're about to pass the cute horse farm.

"Pull in there," I direct Rich.

"Why?"

"I want to ask who the builder was. It's a super cute house."

"Lisa, are you nuts? You're gonna get shot. All of the people up around here hunt. When Bobby and I came up here last week, we stopped in the Wal-Mart to get lunch at the Subway there and the first thing you see when you walk in is nothing but camouflage clothes, shotguns, and ammo. I can't believe you're going to just knock on their door. They're going to open it a crack and stick a shotgun out at you. You'll see."

"Remember, my parents sold their farm in Schoharie this way," I tell him. A nice, young couple looking for a farm in upstate New York knocked on my parents' door several years ago and told my parents to call them before calling a realtor if they ever decided to sell, and about a year later my parents sold the farm to them.

Rich pulls into the driveway. He says he'll stay in the car and call for the paramedics.

I gingerly make my way up the front brick steps and knock on the door. I glance back at Rich; he's holding up his cell phone, ready to dial.

A woman looks through a crack in the door, and then opens it wide when she sees me standing outside. I tell her that we just love her farm and ask her who the builder was. She has no idea because she's the third, or possibly fourth, owner.

She sees Rich sitting in the car. "Too lazy to come in?"

"Nope, too chicken to come in. He says everybody around here owns a shotgun—and uses it."

"Well he's right about that!"

I motion to Rich and he comes in. We tell Lonnie, the home-owner, that we're looking for a house just like hers, and her eyes widen.

"Michael and I have been thinking of selling and going back to Michigan, but were wondering who would buy this place. We have a lot of roof and tree damage."

"Are you seriously considering selling?" I ask, practically falling backward in disbelief.

"Yeah," she says.

Lonnie gives us a tour of the house. The inside of the house is even cuter than the outside. There's a kitchen, dining area, and living room with fireplace. The master bedroom downstairs has a connected bathroom. The screened-in porch across the back of the house looks out over a large pond. There's a big dog yard with a doghouse, which would be perfect for Buddy and Jack. There are two bedrooms upstairs, along with a bathroom and a loft area that overlooks the living room.

Lonnie takes us out to the three stall barn, and tells us that the farm is just under nine acres in size. She points to the property lines as a large truck rattles down the dirt road on one side of the property.

"There's a place down there where they're burning Katrina tree debris," she tells us.

We exchange contact information, and Lonnie tells us that she'll talk to her husband when he gets home from work.

We get home to our boardinghouse and find Howard, a

gastroenterologist, there. Rich has invited him to stay at our house until his flooded house is habitable again. We go out to eat with Howard and our neighbors to the place that has only hamburgers on the menu and an honor bar. Most every restaurant that is open has an honor bar now, I'm told.

Samantha has Claire, Madison, Allain, and Taylor spend the night. Five little lumps on the living room floor. The girls sleeping over have all recently moved back to New Orleans. Taylor is now enrolled at St. Matthew's, her fourth school this year.

DAY 43

Sunday, October 9th

BREAUX MART, THE grocery store in our neighborhood, has reopened but has big empty gaps in the shelves. It's one of a handful of grocery stores that has reopened in the New Orleans area. None of the big chain groceries has come back, and their stores remain shuttered and boarded up. I get the toilet paper we need, and find some chicken and tater tots that I can bake for lunch. I also spot some crisp apples and toss them into my shopping cart, which we call buggies here in NOLA.

The checkout line goes all the way back to the meat department at the rear of the store because only one register is open, and it's cash only.

As I inch forward, I hear the kids behind me crying because their mom has said no candy and no cookies. Her buggy is filled with powdered milk, cereal, potatoes, pasta, and rice. Starch city. Not a single fruit or vegetable. No meat. And of course, no candy or cookies.

I watch as she methodically counts her cash and eyeballs

each item in her buggy, mentally adding them up. I know this look, and have been there myself. I told my mother just this morning that words cannot describe how grateful I am that she sent us the thousand dollars and that Rich was able to land the job in Bogalusa.

I tell the woman behind me that I've forgotten a couple of things and ask her to watch my buggy. I retrieve a gallon of milk, a can of Hershey's chocolate, a bag of apples, and a sack of oranges. We're just a few feet away from the meat counter, so I make a second trip and come back with chicken, ground beef, and bacon. We're about half way up the cookie aisle now, so I throw some Oreos and oatmeal raisin cookies into my buggy. The Keebler Rainbow Chips with chocolate in every bite bring back bad memories, and I have to look away.

At the register, I throw a few assorted candy bars onto the belt and unload my groceries. I keep the extra things I grabbed separate, and as the woman pushes her empty buggy toward the end of the register belt, I start loading it with the extra things I bought. I also wad up one of the $100 bills I have in my purse, from the $500 check that Regina sent, and tell the woman that a friend sent the money to share with people in New Orleans, and that I wanted her to have it. She never looked at how much I gave her; her hands just trembled and tears welled up in her eyes.

"Thank you and thank your friend," she mouthed, barely able to talk.

As we fly out of New Orleans back to Houston, faces are pressed against the windows throughout the plane. The debris pile on the West Bank is huge with mountains of mattresses and furniture. Probably half of the houses near the airport in Kenner have bright blue tarps covering their roofs.

The airport in Houston is bustling with people and food is in abundant supply here. In many ways, I feel like I've just been to a developing country and am now returning to the United States.

DAY 46

Wednesday, October 12th

HURRICANE STAN HAS left 652 dead, 384 wounded, and hundreds of people are still missing. Recovery efforts in Guatemala have been halted because of mudslides. Once again, I am awed at the profound loss of life and irked that this disaster has received perhaps two minutes of national news coverage.

People who live in the Ninth Ward of New Orleans are finally allowed to go back there. It's been over six weeks since people there have seen their homes, and many return to find them gone. In many places, just steps and concrete slabs remain. Those who find their homes still standing find that they're filled with mud and mold.

Civil engineers are beginning to call the devastation in New Orleans a manmade disaster and not a natural disaster. Many of the breaks in the levees are now attributed to engineering flaws. The design of many of the levees that failed relied on the passive pressure of the soil, and were quickly eroded by the onslaught of water.

MSNBC reports that mail service has returned to all New Orleans zip codes. However, the United States Postal Service notes that there is a huge backlog of mail that needs to be delivered because there has not been any mail delivery for the past six weeks. With so many homes damaged beyond repair, it's unclear if the mail can even be delivered in some places. The Postal Service urges NOLA residents who are not residing at their pre-Katrina homes to complete mail-forwarding request forms.

Anderson Cooper is reporting on CNN that "mercy killings" may have occurred at Memorial Hospital, where Samantha was born. Actress Reese Witherspoon also was born at this hospital, back in the day when it was called Southern Baptist Hospital.

One side of the I-10 twin spans over Lake Pontchartrain will reopen tomorrow. The less damaged side of the 5½ mile-long bridge spans, which connect New Orleans with the Slidell area, has been repaired and will have two-way traffic. The pictures are frightening, though, because they show a hodgepodge of repair methods with cement railings in some sections and what appears to be flimsy aluminum guardrails in others.

We are back in Houston, and Samantha scores two of the six goals in a soccer game. She's excited and calls Rich to tell him about it. He's eating dinner at our kitchen table and passes his phone around to Liesel, Paul, Howard, Bobby, Sharon, Sharon's two friends, and Ray, who also congratulate her.

DAY 48

Friday, October 14th

I MAIL A letter off to Regina to tell her how I distributed the $500 she sent. In addition to the $100 I gave to the woman in the grocery store, I gave $100 to our babysitter along with money from us so that she could buy a mattress. The other $300 was distributed directly to people who flooded and had no insurance.

Every one of them was nearly speechless when I handed them the money and told them who it was from.

Hundreds of Louisiana residents are now filing for bankruptcy and 439 claims have been filed *this week*. This is over ten times the number of claims filed at this time last year.

A Gallup poll finds that two-thirds of Katrina survivors that received help from the Red Cross say they'll return home, or have returned home, to the Gulf Coast.

Katrina survivors. I'm happy to see that term. It's been Katrina victims, Katrina evacuees, and Katrina refugees for far too long. Better yet, President Bush is using the term "displaced citizens," saying that "the people we're talking about are not refugees, they are Americans."

However, the Gallup survey also found that the majority of those polled reported that they are depressed, sad, angry, and stressed, even though it's been six weeks since the hurricane.

Over 1.5 million people had to evacuate from Louisiana, Mississippi, and Alabama for Hurricane Katrina, and estimates of the damage caused by Katrina are "a wild guess" according to economists. Congress approves $62 billion in disaster relief aid.

DAY 49

Saturday, October 15th

SAMANTHA HAS A soccer game early in the morning and we head down to Galveston afterward. We need a change of scenery, and it's an easy drive from our apartment in Houston.

The kids do their homework in the car, and Sam again tells me that her IPC course is really hard. We still haven't figured out what IPC stands for, but Sam is pretty sure the "I" is for intermediate.

I park by the sea wall, and Sam and John pull off their shoes and socks and take off across the sand. They run around for a while, and then John lies down on a rock and closes his eyes. Sam lies down next to him and does the same. I join them, and we lie there listening to the waves and sea gulls. It's a warm day, and a gentle breeze blows over us.

"It's nice and peaceful here," notes Samantha.

I take the kids to the Galveston Rainforest Cafe for lunch. Although Rich now has a steady income from the job in Bogalusa and I'm back working as well, we still have a gap in income from the weeks we both didn't work much, and we have a lot of expenses and hurricane repairs. We'll soon start having additional housing expenses if Lonnie and Michael agree to sell the little horse farm to us. We'll then have three of everything: three homes, three electric bills, three water bills, and three natural gas bills.

The kids are now used to splitting dishes and ordering water. It's become a way of life for us, and they intuitively understand the need to conserve. They also continue to order pasta every time we eat out.

DAY 53

Wednesday, October 19th

I'M ON THE Board of Directors of the Oncology Nursing Society and fly to Pittsburgh for a quarterly board meeting. The kids are staying at their friends' houses in Houston, and I can't thank these families enough. They have enabled me to keep working and attend the meetings I need to go to.

I fly out of Bush Intercontinental Airport, about an hour north of our Houston apartment, and sit next to a man who asks if I'm headed home. Going to a meeting in Pittsburgh, I tell him. Home is New Orleans and I hope to move back there one day.

The man's mouth falls open. "You're one of *them?*" he asks.

"You mean a New Orleanian?" I have no idea where this conversation is going.

"Yeah."

"Well then, yes, I'm a New Orleanian."

He proceeds to tell me that the people from New Orleans, in his opinion, are unappreciative of all that Houston has done for them. Just look at how the crime rate has gone up, for God's sake! You people just want a hand-out, he says, and he's Goddamned sick and tired of paying taxes so that people can sit on their asses all day. And people have the nerve to bitch and moan that nobody helped them, that they were abandoned in New Orleans, when they didn't even lift a finger to help themselves! They made no effort at all to get outta there! And then they break into that blue jeans store and are comin' out with stacks of designer jeans—*designer jeans!* His neck veins are bulging now and he's gesticulating all over the place with his hands. Now you tell me, he asks as he leans in toward me, why do those people need to loot a store like that? Designer jeans for Christ's sake! I have no sympathy for 'em, he says, as he waves his thick index finger back and forth as if to say no, no, no.

I tell him that I recently read a magazine article that proposes that perhaps the government helped *too much*, that many people in New Orleans have what's called learned helplessness and wait for assistance rather than seek it out or rely on themselves. I tell him that the issue of "abandonment" is complex, and that many people in New Orleans truly did not have a way to get out of the city. Surely he's seen the photos of the flooded school buses? There was a huge lack of coordination and cooperation in evacuating the city, even though FEMA ran a disaster simulation exercise just one year ago, in the summer of 2004.

In the simulation, "Hurricane Pam" hit New Orleans with winds of 120 mph and dumped 20 inches of rain that created a storm surge that topped the levees. Sound familiar? In that exercise, a million people needed to evacuate and afterwards, pretty much all of the city was destroyed. I tell my seatmate that despite this week-long exercise and the action plan that they came up with in case a future hurricane like Pam hit the area, few of the identified preparedness tasks had been implemented over the next year, and some people would argue that none of them had been implemented. It's shared responsibility, in my opinion, I tell him. As residents living in a hurricane prone area—or any disaster prone area—we need to do as much as we can for ourselves, and our government needs to assist in the evacuation, recovery, and rebuilding process. That's why we pay taxes, in my opinion, I tell him.

I ask if he evacuated for Rita. Hell no, he tells me. He has a brick house that was built in '61, and had enough food and water to sustain his wife and him for three weeks if needed.

"You ain't gonna see me with my hand out," he says.

My hotel room in Pittsburgh has a king size bed. It's huge with just me in it. I'm used to small beds and being kicked by our kids all night long.

At the meeting, a nurse from North Carolina tells me how his hospital received a phone call a few days after Katrina made landfall, instructing them to activate their DMAT (Disaster Medical Assistance Team). The team had forty-eight hours to get down to New Orleans to set up and provide medical care at a yet to be determined location. Right about the time the trucks were fully packed and ready to leave, another phone call instructed the team to stay put, set up, and get ready to receive patients that would be flown up to North Carolina. The team set up in the hospital parking lot and waited for arriving patients. And waited, and waited. Not a single patient ever arrived at this DMAT location.

At the same time, in the first few days after Katrina, four

physicians practicing in the Thibodeaux and Houma area, 60 miles southwest of New Orleans, drove to the New Orleans airport, where medical evacuees were being dropped off. They'd heard that so many patients were being transported to the airport that they were being placed onto baggage carousels and even the bare floor. The four arrived at the airport to find what they later described as "utter chaos." Armed guards at the door halted their entrance, and the physicians were told that a DMAT rep would need to speak with them.

The DMAT rep asked for their DMAT credentials.

"We don't have any," they replied. "We're all physicians and want to volunteer in whatever capacity is needed."

"But you don't have DMAT credentials," the rep repeated. The physicians were able to see past the entrance and saw patients lying everywhere, with no medical personnel anywhere in sight.

"We're here to help. We'll do whatever's needed. Give 'em water, help 'em to the restroom, whatever."

"You don't have credentials."

"We're all licensed physicians with years of experience. You can call the medical staff office at our hospital and verify our credentials."

"But you don't have DMAT credentials and you could be imposters."

"Imposters? Are you kidding me? To come here to volunteer in this shithole?" asked one of the physicians in disbelief.

The group was turned away from volunteering at the airport and drove home in stunned silence.

DAY 57

Sunday, October 23rd

I'M BACK IN Houston, and a flyer catches my eye at the Randalls Food Market checkout register. The state of Texas is offering Louisiana residents a one-way ticket anywhere in the domestic United States. I read the small print; Samantha, John, and I could all get one-way airline tickets. Afraid to fly? The state of Texas will pay for a train or a bus. Just as long as it's one way—out. Hmmm, sounds like the state of Texas has had enough of us "Louisiana people."

A friend of mine who has to drive into New Orleans from Slidell every day sends an email saying that he's been taking the repaired I-10 bridge that recently reopened. He writes that the bridge "shakes, rattles, and rolls," so he rides across the bridge with all of his windows open. He says he's prepared to swim out of his car if he gets pushed off the wobbly bridge or the bridge collapses.

The official map of where bodies were recovered in the New Orleans area immediately post-Katrina is published in several newspapers and posted online. I see that a man's body was found on Douglas Drive, only a couple of blocks from our house.

DAY 60

Wednesday, October 26th

THE KIDS STAY at their friends' houses while I work in New Jersey for three days. I try to rotate the kids around so I don't burden any one of the families. Everyone says it's no problem at all to have our kids stay at their houses, but I don't want to impose.

I receive an email from our bank saying that I need to schedule an appointment to pick up the contents of our safe deposit box. The bank flooded and I'm warned that many of the safe deposit boxes flooded. Huh? I thought they were fireproof and waterproof. Don't those massive metal walls and door protect our stuff? Apparently not, as I read that safe deposit vaults are only theft, water, and fire *resistant.*

The kids' Houston school is selling bricks for its new walkway, and we buy a brick and write:

Thank You
From the Katrina Evacuees
2005

Lillie, our former babysitter and now our dog-sitter, calls

Rich to tell him that Jack climbed the fallen pecan tree in our back yard and he seems to be stuck or won't come down, he's just up there barking, and what does he want her to do? Rich says "send him to a Vietnamese restaurant" and then says just leave the dog in the tree, he'll eventually come down, but Lillie's not so sure.

"He's wedged up in there, Richard," she says.

Rich calls our next door neighbor. Chris comes over, gets a ladder, and extracts the pooch from the pecan tree. "And amazingly I still have all my fingers," he later tells me.

There's an Associated Press story posted online about the Mississippi Coast and the reporter writes that although Bay St. Louis was "virtually erased" by Hurricane Katrina, residents are coming back to rebuild.

One of the posted comments says, "I don't agree with, nor understand, the rebuilding of New Orleans and surrounding areas. My family and I work hard for our money. I disagree with my family's tax dollars, which are needed elsewhere, to go to a doomed community." The writer lives on the New Jersey coast. It's 2015 now, and I find the comment interesting since it's been a couple of years since Superstorm Sandy hit the Jersey shore and other areas in the Northeast. I wonder if the woman still feels the same way today as she did then.

DAY 63

Saturday, October 29th

SAMANTHA'S SOCCER TEAM has a playoff game early in the morning and loses 3-1. Coach Ross tells the girls that they're now in the consolation bracket and he knows they're going to dominate the bracket. Why aren't more coaches like him? He's been positive and encouraging all season, and he's uplifted Samantha's spirits as well as my own. I think back and wonder how well Sam would have coped with a new school if not for soccer. Soccer allowed her to do something that she really enjoyed, kept her mind off of other things, and gave our family a sense of normalcy in a time when everything was anything but normal. The heart of Coach Ross and the spirit of this little team will forever stay with me.

We fly home to New Orleans after the game. The plane is full of people we know. There are our neighbors. There's a woman who teaches in the LSU nursing program. There's a family whose kids go to our New Orleans school.

I make the rounds to say hello at the gate and in the air,

and ask how everyone's doing. The other question everyone asks now is, "How's your house?"

"Not doing too good," says the nursing instructor. She's been going back and forth from Houston to New Orleans. The nursing school is in Baton Rouge now, at a movie theater. All classes are in the early morning so that they'll be out by noon when the theater starts to show the matinees. She knows it's time to finish up her lecture when she starts to smell popcorn. Some of the students are essentially living out of their cars, and others are on the Finnish ferry boat that was brought in to provide housing for students and faculty. She's stayed on the boat but doesn't like going up and down the little gangplank when it rises and falls with the tide.

I ask our neighbors how they're doing. "Mold," they answer.

The mother of the kids who attended the same school in New Orleans as our kids tells me that our school abandoned us, that there was absolutely no communication from the school and that a school should have been set up somewhere *immediately*, and thank God that their private Houston school has waived tuition because good Lord, there is no way that they could have paid two tuition bills this year.

The New Orleans airport is basically deserted when we arrive. Ticket counters are about the only thing open.

John walks into the house and walks past Jack without saying a word. He hugs Buddy and says he's so glad to see him. Little Jack snaps at Samantha's fingers when she reaches down toward him, and she quickly retracts her hand. When we sit down for a late lunch, John announces that he has changed Jack's name, and it's now Jack Russell Terror.

Rich and I drive up to the little horse farm, which Lonnie and Michael have agreed to sell to us. Lonnie shuffles the papers she's printed out on how to sell and buy a house. She thinks we can do this ourselves and reads each step aloud.

"Okay, now," Lonnie says after we've all signed a few of the papers, "It says here that I need to collect earnest money from you."

Rich and I nod our heads. That's all right with us.

"Give me a dollar," she says to Rich.

Rich opens his wallet and extracts a dollar bill.

We go over the things that need to be done, such as repairing the fence and replacing the barn roof and an air conditioner, and agree to split the cost fifty-fifty. Lonnie and Michael are easy to negotiate with.

"We do have a couple of requests," she says. "We'd like to do the Act of Sale around the middle of December so it gives us time to find a place for us and our horses to move to." She tells us that they plan to stay in the area for a few weeks, or perhaps a few months, and the long-term plan is to move back to Michigan.

"Our only other request is that you don't disturb the blueberry garden. Two of our dogs are buried in there."

We readily agree to both requests, shake hands, and head out the door.

Rich worked his first week at the LSU Hospital in Bogalusa last week, and I ask him how it went as we drive back to New Orleans.

"There's one surgeon up there who's been there for a few years, but he's pretty much overwhelmed by all of the people who've moved up that way, so when I went to clinic on day one, they already had ten people for me to see. A lot of big hernias. They've probably had them awhile and cleaning up tree debris just made them worse, or made it hard to clean up the tree debris."

He tells me that his office is staffed by Denise, an RN who had a quadruple bypass, and a receptionist, who looks to be twelve but apparently is older. They both like their new jobs that allow them to work only on weekdays, and want Rich and Bobby to succeed. They use the overhead paging system at the hospital a lot. "Doctor Karlin, please call your office," they'll say, but when Rich calls, they say it's a PR page and he's not needed. They just want the other doctors and staff to know that there are new surgeons in town.

Rich says he's been introducing himself to the medical and hospital staff. People seem surprised, he says, that two well-educated and highly trained general surgeons are now practicing in small town Bogalusa. Most of the staff members have worked at the hospital for decades; there are no other healthcare facilities for miles around, so the Bogalusa hospital staff stays put.

The hospital is a major employer in town, as is the paper mill. The other businesses in Bogalusa are Wal-Mart, Winn Dixie and Piggly Wiggly grocery stores, a CVS pharmacy, a video store, the Donut Palace, a handful of restaurants and fast food places, a couple of gas stations, and Culpepper's Miniature Donkey Farm.

Rich describes the hospital staff as "good old boys" and it only took him five minutes of working there to realize that everybody knows everybody, and everybody knows everything that goes on in the hospital and in the town.

Samantha calls and asks to be picked up from Molly's second house. Many of her friends have a "second house" now, which is where they're living post-Katrina while their pre-Katrina or "main houses" are being repaired or rebuilt. Molly's main house flooded from the levee breaches and has major structural damage. People are also calling their pre-Katrina houses their "Pre-K houses."

The only people staying at our house now are Howard, Ray, and Liesel and her husband Paul, who stay at our house when they're in town to work on the two houses they own. Sharon's two friends have left, and Bobby and Sharon moved back into their Metairie house after they removed a tree from their bedroom. They also have the pink house in Bogalusa where they'll live while Bobby has his "week on" there. Every Monday morning at 7 a.m., the Bogalusa doc leaves for New Orleans, and the doc in New Orleans leaves for Bogalusa.

The medical office building next door to East Jefferson General Hospital, where Rich and Bobby have their office, has reopened. All of the girls in the office have come back to work there, except for one who left to work at Burger King, which is now paying $13 an hour.

DAY 64

Sunday, October 30th

IT'S A BEAUTIFUL day in New Orleans. We set the clocks back, pick up Sam's friends Taylor and Allain, and drive down to the French Quarter. There are not many people around. A few restaurants have reopened and a sign exclaims that "Beignets are Back!" at Café du Monde by the river. A sprinkling of stores and art galleries are now open, and the surrounding parking lots are being used to house and feed relief workers.

We eat red beans and rice at the place on the corner and head to the Moonwalk by the river. Rich and I sit awhile on one of the benches while the kids explore the rocks, looking for treasures. In the northeast where I grew up, they'd call this kind of day Indian summer, just a wonderful day to sit and contemplate life. When Rich brings up our finances, I refuse to talk to him about it. I don't want to ruin an otherwise perfect day.

Rich takes us directly to the airport to fly back to Houston. While I'm sitting at the gate waiting for our flight, a friend on the east coast calls to ask how I'm doing. She gets the short answer that we're doing just fine, thank you. She tells me about her pilates class and how it's going to be the next best new way to limber up and lose weight. I want to tell her to try the Katrina diet, which has been working far too well for many of us. She chatters on about her kids and when she mentions their upcoming trip to Disney World, I tell her that they're boarding the flight and I need to go.

DAY 65

Monday, October 31st

SAMANTHA IS VISIBLY upset when I pick her up from school. What's wrong?

"My history teacher said he didn't feel well during class and then he just keeled over onto the floor. We all just sat there, petrified. Then somebody ran out of the room to get another teacher. Our teacher was having a seizure and we were all afraid to go up to him. He had foam coming out his nose and mouth, and then he puked all over the place. And then a teacher came in and said oh my God and ran back out. They took our teacher away by ambulance."

I tell her that I hope he's all right. She tells me that she just can't comprehend how dad and I take care of sick people all the time. She says she will never, ever, *ever* become a nurse or doctor.

Interesting tidbit in the news today; two hundred of the two hundred fifty sex offenders in four Louisiana parishes affected by Katrina have now been accounted for. The others haven't reported in or have not been found. Rounding up the sex offenders is not something I would have thought about when accounting for people's whereabouts after Katrina.

It's Halloween, and a torrential downpour occurs right around dinnertime. The power goes out an hour later. "Why does this keep happening to us?" the kids ask. There's no trick-or-treating tonight, but the kids weren't all that interested in going around the apartment complex for treats anyway. We're thankful when the power comes back on around ten.

DAY 66

Tuesday, November 1st

THE UNITED STATES Department of Education has started a "What do You Need List?" on its website for Gulf Coast and New Orleans area schools.

The Archdiocese of New Orleans has twenty-seven elementary schools, three middle schools, and twenty-two high schools in the New Orleans area. Most remain closed, but some are planning to re-open in January. The Archdiocese posts its wish list: inspirational posters, calculators, orange safety cones, footballs, white socks, loose leaf paper, file cabinets, computers, book bags, pens and pencils, toner cartridges, and cleaning supplies.

Rummel T, the transition school, has "feminine supplies" on its list with a note that says, "As an all-boys school taking in females for the very first time, we have virtually nothing to provide to the young ladies in this regard. Whatever you can provide at whatever numbers would be most appreciated. We expect about 500 girls."

Haynes Middle School in Metairie asks for "three flutes,

two oboes, a tuba, combination locks, chalk, batteries, sticky notes, and pocket folders with prongs."

A counselor at Riverdale High School writes, "Would appreciate any info on teaching students who have post-traumatic stress disorder, any info on counseling students who have great loss in their lives, and any staff development info on dealing with a personal crisis while maintaining jobs and handling catastrophic situations. Would also appreciate reading books and magazines. Our students have nothing to read outside of school."

The "What Can You Give?" list on the site has a note from Jennifer and Steve Hynek. "We're doing a backpack and school supply drive in Idaho. We have a goal of 1,000 packed backpacks. We are willing to personalize the backpacks if it would help the kids."

The Little Shop of Stories, a children's bookstore in Decatur, Georgia, has about 1,000 new and gently-used books that have been donated and are ready to be sent somewhere.

Meghan Schultz, a high school senior, writes that she wants to run a new and used book drive for schools or public libraries as part of her National Honor Society project.

RAVSAK, the Jewish Day School network, says "we will provide unlimited school supplies and personal items to any Jewish Day School absorbing displaced children."

St. Michael's Country Day School in Newport, Rhode Island, has collected 240 children's backpacks and filled them with school supplies. "Every child here from three years old to eighth grade filled a backpack and wrote a personal note. We want these to go to school children in need of these items. Please help us find someone to help."

Sundance Publishing is offering 200 brand new hardcover library books.

Time for Kids, a subsidiary of Time, Inc., has *Time for Kids* almanacs, *Guinness World Record* books, and lunch bags to send somewhere.

A member of Phi Kappa Phi at UNC Charlotte writes that she has a 1995 Dell computer to send wherever it's needed. "It's old, but it works."

Books 4 Kids writes that they have collected over 900 new and gently used books. "Our goal is every child affected by the hurricane has a book to call their own."

The Hogan/Totzke Fund has 100 new pearl and bead headbands and some butterfly barrettes to donate.

Georgetown Day School offers to help clean or rebuild a school in late March, during their spring break.

Writer's Block International wants to send notebooks, pens, and pencils wherever they are needed.

Mrs. Vining's sixth grade class at Fort Colville Elementary School has books to send.

And then I see the Hartwick College student's post that she has music textbooks to donate. This sends me into a half-hour crying jag because it's the college where I obtained my nursing degree. It's a tiny school, with 1,500 students, in upstate New York. Seeing this message affects me in a very profound way as memories of my years there, a happy time, come flooding back. It's very touching to see the student's offer amid all of the wonderful offers of support to the children of the ravaged Gulf Coast.

DAY 69

Friday, November, 4th

PRINCE CHARLES AND his wife Camilla tour the Lower Ninth Ward. They stopped in New Orleans after being in Washington DC, and are on their way to San Francisco. The stop in New Orleans only recently was added to their itinerary, and they stand on a patched levee that looks over the Lower Ninth Ward and simply shake their heads.

DAY 72

Monday, November 7th

I'M ABOUT TO head out to pick up the kids from school when my cell phone rings. It's Carol, and she asks if our TV is on. No, I tell her. She tells me to put it on.

"What channel?" I ask.

"Any channel," she says and hangs up.

The local channels are showing aerial shots of Spring Branch Middle School. An armed gunman is thought to be on the loose somewhere in or around the school. Preliminary reports say that this guy shot at someone in the neighborhood during a presumed robbery attempt. However, police are not sure where the gunman is, so search teams with barking dogs have descended upon the school and surrounding residential neighborhood.

I sink into the sofa and let my car keys and purse drop to the floor.

Dear God, dear God, dear God. My poor kids have been through enough already. Let them be okay and get them out of there safely.

I keep switching from channel to channel but the reporting is all the same. My cell phone rings again, and this time it's an automated call from the school saying that the school is on lockdown, and all children and staff are safe. We'll receive another call when the students are released.

I sit and sit and sit by the TV, and the same scenes are shown again and again. I try to imagine our kids ducked under desks, waiting it out.

After two hours, Carol's calling on my cell phone. "We can go get them," she says.

"I just got the call too," I tell her.

"But they haven't found the guy yet," Carol tells me.

"I know, I find that weird that they're letting the kids out now."

"Oh, wait, channel 7's showing how the police are escorting them out bunch by bunch."

"Okay then, I feel better."

"That's going to take forever," she says. "There's twelve hundred kids in the school."

"Yeah, I hadn't thought of that." As soon as I finish my sentence, my cell phone beeps in and it's Samantha calling. "Sam's calling me," I tell Carol.

Samantha says she's fine but has to pee really badly. They won't let her stop in a restroom, so can I come get her?

Of course, I tell her, I'm on my way.

I get Sam in my car and police officers direct me to keep moving out of the school pick-up area. I take Sam to the Shell station on the corner. The restroom has an outside entrance on the back of the building, and has a sign saying it's locked after 9 p.m., so it's unlocked now. Since we're not far from the school, I blast open the door like they do on TV in those police shows. No one's inside. Good.

We wait at the Shell station, and after a few minutes, I get the automated call that all children can be picked up now. Sam and I head back to the school. This time, kids are sauntering out just like they do on any other day.

John gets in the car and says he's hungry. It's been a crazy day and I haven't been able to make anything for dinner, so I ask the kids where they want to go to eat.

"Macaroni Grill," they chime in unison.

Our server hears our kids talking about the school lockdown and brings two Shirley Temples to our table, with extra cherries.

"On the house," she says as she puts a drink in front of each of them. "You've had quite a day. That must have been scary in there. It was on the TV in the bar all afternoon." She looks at me and asks, "So Momma, what are you drinkin' tonight? First one's on the house."

I'm practically chugging my Merlot as Samantha describes what happened.

"All of a sudden, the loudspeaker thing came on and said, 'This is not a drill. Will Charles Manson come to the office?' So my teacher, he like freaked out and ran over to the door and locked it, and then yelled at us to get under our desks, and then he turned off all the lights, and then he told us to be super quiet, and then he told us to shut up when we started asking him what was going on, and then he yelled YOU KIDS SHUT UP RIGHT NOW, THIS IS NOT A DRILL, and then he whispered that everything is going to be okay if we all keep quiet, and then he was running around dropping the blinds over the windows, and then he got down behind his desk, but then he popped up again and took a bunch of our homework papers and started taping them to the window on the door of the classroom, and then we just sat there forever."

This is perhaps the longest run-on sentence ever spoken by our daughter. She's breathless and takes a long sip of her Shirley Temple.

John removes a cherry stem from his mouth and tells us that his teacher had his classmates do the same thing and told them that it's probably nothing, that you know how schools are these days, always taking precautions even if there's even the slightest possibility of something going on. She had them group desks together and turned the ones facing the door onto their sides. John says he and a couple of other boys made themselves a really nice fort. But it was really, really boring sitting there for so long.

Both kids have ordered pasta, and our meals arrive with crisp garlic bread and another glass of Merlot for me.

After I've taken a couple of bites of my chicken, my cell phone rings. It's FEMA asking if we need a trailer.

What a whack-a-doodle day.

We are back at our apartment when John casually asks why the principal, or whoever was on the loudspeaker at school, would call a kid to the office when a gunman was running around the school. He surmises that the kid must have done something really, really bad. Samantha pipes up that it was Charles Manson who was called to the office, and she too, wonders why he was summoned.

Charles Manson was a bad guy, I tell them, not a kid at

the school, and what they heard on the loudspeaker was a code for the teachers so they'd know what was going on and what to do.

"That's pretty smart," says John as he nods his head approvingly.

DAY 82

Thursday, November 17th

I TAKE MY Tahoe to a Chevy dealer to get the heated seat situation fixed. I've tried padding the driver's seat with a towel and then tried a thick blanket, but the heat penetrated through the cloth. I'm now using a broken-down cardboard box from Randalls Food Market to protect me from the heat, and went to soccer practice one day with what once was *Northern Bath Tissue* imprinted on the back of my thighs. In view of the upcoming long drive to Louisiana for Thanksgiving break, I need to get the seat fixed.

"How can I help you?" asks the service advisor.

"My heated driver's seat, both the seat and the back portion, continually stay hot."

"Have you tried pushing the heated seat buttons down by the floor?" he asks as he gives me a little wink.

I want to say yes I have you asshole. "Yes. Multiple times. And a guy at a gas station said it's not the fuse."

"Well then, we'll take a look at it," he says as he starts the paperwork.

About an hour later, right in the middle of *The Price is Right* on the TV that is mounted so high in the customer waiting room that we're all straining our necks to see it, I hear my name called on the intercom.

"Did your Tahoe flood?" I'm asked by the service advisor. The mechanic standing next to him says he noticed the Louisiana plates and says I have a lot of corrosion that caused the driver's seat wires to be shot. Apparently my seat doesn't move at all, but I never had the need to change any of the settings, so I was unaware of this. I think back to where my Tahoe was parked in our driveway during Katrina, and it's entirely possible that it sat in water since the houses on the adjacent street flooded and we have a pretty high water line on the parts of our fence that are still standing.

The service advisor then says that I shouldn't be riding around sitting on cardboard, and says he's giving me the Louisiana pretty girl discount.

DAY 83

Friday, November 18th

ENTERGY, THE POWER company supplying New Orleans with electricity, announces its "neighborhood plan" to restore power. Entergy filed for bankruptcy protection shortly after Katrina hit, and added a hefty hurricane recovery fee to utility bills. I joke around with Rich and tell him to add a recovery fee to his bills when he takes out somebody's gallbladder.

Entergy's plan is to restore power to the Ninth Ward within 16 days, Venetian Isles within 17 days, Gentilly within 21 days, and Lakeview within 29 days. However, this timeline excludes the devastated portions of Lakeview and the Lower Ninth Ward.

I've been keeping up my journal entries, and calculate that parts of Lakeview should have power restored 112 days after it went out.

"Hey y'all," I yell. "What's 112 divided by 7?"

"Sixteen," John yells back. Holy cow, that's four months without electricity.

DAYS 84 to 92

Saturday, November 19th to Sunday, November 27th

AT 9 A.M. Saturday morning, the kids are up and my Tahoe is packed for what I hope is a six to seven hour drive to Bogalusa. Samantha and John have a week off from school for Thanksgiving break.

The traffic through Baton Rouge is still horrendous and we creep through the state capital until we reach I-12 and drive east toward Hammond. We get to Covington and take the Highway 21 exit and head north. It's Rich's week to work at the LSU Bogalusa Hospital, so we're headed up to stay at Bobby's house until Monday morning.

I slow down to point to the farm we're buying as we drive by it, and tell the kids we'll be moving in there on December 17th. Although the kids have seen pictures of the farm taken with my Cool Pix camera, they lower a back window to get a better look.

"Can we get horses?" asks Samantha hopefully.

"No."

"Why not?"

"No is a complete sentence," I tell her.

"A trampoline then?" she asks.

"We should get four wheelers," says John emphatically.

"Absolutely not! They are the most dangerous things around. You can get paralyzed on those things!" I tell him.

"Well then, we should get a trampoline," says Sam. When she was in second grade, she sent Rich and me a PowerPoint presentation titled "Why I Need a Trampoline." She has wanted a trampoline for a long time.

We arrive at Bobby's house right at 5 p.m. (happy hour!) and inflate the two air mattresses we've brought with us. The kids put their mattresses in the room with the bed. Although there are two empty bedrooms, they've chosen to sleep in the "bedroom slash TV room slash living room slash family room" as Sam calls it.

Bobby and Sharon have outfitted their Bogalusa house with the basics: stove, refrigerator, kitchen table and chairs, and a queen sized bed and TV in one of the upstairs bedrooms.

Samantha scribbles in her journal and announces that this is the 27th place she's stayed overnight since Katrina. She's kept a tally of all of the motels and friends' houses where she's been staying. "Oh, and if you count our couch and floor at home because Doctor Ray is in my bed, then it would be more," she adds.

We take a walk around Bogalusa and get some groceries at the Piggly Wiggly. I buy a bunch of cleaning supplies that I plan to leave at Bobby and Sharon's house, and plan to clean their house on Sunday night.

"What's that smell?" the kids ask.

"That's the paper mill."

"Smells like chemicals," says John. I still think it smells just like ant powder.

Rich gets home from the hospital and we eat dinner. I drink an entire bottle of wine. John and Samantha both reenact how their teachers were running around their classrooms when the school was locked down. Sam lies down on the floor and demonstrates how her history teacher writhed during the seizure he had in class. And how he threw up all over the place when it finally stopped.

I'm so exhausted from driving all day, not to mention the wine, and I fall right off to sleep.

We follow Rich across the Causeway on Monday morning and make our way home. Our neighbors Dan and Michelle come over at dinnertime and ask how I've spent my time in Houston when I'm not flying off for work. I tell them I spend a lot of time on the computer keeping up with the news, I've filled out a ton of forms for the insurance company and have helped our babysitter and others with their paperwork, I write in my journal, and I clean the apartment, which I find very therapeutic. Lately, I've found amusement in the cottage industry of slogans and sayings that are popping up on shirts, tote bags, and bumper stickers and flip open my journal to read them some.

New Orleans: It will take a nation to rebuild a village.

New Orleans Swim Team. Est. 2005

Hurricane Katrina came to New Orleans and all I got was a brand new plasma TV.

Don't Evacu-Hate

New Orleans: Wading Home

I'm qualified to run FEMA!

No one drowned when Bill was around.

Make levees, not war.

My heart belongs to New Orleans.

Want gumbo? Save New Orleans.

Rebuilding New Orleans one street at a time.

FEMA: the new F word.

New Orleans: Bring back the music.

Long Live New Orleans

FEMA: **F**ailure to **E**vacuate **M**inority **A**reas

Got mold?

Remember Hurricane Dubya 8/29/05

My freezer smells worse than your freezer.

I survived FEMA.

There's no place like home.

Be a New Orleanian Wherever You Are!

I tell Dan and Michelle that the kids and I will be moving back in mid-December, right after John and Samantha finish the fall term at their Houston school. Their New Orleans school is in the process of being repaired, and it's unknown how many students are expected to return to the school in January.

As soon as I'm back from the grocery store on Tuesday, Samantha tells me that Jack got out of the back yard. It's not hard to envision how he escaped since our entire fence is patched with plywood and cardboard. Sam was in the front yard talking to Taylor, who had walked over, when they saw Jack rip across the yard toward the street. Sam ran for his leash—and my oven mitts—while Taylor tracked the direction Jack was headed. Fortunately, Jack stopped to sniff around the mailbox, so he was quickly apprehended.

"I hate that dog," says Samantha. She tells me he was barking and biting when she retrieved him. John won't even go near him now, and Buddy keeps his distance. Somehow the littlest member of our family has become the Alpha Dog.

On Wednesday, November 23rd, I go to our bank for my scheduled appointment to clear out our safe deposit box. The bank flooded from the bottom up when the levees broke, and flooded from the top down when part of the roof blew off.

I park amid the many construction trucks in the parking lot. There's a security guard at the door and he asks for my ID. He scratches my name off a list on a clipboard, tells me I'm a little early, and points to two metal folding chairs where I can wait. The guard then hands me a four page waiver to read and sign because I'm entering a building that is under construction. I now vaguely recall the instructions on the phone that no children will be allowed in, and be sure to wear closed toe shoes.

After a few minutes, the people who had the appointment

before me are ushered out. Both look ashen and look down as they pass me. The woman from the bank introduces herself, and tells me that the man with the two cameras around his neck is from their insurance company. She hands me a hard hat and paper facemask, and leads me through a maze of clear plastic nailed to the studs. The first floor of the bank has been cleared, the sheetrock and flooring have been removed, and it no longer resembles a bank.

"They're doing the ducts for the AC today so it might be noisy back here," the woman says with a flip of her hand.

We enter the bank vault, and the woman is surprised to see that I have a key to our safe deposit box. She tells me they usually have to drill out the locks. We put the two keys into our box, which is about two feet off the floor.

Wait a sec, the insurance guy says, as he focuses his video camera on the box and starts to film. As I pull our box out, water drains onto the floor.

The woman from the bank and I lift the safe deposit box onto a folding table outside the vault. There's already water on the cement slab below, so I'm not the first to have a flooded box. We have to jiggle the latch several times in order to get the box open.

I'm handed latex gloves and asked to describe each item as I remove it from the box and place it in a plastic bin on the table.

"I don't know, I'm trying to remember what we had in here," I tell them. The videographer tells me to speak up, which is difficult with the face mask. "I know our car titles are in here, and the kids' birth certificates are in here." I'm removing handfuls of mushy paper, and cannot tell what's what. Navy blue folders with a rubber band around them;

oh yeah, our passports. "Oh, and we have a bunch of savings bonds in here for our kids as well as our nieces and nephews that we were going to give to them when they graduate from high school so it will help them with college." What am I saying? Way too much information. "Our marriage license should be in here. And the deed to our house. I forgot all about that." I shouldn't have forgotten about the deed; we had paid off our mortgage just three months before Katrina hit. "And here's Rich's coin collection that his dad gave him when he was little." The cardboard folders holding the coins at the bottom of the box appear to be intact until I lift them and they fall apart.

The stack of wet paper reminds me of when some other mothers and I brought our blenders into Mrs. Miller's second grade classroom to make papyrus so that the kids could learn how paper is made. The stuff from our bank box looks exactly like papyrus. I also remember how none of our blenders worked after we used them in the classroom.

"Okay then," says the woman from the bank as she picks up the plastic bin and motions me to follow her. We pass a couple waiting in the folding chairs at the entrance and go outside to a trailer at the far end of the parking lot.

The woman ushers me to a cube inside the trailer where another woman is sitting at a folding table with a laptop. "To the best of your knowledge, list everything you had in your box," she says.

With each item mentioned, she stops me, and pulls papers from an accordion file for me to sign. She explains that the bank will assist in the replacement process but tells me to be patient. A lot of documents were lost during Katrina, she says.

I call my sister to get her kids' social security numbers so their savings bonds can be reissued. I call Rich to get the VIN number for his Expedition from his insurance card so we can get a replacement car title. I don't have our passport numbers, but apparently that's not a problem as long as our social security numbers are submitted. The bank held our mortgage, so getting a certified copy of the deed is no problem at all. The woman tells me I'll be hearing from their insurance adjuster, and asks if we want a safe deposit box at another branch or would we rather wait three to four months for this branch to reopen?

I ask her where other branches are and she rattles off a few locations. I pick a location on high ground that is fairly easy for me to get to.

"What I'm going to do," she says, "is put in a request for a box high up, like near the ceiling so you don't have to go through something like this again." Fine with me.

We get a safe deposit box that's about five feet off the ground, and over the next couple of years, I place the reissued savings bonds, house deed, all of the paperwork for our Bogalusa house, our marriage license, birth certificates, the car titles, our passports, and Rich's childhood coin collection in the box.

In 2012, Rich is watching TV and I'm reading a novel on my Kindle when a breaking news story interrupts the program he's watching.

"Our bank is on fire," announces Rich.

"You gotta be kidding me," I tell him. "Our safe deposit box is in there."

The bank is engulfed in flames, and the on-site news

reporter says, "As you can see from the looks of things, this branch isn't going to re-open anytime soon."

The building has smoke and fire damage, as well as extensive water damage from the sprinklers going off throughout the building. A few weeks later, I receive a letter saying that I can come in to retrieve whatever's left in our safe deposit box.

DAY 96

Thursday, December 1st

WE'VE BEEN BACK in Houston for four days. The kids each hand me a note from the school that says that an alumnus of the school, who is now an executive at Deutsche Bank, is giving each Katrina kid in his former school district a $100 Wal-Mart gift card for Christmas. A parent needs to come in to the school counselors' office to pick it up.

Samantha has retreated to her room to start her IPC homework, and John has gone outside to throw his football against the fence by the dumpster. I'm so glad they left the room because I start to cry big time. What a beautiful, gracious act of kindness by this banker. Santa Claus really exists.

Most of the conversations that I had with Rich over Thanksgiving break were about money, bills, payroll, health insurance, taxes, and our sanity. I had calculated our budget over and over again, and even with Rich's Bogalusa job, we had drained our savings and our retirement and college funds were nearly gone. I'd already told the kids and my family that this Hanukkah and Christmas were going to be "no frills" holidays. We'd all be together in New Orleans, so togetherness is our gift to each other this year.

DAYS 97-98

Friday, December 2nd to Saturday, December 3rd

IT AMAZES ME how much our kids look like their school counselors, which reminds me of how dogs often look like their owners. John and Sam pick up their Wal-Mart gift cards while the counselors and I wipe away tears.

The kids are super excited to go shopping with their gift cards and skip across the parking lot toward the store. Both are blown away by the $100 amount; it's a huge amount of money for our kids. I plan to snap some photos so I can include them in the thank you notes the kids will write. I don't know if words can adequately convey our gratitude, and hope that the smiles on our kids' faces will help the kind donor see how appreciative we are.

Samantha and John have not been in a store, except for the grocery store, since right after Katrina when we went to the Wal-Mart in Oxford, Mississippi. There's just way too much temptation. Or perhaps it's that it would break my heart to repeatedly say no to them, so I've kept them out of the stores and malls.

I let the kids decide where to go when we enter the Wal-Mart. They walk down the main aisle and swivel their heads from side to side, taking it all in. I hear Samantha saying she wants to go to the bedding section and John says let's go to electronics too. They're walking along side by side when John suddenly veers to the left, stops, and stares at something on the shelf that's at his eye level. Now he's holding it in his arms.

It's a gingerbread house kit. He studies the packaging, turns the box over, looks up at the $8.89 price posted above, and puts it in our buggy.

His unexpected purchase sends tears down my cheeks, which I wipe away quickly before the kids see them. With the thousands of things in this store, why a gingerbread house I wonder?

We move on to bedding. Sam spots a purple comforter set for her new room at our farm and likes the coordinating sheets too. She and John do the math and she has enough for both, and she has money leftover! She's smiling broadly as she puts the comforter set and sheets in the buggy. Be careful of my gingerbread house, John tells her.

We move on to electronics where John intently studies the video games. Samantha and John play Frogger for a while using the controllers mounted to the display cabinet. John tells me that he wants to wait in buying something, that a video game is not a smart choice right now since he doesn't need it.

Our kids' mindset has shifted from wanting things to needing things. Every decision now is need-based. Impulse buys are a thing of the past, even for things like sodas and candy bars. The word "want" has been struck from our vocabulary.

The kids tell me to go look at things I'd like to look at, and at first I don't understand, but then realize that they want to shop for a Christmas present for me.

On the way to check out, the kids veer again, toward the heated display case filled with fried chicken. They study the pack, add it to our buggy, and invite me to join them for lunch in a Formica booth at the front of the store.

DAY 101

Tuesday, December 6th

SAMANTHA COMES HOME from school, excited about two things. She did well on her IPC test and delivered the morning announcements at school. Each day, a student is asked to read the announcements over the loudspeakers and *the whole entire school hears it!* No wonder she worked on her hair for an hour this morning.

Rich calls and says that he walked out to his Expedition in the Bogalusa hospital parking lot to find life-like plastic bull testicles hanging from the trailer hitch. Likely a gift from the OR staff, who enjoy poking fun at the two "city docs." Rich also tells me about a restaurant owner we know who has just died from a vibrio infection, likely acquired from Katrina sea water.

DAY 109

Wednesday, December 14th

IT IS FINALS week at school, and Samantha wakes up with a fever and sore throat. She croaks that her IPC paper has to be turned in today, and there are no exceptions for getting it in late. I tell her I'll take it in to her teacher when I drop John off at school.

As I walk through the 1,200-student campus, I now understand why John kept a list of classrooms and his primitive hand-drawn map in his pants' pocket for so long. I have to ask for directions twice to find Samantha's teacher's classroom.

I introduce myself and hand over Samantha's paper. The teacher says he hopes Samantha feels better. "I just want you to know," he adds, "that your daughter came into my class almost a month after it started and outperformed most everyone else in this class."

"Actually I'm not surprised," I tell him. "She spent a lot of time studying and doing homework, and said it was a challenging course. By the way, neither of us knows for sure what IPC stands for. It's intermediate what?"

"IPC is Integrated Physics and Chemistry," he says.

"Oh wow, no wonder it's a hard course," is all I can say.

DAY 111

Friday, December 16th

I SEND THE kids to school with thank you cards attached to boxes of pralines from New Orleans. I want the kids' teachers and counselors to know that we will never forget them.

I made a deal with two guys from Randalls to help me pack the small U-Haul truck I've rented for the trip to our new farmhouse, and they fill the truck with my mattress set, our couch, two end tables, my computer and the plastic table it's been sitting on, the TV, the table and chairs, and boxes and bags filled with kitchen items and our clothing.

I make one last "look see" around the apartment for overlooked items, which doesn't take long considering how little we had in the apartment. I check John's "room," the walk-in closet in the master bedroom, and spot something in the back corner of the top shelf. It's Sharky, the stuffed animal that spent the first few days after Katrina tucked under John's arm; inseparable then and now no longer needed.

The kids and I sit on the floor and eat up leftovers, and then share a pint of chocolate ice cream to commemorate our last night in the apartment. We play cards for a while and then I push Samantha's air mattress next to John's and the three of us lie across them sideways to sleep.

DAY 112

Saturday, December 17th

RICH FLIES INTO Houston early in the morning and is picked up by his brother and deposited at our apartment. I check the mailbox one last time, turn in our keys, and ask how soon we'll get our security deposit back.

I pack up my Tahoe with the air mattresses and the few remaining things in the apartment, including John's gingerbread house kit, which he plans to assemble once we get home. Samantha makes herself a nest of pillows and blankets in the back seat.

The U-Haul roars to life and John and Rich wave goodbye. We're each going to go our own speed and meet up at our Bogalusa farmhouse.

It's cold, pitch-black, and raining steadily when I turn into the driveway of our new house. It's colder inside the house than outside, and I crank up the heat. The raised Acadian house is set on pillars, and I can feel the cold air coming up through the hardwood floor.

As Samantha and I are inflating the air mattresses, we hear a honk, and it's Rich and John. I'm amazed that they're here already.

John excitedly tells me that Rich nearly took the top off of the U-Haul when he absent-mindedly went into a drive-thru lane, and if it wasn't for the car behind them honking wildly and pointing up to the sky, Rich probably would have driven right into the bar by its entrance.

It's eight at night, and I get some turkey and cheese out of our cooler and make sandwiches to eat. We leave everything in the U-Haul for the morning. Cheryl and Wayne and their boys are coming to help us unload.

I drape a king sized comforter over our couch cushions and the two air mattresses that we've pushed together. The four of us collapse on our make-shift bed, a Louisiana super-king I call it, and we fall asleep to the sound of rain hitting the tin roof.

DAYS 113-119

Sunday, December 18th to Saturday, December 24th

WE UNLOAD THE U-Haul with the help of Cheryl and her family, and they pronounce our horse farm "very cute." They've moved back to Slidell from San Antonio, are working on getting their chimney and roof fixed, and the boys are back at their Slidell school, which has now merged with the other Slidell high school that flooded when Katrina struck.

Cheryl and her family get into their van to go home, Rich climbs into the U-Haul, and the kids and I get into my Tahoe. We're going to return the U-Haul, and then go to our New Orleans house to pick up Buddy and Jack and bring them back to the farmhouse. It's another four hours of driving there and back. I haven't driven this much in years.

I follow Rich to the U-Haul drop-off location at the foot of the Causeway Bridge and circle the block twice looking for a place to park. The U-Haul lot is overflowing with trucks and trailers, and many are parked along the side streets.

Returned U-Hauls mean that people have returned, so this is a good sign.

Driving around New Orleans continues to be challenging because of the lack of functioning traffic lights. In many intersections, the traffic lights are no longer there. People familiar with these intersections know to stop, or at least slow down, but construction workers and relief volunteers do not, and I feel like I'm taking my life in my hands every time I get behind the wheel. To add to the driving challenge, most of the street signs are gone, so people have been hand-painting street names on scraps of wood and even things like cabinet doors.

We have two close calls as we make our way to our New Orleans house. Our former babysitter, Lillie, is now our dog sitter. Lillie has been coming to our house twice a day to feed Buddy and Jack, and let them out.

"Call Lillie," says Rich as we head to our New Orleans house after dropping off the U-Haul.

"Why?" I ask.

"To see if her nose is still attached," says John from the back seat.

"Well, yeah, that's exactly what I was thinking," says Rich. "We should make sure she's okay and thank her for watching our house and taking care of the dogs."

Lillie tells me she had no trouble at all with cute little Jack. In fact, he sat on her lap and watched TV with her for hours every day. She still does not have cable at her house.

"Ask Lillie if she wants to adopt Jack," says John.

I tell Lillie that Jack is now up for adoption, and she tells me that she'll take Jack on a trial run for forty-eight hours to see how well he gets along with her Pit Bull.

"Tell her we'll send him with six months of dog food to sweeten the pot," says Rich.

"No, a year," says John.

Over the next week, Rich and the kids and I patch the places where Katrina rainwater has come into the farmhouse, and we paint the kids' bedrooms. Samantha decides on pale pink and John picks a neutral color called Raffia for his room. As we're painting, Rich tells me he's glad that togetherness is our present to each other this year.

"Yeah, so you don't have to be the guy looking for presents at Walgreen's at ten at night on Christmas Eve," I tell him. "Yup, you're in luck this year."

Rich and the kids are Jewish and I was confirmed a Lutheran, so we celebrate Christmas as well as Hanukkah each year. I want to decorate for Christmas, but there are no Christmas trees for sale anywhere. The Northshore population has grown significantly, and the tree farms and tree stands have been picked clean.

Samantha draws a Christmas tree on poster board and places it by the fireplace, and puts the menorah on the mantle.

DAY 120

Sunday, December 25th

PRESENTS FOR THE kids that I bought in Houston traveled to Bogalusa in a box marked "cleaning supplies," which pretty much guaranteed that John and Sam would leave the box alone. The kids understood we were having "no frills" holidays this year, but I wanted them to have a few things to open. My parents and sisters showered our kids with presents, so each had about ten presents to open on Christmas Day, and I had little things for each to open on the eight nights of Hanukkah. My family also sent presents for me and Rich, and all were farm- or home improvement-related. My parents gave me a cordless drill, and my sister Erica gave me Beekman 1802 heirloom vegetable seed packets so that I could plant a garden in the spring.

The last present under the cardboard tree was for me, and in it was a small meditation fountain. Samantha and John bought it in Houston, on the day we shopped with their Wal-Mart gift cards.

In the afternoon, we headed outside to pull downed

branches to a pile at the back of the property. Lonnie and Michael already had a bulldozer push downed trees to the pile, but there still are hundreds of small branches on the ground all over the nine-acre farm. The kids poop out quickly, and Samantha points out places that would be perfect spots for a trampoline.

DAY 128

Monday, January 2, 2006

WE RIDE BACK to our New Orleans house so that Rich can start his week at his Metairie office. The office is closed for the New Year's Day holiday, so we decide to take a ride to the Mississippi Gulf Coast to see how things are coming along there.

Samantha was born in February 1992, and in the summer of 1992, we took our first family vacation to the President Casino and Broadwater Resort in Biloxi. The hotel and its surrounding cabins originally opened in 1939, and a riverboat casino parked next to a barge on the gulf was added in 1992 after legislation allowing dockside gambling was enacted in Mississippi to revive a slumping economy.

Our family went back to the Coast for a few days every summer. We'd stay at different places and often stayed at the Grand Casino and Hotel in Gulfport, which had a lazy river pool, a Kids Quest play area for John and Sam, and over a thousand slot machines for me.

Hurricane Katrina's winds and 28-foot storm surge hit

the Mississippi coastline in the afternoon of August 28th and obliterated many coastal towns. Even the three emergency command centers, thirty feet above sea level, flooded. Hurricane-force winds lasted for seventeen hours and spawned eleven tornadoes. Over a hundred people were rescued from roof tops and trees. Afterward, all counties in Mississippi were declared disaster areas.

Katrina left 236 people dead in Mississippi, 67 missing, and an estimated $125 billion in damages. Mississippi Governor Haley Barbour called the scene indescribable, saying "I can only imagine that this is what Hiroshima looked like sixty years ago."

Several casinos, which floated on barges to comply with gambling laws, were washed hundreds of yards inland. A number of streets and bridges washed away, including the bridge between the towns of Bay St. Louis and Pass Christian. The Biloxi beachfront *Beauvoir* mansion, home of Jefferson Davis, sustained major damage, and hundreds of irreplaceable Civil War-era artifacts were either lost or destroyed.

More than half a million people in Mississippi, which has a population of 2.9 million, applied for FEMA assistance. Its coast was dotted with FEMA trailers for years, and the process of rebuilding the Gulf Coast continues even today. Following Katrina, gambling regulations were changed to allow casinos to be built on land in taller buildings, and no longer forced the use of massive floating casino barges or riverboats. Casinos began to reopen in the summer of 2006 and ten are now open along the Gulf Coast.

The two things I need for the "Mississippi misery tour" are my camera and tissues. Rich and I cross the repaired I-10 twin span and I open all the windows, just like my friend who drives this rickety bridge every day. We continue to take I-10 to the I-59 split where we were forced to go northward during our evacuation just four months ago. We stay on I-10, take the Biloxi exit, and drive down to Highway 90, which parallels the beach.

Much of the big debris has been removed or pushed into piles, and skeletons of buildings remain standing in a few places. Rich pulls into the Waffle House parking lot "out of respect for the past" he says, but says he'll stay in the car. During our annual vacations, we would stay at different motels, but always ate at least one breakfast at the Waffle House. Walking on the cement slab, with nothing left other than the steel posts where the counter stools once stood, brings back a flood of happy memories but leaves me weeping.

Rich is holding the box of tissues out of his window as I walk back to his SUV. He knows me too well. This is so sad, I tell him.

We stop at another parking lot and I look up and down the highway, trying to remember what was here. All of the landmarks I remember are gone, and one cement slab is indistinguishable from the next. We pass slabs that have cement or stone walls around their garden areas and see that the owners have spray-painted their names on them. Several have American flags flying.

I ask Rich to pull into another driveway. Household items litter this area. There are broken dishes and pot lids amid pieces of sheetrock. And then there's a perfectly intact green vase in a pile of rubble and bricks.

I wonder about the people whose treasures are now at my feet. Where are they now?

I look in the distance and see the shell of a motel. Its sliding glass doors are ripped away and allow a glimpse inside. Industrial washers and dryers are still standing on the first floor.

We make our way down Highway 90, passing the deserted Wal-Mart and McDonald's slabs. We're now along the part of the highway where beautiful old Southern homes once stood.

Rich follows my commands to pull in here and there, and I find myself on the foundation of what was once a house. The tile by the front steps is intact and leads me to a big marble-floored area. There's a small rectangle of white octagonal tiles to the right with cut-off plumbing pipes, which must have been a bathroom. I walk the hallway to the back and find kitchen tile and a lonesome-looking in-ground pool beyond. The water in the pool is black and the grass around the pool is dark brown; there's no sign of vegetation or life anywhere.

Rich doesn't feel the need to see things up close like I do, and stays in the car listening to NPR. I cross the street and stand at the edge of the beach. The sand resembles snowbanks carved by the wind, and there are peaks in some places that are at least six feet high. The smooth, flat beach that I remember is no longer here. The kids and the beach balls and summer fun that spring to mind are gone, and I wonder how long it will be before they are back.

Lillie comes to pick up Jack for his two-day trial run with her Pit Bull, and we send them off with a large bag of dog chow, probably more than Jack could eat in a year. There's relief in the house that Jack is gone, and no one seems to miss him.

A day later, Lillie is on the phone saying that she's bringing Jack back. He's bitten her dog, first in the nuts, and then his legs. Her Pit Bull won't leave the couch.

Lillie tells us about a couple she knows—retired military and retired nurse—whose dog drowned in Katrina. She remembers them saying they'd like to get a rescue dog when they move back to New Orleans around the first of the year. She thinks they may have moved backed by now, and says she'll give them a call if it's all right with us.

Jack went to live with the retired couple and to this day enjoys his reign as Alpha Dog there. With no other dogs around, Jack returned to the frisky but gentle dog that we first knew and loved. From time to time, Lillie would update us on how Jack was doing in his new home. Jack took a liking to driving around, and sat on his new owner's lap with his front paws on the bottom of the steering wheel. Jack spent the summer of 2006 vacationing in Maine and went on a cruise the following year.

DAY 133

Saturday, January 7, 2006

RICH AND I walk Buddy around our New Orleans neighborhood. It's infinitely easier to walk one dog instead of two, and we take the longer loop down Walter Road over to Orchard Road and back. Near the end of Walter Road, there's a one-story brick house where who-knows-how-many college boys used to live. We know this house from many pre-Katrina walks when we'd find a bunch of cars haphazardly parked in front and beer cans littering the lawn. Sometimes, when I'd walk by with the dogs, the boys would be working on their computers while soaking up the sun, and there were a couple of early mornings when I'd find someone passed out on the lawn.

I wonder where those boys are now. There's been no sign of life at this house since Katrina, but there are still several houses in the neighborhood that remain empty and silent. It's hard to tell what's going on with these houses.

I hand Rich the leash and head up the driveway. Through the kitchen window I see that books are open on the table, dirty dishes are stacked on the counter, and a sweatshirt hangs over the back of one of the chairs. It's as if time has stopped here and like *The Twilight Zone*, the boys who once lived here have simply vanished.

A rep for a liquor distributor tells me hello as I round the corner in Breaux Mart. I park my buggy to the side and ask where his daughter, who played soccer with Samantha, is in school. I hear his family's evacuation story and learn that his daughter is in Baton Rouge with her mom, who has been transferred there for work. He goes up nearly every weekend, and would go up every weekend if he could, but his company is down two reps and business is booming. I tell him that I'm not surprised. I used to drink a glass or two of wine every now and then but now can drink a bottle. He tells me that alcohol sales in New Orleans are up—way, way up!—in part because of Katrina distress, but also because of all the construction workers in town, and you know how they like to drink, he says, as he pantomimes chugging motions with his hand and mouth. And apparently, we're all drinking the "hard stuff" a lot more now. Less than a case of champagne was sold in Breaux Mart for New Year's, but the shelves with the bourbon, rum, gin, and vodka were pretty much emptied out. He adds that the store is planning to expand the liquor section and make the produce aisles smaller, and by the way, "Have you heard about the guy who has been exposing himself in the bread aisle?" he asks.

My friend Mary tells me she went back to the office where she used to work to pick up some of her things. It's the first time she's been back to New Orleans East since evacuating for Katrina, and she found that someone had opened the bottom drawer of her desk and defecated into it. At some point post-Katrina, the office building was ransacked and nothing of value remains. She says the entire area looks like a bombed-out wasteland.

DAY 135

Monday, January 9, 2006

RICH LEAVES FOR his week working up in Bogalusa and our kids return to their New Orleans school. Five hundred forty of the 720 students in the school have come back, with many living with relatives, in FEMA trailers, or in houses that are being repaired. The school, which had several feet of water in it in some places, is still a major construction zone.

As people in the neighborhood surrounding the school have begun to return, they're cleaning out their flooded houses and piling the discards at the street. Nearly every house has one of these growing piles now, and the streets are peppered with refrigerators taped shut with duct tape. Warning notes say things like "DO NOT OPEN. Rotten food and mold!!" My favorite was "C'mon, I dare you...Open me up!"

There's furniture, carpet, clothing, shoes, books, and toys in the piles. Not much was salvageable in this neighborhood. I drive by the piles when I take the kids to school and when I pick them up. They look like the piles on the street adjacent to ours, and remind me of the piles we had in front of our house when it flooded ten years ago.

A family's life story can often be told simply by looking at the debris pile in front of the house. Toys mean kids live there, books are indicators that the homeowners like to read, and a green bathroom sink says they haven't updated in quite a while. Photo albums in the piles are hard for me to look at, and remind me that I need to look at photos that I have at home. I want to make copies of photos that include kids who live in these houses so that I can give them to their parents.

There's an "old lady" pile that has a pink chenille bedspread next to a bedside commode. Across the street, there's a crib with a water line half way up the rails. At the corner of Northline and Park Road, a lone sunflower grows amid the barren dirt and debris and serves as a reminder to me that there is hope amid the rubble.

John is happy to be back at his New Orleans school with Colin, William, and his other close friends. Samantha is glad to be back but says she feels like she's at a one-room schoolhouse now. Less than half of the fifty kids in her grade have come back. She also tells me that her classmate Katrina has changed her name to Katie.

People in New Orleans are now using the word "plus" a lot. In the carpool pickup line, the woman in the car in front of me gets out to talk. Her son is in the 6th grade with John, and she tells me, "We've gutted the entire first floor down to the studs; plus we have some mold upstairs, so that sheetrock is coming out; plus I'm driving my husband to work because his car flooded; plus we're staying with my brother-in-law's family, so you know how that is; plus I started smoking again. I'm so depressed with everything right now!"

It's times like these, when there are no words to say, we just nod our heads and listen, and give each other hugs.

There's a bright yellow flyer on our front door handle when we get home. The gas grid to our area has been restored and the flyer lists instructions on how to relight stoves, outdoor grills, and water heaters. I practically jump up and down because this means that we do not have to bathe at the kitchen sink any longer, and I can stop baking or microwaving everything. I try our gas cooktop with its electric igniters and it works! I plan to go to the store and get some eggs; we'll have scrambled eggs for dinner, something we've not had in a long time. I head outside to our grill and hear the hiss of gas as I turn it on. Yay! I switch on the heat in our house and the furnace kicks on. I can put away the space heaters and multiple layers of comforters and blankets that we've been sleeping under. I then relight our hot water heater and applaud when I hear a "vroom." I go back a few minutes later and the tank is getting warm. We now have three microwaves on our counter, along with my built-in microwave over the stove where we've been heating water in big glass bowls, and now I can retire and return the tabletop microwaves. I'm not even sure who they belong to at this point.

DAY 140

Saturday, January 14, 2006

JOHN AND HIS friend Colin join the middle school boys' soccer team, along with several of their friends. It's the first game of the season today, and we drive down River Road in to New Orleans and park at the Fly along the Mississippi River. The kids talk about how their school has been patched up and partially reopened, and some of the classrooms have been combined, which leave the remainder locked and dark. Volunteers are attempting to freeze-dry the books in the library, a process that removes water from the drenched books and has had some success in preserving what was once the largest children's book library in the South. The school continues to be a construction zone as flooded areas are repaired and restored. The absence of many of the previous students is felt in the carpool line as well as the classroom. I miss talking to the moms who have moved away or have not yet come back.

The boys' soccer team has had four days of after-school practice. A whistle blows, and it's the coach waving the team toward a big cardboard box. The coach starts handing out brand new long-sleeved soccer jerseys, and tells the boys he needs them back at the end of the game. The boys play against another school, who like theirs, barely has enough players to play. When the game ends, the boys huddle with the coach, peel off their jerseys, and put them back into the box.

The girls' varsity soccer team appears. Each girl takes a sweaty jersey from the box and pops it over her head without hesitation, in the spirit of making do with what you have, and sprints onto the field.

Rich has been working in Bogalusa, so after the game, the kids and I pack up our stuff, put Buddy in my Tahoe, and head up to our little farm. It's a fairly warm day and we spend a couple of hours pulling branches and broken pieces of the fence to our debris pile in back. Between the bulldozing of the downed trees and the branches and fence pieces that we've added, the debris pile is now roughly the size of a small two-story house.

We've been told that FEMA will eventually come by and pick it all up, and take it somewhere to burn. "Somewhere" is likely to be what we've been calling "the inferno" at the end of the dirt road adjacent to our property. We've gone back there a few times. The area once was a deep sand pit an acre or two in size. Truck after truck now rattle down the dirt road, filled with "clean" tree debris, dump their loads, and rattle back up the road, kicking up dust all along the way. The tree debris fire continually burns and sends big black plumes of smoke up into the sky.

The Backwoods Mercantile is a little store, not far from our farm, that primarily sells cigarettes, beer, and lottery tickets. It's become a stopping point for many of the truckers, who buy a Red Bull, eat some pizza, and use the restroom.

Via Pete, the owner of the store, we learn that the FEMA clean-up money was awarded to a large corporation, which subcontracted with a middle man who subcontracted with another middle man who subcontracted with yet another middle man, and finally in the end, anyone with a truck or trailer could find work hauling way tree debris. The pay is good and the work is easy, so trucks with license plates from all over the country are buzzing up and down our dirt road.

Rich has been up at the hospital making rounds and pulls into the driveway.

I notice the huge white box in the back of his Expedition. "Oh no you didn't," I tell him.

"Oh yes I did," he says.

He's smiling and says it was on sale. Such a good sale, in fact, that he bought it on the spot and brought it right home.

Samantha and John walk up from the debris pile and see the box in Rich's car. They sprint to the back windows and cup their hands on the glass to peer in.

"OH MY GOD, IT'S A TRAMPOLINE!" squeals Samantha.

Even John is excited. It's something else to do other than haul branches or sit in a barren farmhouse.

It takes all afternoon to assemble the darn thing, but it's worth the expense and the aggravation of putting it together when we see Sam and John laughing as they bounce around.

DAY 160

Friday, February 3, 2006

I START MY day in New Orleans by dropping the kids off at school and then head to the CVS pharmacy, which is now in a trailer in a parking lot near Lakeside Mall. I head over to a branch of our bank that is now open, and it too is in a trailer, although this one seems bigger and might be a double-wide. The post office is operating out of three long trailers that are parked end-to-end, but their configuration necessitates going outside of one in order to enter the next.

Volunteers from all over the United States and beyond have descended on New Orleans and the Gulf Coast, and despite how cold it is, I keep my window down so I can wave my THANK YOU sign to them as I drive by. It's attached to a paint stirring stick with two other sticks crisscrossed in the back so I don't have to worry about the wind bending it. It's gotten to the point that if a car doesn't wave a sign or have painted windows saying "THANK Y'ALL!" then they're not from around here.

I'm so overdue for a mammogram that I've finally

scheduled it for today and head to East Jefferson Hospital to have it done. The receptionist praises me for coming in and says that their mammogram return rate is way, way down since Katrina.

"I'm worried about the ladies out there who aren't coming in," she says. "But I understand how everybody has bigger fish to fry these days."

On the way home, I hear the familiar rumble of yet another flat tire, this time the left front. I curse the debris on the roads and the construction workers who seem to drop nails everywhere. Everyone I know has had a flat tire or two. It's my third flat since moving back, and the second flat for this tire. I stop at Southern Tires, where my account is quickly pulled up, and settle in to watch *Judge Judy*. A few minutes into the show, a mechanic comes in from the back and holds up a shiny silver nail.

"But that ain't all," he says excitedly. "You had two nails in that tire!" He opens his other hand to show me an even longer nail.

I ask the man at the cash register if I get a prize for having so many flat tires. He laughs and says no, but I can keep the nails if I want.

I get home just before the tree guys arrive. It's been twenty-three weeks since Katrina, and today's the day that the massive pine tree in our pool comes out. The pool was drained several weeks ago so that the tree could dry out, and the crew is now able to stand at the bottom of the empty pool and cut up the tree. It takes two full days, but the tree is finally removed from our pool, and repairs to the pool and surrounding fence can begin.

DAY 185

Tuesday, February 28, 2006

ALTHOUGH THE CITY has been divided about whether or not to have its 150th Mardi Gras celebration, city officials and Carnival organizations decide the show must go on. The population of New Orleans is now around 156,000, down from nearly half a million.

During the last eight days, twenty-eight parades have rolled, many of them shorter in length than in years past. News reporters look surprised to learn that in 2005, thirty-four parades rolled over eleven days, so this year's schedule is not as much of a cutback as many expected.

As predicted, attendance is down about 40% to around 400,000, and because the French Quarter and downtown areas were among the areas least affected by Katrina, 23,000 of 28,000 hotel rooms are operable. Two-thirds of them are available to tourists since many relief workers and volunteers are now housed in apartments, churches, tents, and trailers.

Mardi Gras Day looks pretty much the same as previous Mardi Gras Days from our vantage point on St. Charles

Avenue. John gets a prized coconut and a spear from Zulu riders and is thrilled. This probably wouldn't have happened if last year's crowds were here.

DAY 189

Saturday, March 4, 2006

JOHN TURNS TWELVE tomorrow, and we're having his birthday party at the farm. Rich and I caravan the eight boys across the Causeway and let them loose. Hide and seek on nine acres is a whole different game than playing hide and seek in someone's back yard.

Rich and I sit on the screened-in back porch with our cocktails. We have a little metal sign in our kitchen that says it's five o'clock somewhere, and it's always five o'clock on the farm.

Cocktail number two is served, and some of the boys are now in the rowboat on the pond. Colin thinks he's seen a snake, so the others are investigating with him.

"You're done with your drink already?" Rich asks.

"Yup."

"You sucked those right down. How much are you drinking these days?" he asks.

"I don't drink every day if that's what you're asking."

"I see you with a drink every day."

"No you don't. I don't drink on Mondays or Thursdays."

"So you drink five days a week."

"But not sequentially."

"Well, yeah, you take two days off a week. Do you think you have a problem?"

"What are you now, the AA police?"

"Good God, no. I'd drink every day if I wasn't on call."

"I drink to escape, but I don't think I drink that much. Just enough to calm the nerves and help me get to sleep. I don't think I'm drinking any more than anyone else."

"Well, you just be careful not to overdo it."

Rich and I talk about bills, money, and our sanity yet again. Our insurance company has just paid our claim and the amount has been way less than expected. Trees that fall on the ground instead of on houses are not covered. Nor is replacing the trees that fell. We're planning on having our back fence replaced in April by a company from Alabama. The fence is not covered by our policy either. The owner of the fence company and his crew of six are living in a one-bedroom apartment in Elmwood near where we live.

I haven't yet been able to find someone to repair the three rooms with water damage. Most of the crews want the bigger jobs and aren't interested in something so small.

Rich checks our bank balance daily, if not hourly. We're worried about how we're going to be able to send the kids to college. I'm even worrying about how we'll pay our bills in the coming months. I worry about my Tahoe and how long it's going to keep running. I wonder about the toll on our health—physical as well as mental. I know that there are many, many people on the Gulf Coast who are in much worse of a situation, and I can't imagine how they're managing.

DAY 200

Wednesday, March 15, 2006

I'VE CONTINUED WORKING on our farmhouse, tending to all of the little fixer-upper details, like adding some hooks in the broom closet and repairing the blinds in John's room. Our kitchen cabinets and drawers didn't have knobs when we bought the place, and we haven't yet mastered the art of opening them with just our fingertips. It's especially difficult in humid weather when the doors and drawers seem to seal themselves shut.

I stop at our local Home Depot in Harahan to see if they have enough knobs and matching drawer pulls for our kitchen. I've stopped in every other week or so for a couple of months now, but each time, there either wasn't enough of something I liked, or the drawers would be filled with a mixture of knobs and pulls and sorting it all out would take hours. I understand the chaos here; the store barely has enough employees to keep three checkout lines open, and there are a ton of people in here all buying all sorts of things to repair their homes. The parking lot has a large fenced-in area filled with roofing materials, plywood, and pipe, so the larger items are being sold outside, often straight from a tractor trailer right into someone's pickup.

No drawer pulls today, so I head out through the garden department, which has just received one of the first shipments of spring flowers and plants. I'm reminded of the flower beds in front of our house, where nothing appears to have survived the Katrina flooding in that part of our yard. Pink vinca flowers look bright and cheery, and are fairly inexpensive, so I pick them up and head to the cash register.

The cashier asks if I need soil, and tells me stories of how people have tried to grow plants in soil that was covered by floodwater for days to weeks. "Nothing grows there," she informs me. I don't know how long our flowerbeds were under water, and think back to the water line on our fence and the corrosion on the underside of my Tahoe. I buy several bags of soil, just in case our soil is as bad as they say.

I need to get my eyesight checked, so I call my optometrist to make an appointment. I always like to get the first appointment of the day, and I'm told the first appointment is now at 9:30 a.m.

"What happened to eight o'clock?" I ask.

"The doctor lives in Baton Rouge now and drives in, and then he drives back up every day, so our appointments are from 9:30 to 3:30 p.m."

I tell her that 9:30 a.m. is just fine.

Like so many people along the Gulf Coast, I learn that some of my doctors have returned, some will return at a later date, and some will not return at all. It's often a topic of conversation in the carpool lines at the two schools our kids attend. Who's back? Who's coming back? And when?

Years later, I learn that my eye doctor commuted in from Baton Rouge for two years following Katrina. Two hours each way.

I also eventually found matching drawer pulls and cabinet knobs, at a Home Depot in Minneapolis, during one of my out-of-town work trips.

DAY 209

Friday, March 24, 2006

TIME FOR ANOTHER Oncology Nursing Society Board meeting in Pittsburgh. Because US Airways has not resumed many flights into and out of New Orleans, I fly on Delta from New Orleans to Atlanta, Atlanta to Cincinnati, and finally Cincinnati to Pittsburgh. Everyone asks how we're doing and how things are coming along in New Orleans.

Our annual nursing meeting was scheduled to be held in New Orleans in May, but Katrina scratched that, so it's being held in Boston instead. Parts of the New Orleans Morial Convention Center are being used as a temporary clinic, called Spirit of Charity.

"Big Charity" Hospital remains closed and the extent of its damage is being disputed. The Foundation for Historical Louisiana hired the architectural firm RMJM Hiller to determine if the hospital could be repaired, and the firm found that the building was structurally sound. The Hiller firm also noted that the hospital's Art Deco design is architecturally significant. In addition to Big Charity staff, who cleaned up the hospital soon after Katrina, Louisiana Treasurer John Kennedy advocated for repair of the hospital, citing it would be the most cost-effective way to return quality healthcare and a teaching hospital to New Orleans. However, the Louisiana political process being what it is, replacement of the hospital was favored over repair. A new teaching hospital and Veterans Administration Hospital are being built in the Mid-City area of New Orleans and are projected to open in the summer of 2015, a decade after Katrina hit.

In May 2008, the National Trust for Historic Preservation added Big Charity to its list of America's most endangered places. The documentary film *Big Charity: The Death of America's Oldest Hospital* was released on October 21, 2014, and recounts the history of the hospital from its opening in 1736 until its controversial closing in 2005.

After Big Charity closed, University Hospital was renamed the LSU Interim Hospital. The hospital has gradually increased its capacity following Katrina and now has 235 staffed beds. Big Charity remains empty, surrounded by a locked chain link fence.

DAY 216

Friday, March 31, 2006

I FIND A place near the barn that gets the morning sun and seems to drain well when it rains. It's the perfect place for a vegetable garden. I get the tiller started and turn over the hard ground. I walk back and forth in one direction and then push the tiller perpendicularly until the soil looks like it may be ready for seeds.

I had decided that each time I come to the farm, I should spend at least an hour enjoying it, so I take the pool chaise out of my Tahoe and put it in a sunny spot in the back yard. It's a nice, warm day, so I sit outside and eat my tuna sandwich.

From this vantage point, I see all of the remaining debris on the ground that could mean death to a lawnmower. The grass is now greener and growing faster, and will need to start being cut in a few weeks.

There are sticks and shingles from the barn roof everywhere, so I look at my watch and calculate that I can pick up debris for about an hour before I have to pick up John from school and Samantha from soccer practice.

I grab my gloves and the two rolling trash cans, and walk toward the corner of our property where our driveway comes in from the road. I'll start over here and work my way across the nine acres in the coming weeks.

I'm wearing a sports bra and running shorts, and a couple of the debris truck drivers honk at me as they go by. I wave and keep picking up the roof shingles, along with a dirty diaper that someone apparently pitched from a car.

I roll the trash cans down the dirt road toward our debris pile at the back of the property and hear a pickup truck coming up behind me. I move to the far right side of the road so the truck can pass. It's now going exceptionally slowly, following me. I look out of the corner of my eye to see if he's about to pass me, but he stays behind me. I quickly look to see which way I should run when he gets out of the pickup to attack me, and decide that I'll push the trash cans into him and take off for the highway in front of our house. My adrenaline is pumping, so I should be able to run pretty fast.

The pickup has come to a stop and the driver is opening his door. We have truck after truck coming down this road with debris every minute of the day it seems, but where are they now? There are no trucks coming in either direction.

The man is about my age and appears tall and strong. He's looking me up and down as he walks toward me.

"Let me help you with that, ma'am," he says as he tips his cowboy hat and reaches for the trash cans in front of me. I can't speak or move for a moment or two; I was that scared when he was coming toward me. My heart is still thumping in my chest as I blurt out a weak "thank you."

The man empties the trash cans onto our debris pile, tips his hat again, and gets back into his pickup and drives on down the road.

DAY 223

Friday, April 7, 2006

MY ROUTINE NOW is that every Friday, I drop the kids at school by 8 a.m. and head to the farm on the Northshore whether or not Rich is working in Bogalusa that week. The kids and Buddy and I also go up on the weekends when Rich is working up there. I plan my out-of-town work for the beginning of each week, so I can head up to the farm at the end of the week. Rich is with the kids when he's working in Metairie, and Lillie stays with the kids when Rich is working up in Bogalusa and I'm working out-of-town.

Every Friday, I stop at the Ritz gas station at the corner of Causeway Boulevard and West Esplanade to use the restroom and get a cup of coffee before I ride across the 24-mile long bridge. I usually get to the farm by 9:30 a.m. and start working in the garden before it gets too hot.

Today, I'm planting the Beekman 1802 heirloom vegetable seeds that Erica gave me for Christmas, along with six tomato plants. The peas that I planted last week have sprouted, and so far, the deer haven't eaten anything.

I flip on the TV while I eat lunch and hear that all of the 2006 Saints' home games will be played in the Superdome. It's undergone a $185 million renovation and is almost finished. When the newscaster says "You'll remember how the Dome looked back in August…." and Katrina footage is shown, I click the TV off. I don't need this painful reminder today.

DAYS 250-253

Thursday, May 4, 2006 - Sunday, May 7, 2006

I FLY TO Boston for the annual Oncology Nursing Society meeting, which was previously scheduled to be held in New Orleans. The meeting always begins with an opening ceremony that consists of the organization's President and Board of Directors walking in from the back of the convention hall. This year, ONS members from New Orleans and the Gulf Coast are invited to join the processional, and I decide to walk in with my NOLA colleagues rather than the Board. Over 6,000 nurses stand up as we walk arm-in-arm down the long aisle to our seats in the front. None of us were expecting this touching show of support.

At the meeting, I hear story after story about patients who traveled to, or were sent to, places all over the country in the days following Katrina. They needed to continue their cancer treatments, but did not have their medical records with them, and there was no one in New Orleans that could be contacted for information. Many of these patients underwent scans and tests for restaging, and their new oncologists did the best they could to continue treatment. The nurses who told me these stories often started crying as they talked to me, and many ended their stories by saying, "I'm never going to forget that patient and all he went through."

Gabe from Birch Trail Camp in Minong, Wisconsin, calls me to say that they are expecting Samantha at camp this summer, free of charge. I'm momentarily stunned into silence, and he has to ask if I'm still on the line. We've been saving up so that Sam could go to the camp again this year, so I decline his kind offer but tell him how very much appreciated it is.

DAY 268

Monday, May 22, 2006

MORNING NEWSCASTERS ANNOUNCE that the nineteen penguins and two sea otters that were flown to Monterey, California by Betty White back in September are returning to New Orleans today, and the aquarium is scheduled to reopen on Memorial Day weekend. FedEx donated the chartered flight and $100,000 to the aquarium.

Since I fly a lot, I know how to track planes on the computer. I see a flight that's coming in from the west and it's a FedEx plane. I yell to John and his friend William, who has spent the night, that we're going to the airport to see the penguins come home. They barrel down the stairs in no time at all.

I park in the cargo area of the airport and see a brass band and several newscasters with their cameras mounted on tripods. We're about to enter the gate when an airport security guard stops us and says that the event is for the media only. I have to explain to the boys what this means and their faces fall.

A woman in a FedEx shirt has been watching from the check-in table just beyond the gate, comes over, looks at the crestfallen twelve-year-old boys, and invites us in. She gives us all ear plugs and takes us to a place where we can stand, and the boys can see.

The big FedEx plane lands and parks in front of us. Stairs are pushed up to the plane and a purple carpet is rolled out, leading to the refrigerated FedEx Special Delivery truck. The band is playing "When the Saints Come Marching In," the door pops open, and Ron Forman, head of the Audubon Nature Institute, comes out holding a tiny penguin.

One by one, the penguins are brought off the plane, carried down the stairs, and placed on the purple carpet. A guy from the aquarium in New Orleans is at the end of the carpet calling each by name. We're majorly impressed that he recognizes each of the penguins he hasn't seen in months, and he's getting emotional seeing them again.

One of the penguins is veering off a bit, heading toward the pavement.

"Emma, come here. Come here Emma," says the aquarium guy. Emma tilts her head back and forth a few times, looks right at the guy as if to say oh there you are, and then heads straight for him. She picks up her pace as she gets closer and closer. It was just like one of those reunion scenes in the movies, except of course that this was a penguin strutting into the arms of a man crouching on purple carpet. He scooped her up into his arms, the spectators applauded, and Emma was whisked into the FedEx truck for a very special delivery home.

DAY 282

Monday, June 5, 2006

THE LOCALS WHO hang out at the Backwoods Mercantile say that it's not a good year for blueberries because of Katrina, but not knowing how last year's crop was, I'm pleased with the three huge bowls I've picked just this morning from our bushes out back. It's hurricane season again, so we keep a minimum amount of food in the freezer here on the farm and in the freezer at our New Orleans house. I line baking trays with the blueberries and stack them in the freezer to freeze.

My little garden has produced copious amounts of lettuce, tomatoes, cucumbers, peas, and string beans so far this year. I've got pumpkins growing, along with watermelon and cantaloupes. I'm not sure about the onions, and the corn is looking a little wilted. The flowerbed along the south side of the house has Beekman 1802 zinnias in full bloom, grown from the historic zinnia seed collection packs that Erica gave me for my birthday.

The trucks continue to bring tree debris to the inferno at the end of the dirt road by our house, but there have been fewer and fewer of them. The Mercantile is a great place for news, and I hear that the dump on Highway 1083, which is where household debris is being deposited, has been contaminating wells over that way because of the lead in the debris.

ONE YEAR AFTER HURRICANE KATRINA

August 29, 2006

JOHN CONTINUES ON at the flooded Metairie school, to be with his friends. Samantha applied to the Academy of the Sacred Heart, an all girls' Catholic school on St. Charles Avenue in New Orleans, partly because it hadn't flooded at all and partly because one of her best friends and neighbor, Taylor, had been attending Sacred Heart since preschool. She knows a number of the girls there through Taylor and has quickly acclimated to her new school.

In retrospect, I'm not sure if Samantha the Jew would have been so readily admitted to a Catholic school if not for Katrina. Hurricane Katrina made people in New Orleans a whole lot nicer to one another and a lot less judgmental. Especially today, the one-year anniversary of the devastating hurricane. It's a very sad day for those who lost loved ones, and a reaffirming day for the rest of us. We all know what today is, and give nods of understanding and hugs to one another. Many of us reflect on how far we've come, while others think about how far they still need to go.

A number of memorial programs are being held around the Gulf Coast, including programs at both our kids' schools. The names of Katrina casualties and those still missing are read during a service in New Orleans. The remains of 1,079 people have been recovered in Louisiana and an additional 231 were found in Mississippi. However, Louisiana officials have information on 700 people whose loved ones continue to search for them, and 90 unidentified bodies remain in the morgue.

Exactly one year after Katrina, the National Institute of Mental Health released its study findings on disaster behaviors and effects of the hurricane on 1,043 adults living in Louisiana, Mississippi, and Alabama. The study group's composition roughly mirrored the demographics of the population living in these areas in August 2005.

The Institute of Mental Health found that three-fourths of those surveyed evacuated. Half of the people who did not leave said they were unable to go because they lacked the money needed to evacuate, and the other half reported that they chose not to leave because they did not think the storm would be that bad or felt they needed to stay with family or friends. Choosing to stay or leave was not related to gender, race/ethnicity, education, marital status, or income.

Nearly all of the respondents reported experiencing significant stressors that included death of a loved one, major financial loss, extreme physical adversity, and extreme psychological adversity. All of these stressors were as common among the socially advantaged as the socially disadvantaged.

Interestingly, the survey also found that 88.5% of respondents reported post-traumatic *growth* and said that their hurricane experiences helped them develop a deeper sense of meaning or purpose in life. About 85% found that Katrina made them realize that they had inner strengths that they did not previously know they had. In other words, this perception of strength was not thought to be there all along, it was something that people experiencing Katrina discovered in themselves because of Katrina.

A year after Katrina, many of the streets of New Orleans are still filled with debris, half of the shopping malls in and around the city remain closed, and tourism is in steep decline. The city's population before the storm was 484,674 and it's now 217,279, according to The Brookings Institution. Despite the large amount of recovery work in progress, the unemployment rate is 7.2%, which is higher than the 6.8% pre-Katrina rate. Hurricane Katrina disproportionately displaced residents who were black and poor, and the city is now 57.6% black and 37.8% white, and 4.5% self-identified themselves as "other" races. Prior to Katrina, New Orleans was 67.3% black and 28.1% white, and 4.7% "other." Half of the hospitals are now up and running, and 29% of the schools have reopened, yet 40% of the population still does not have power in their homes. Rent for a two bedroom apartment now averages $940 a month, compared to just $676 a year ago, and 4,433 homes are for sale.

FALL 2006

IT'S ANNOUNCED THAT a company in Baton Rouge is sending recycling trucks to New Orleans once a month so that we can drop off our recyclables. For the past year, everything has been going into the regular trash. On the first collection day, we pack Rich's Expedition with our recyclables and have so much that I sit in the passenger seat with a huge bag of cans on my lap.

We get in line at the drop off location in the Elmwood shopping center, and there are at least fifty cars in front of us, all patiently waiting for a turn at a collection truck. We've all learned to be incredibly patient in the months, and years, following Hurricane Katrina, and we eventually arrive at the truck, empty our recyclables, and head home. We repeated this process every month until May 2011, when curbside recycling was finally reinstated.

On September 19th, Saints owner Tom Benson announced that the team had sold out the Louisiana Superdome for the entire 2006 season with season tickets alone, a first in franchise history. The first post-Katrina home game on September 25, 2006 was an emotionally-charged *Monday Night Football* game against the Atlanta Falcons. The Saints, under rookie head coach Sean Payton and a new quarterback named Drew Brees, defeated the Falcons 23–3. Attendance for the game was a sellout crowd. Green Day and U2 performed "Wake Me Up When September Ends" and "The Saints Are Coming" before the game, and the game later received a 2007 ESPY award for "Best Moment in Sports." The game also is remembered by Saints fans for Steve Gleason's blocked punt on the opening series that resulted in a touchdown for New Orleans. In 2011, Gleason was diagnosed with ALS and has since started Team Gleason to increase ALS awareness.

On December 17, 2006, the Saints clinched their third division title and their first NFC South title in franchise history. Things were looking good for the Saints. Wal-Mart doubled its Saints apparel area, and it was not uncommon to see massive numbers of New Orleanians decked out in Saints-wear. In addition to T-shirts and hats, just about anything now can be found with the Saint's team name or logo, a fleur de lis, in the team's colors of black and gold.

After a first-round bye, the Saints beat the Philadelphia Eagles 27–24 in the 2006 Divisional Playoffs. No team had ever had such a poor record in the prior year (3–13) and then gone on to a league or conference championship game since the 1999 St. Louis Rams. Unfortunately, the season ended on January 21, 2007, when the Saints lost to the Chicago Bears in the NFC Championship game.

Paul Soniat comes to pick up his son from our house and hands me *Below the Water Line,* a CD containing thirteen songs he wrote and performed. Paul is a self-taught musician who was born and raised in New Orleans, unlike people like me who say that we weren't born here but got here as fast as we could. Paul grew up on Soniat Street, long ago named after his family, and is the Director of City Park's Botanical Garden. After Katrina, City Park was submerged in three feet of water for a couple of weeks, which wiped out the majority of plants in the garden. In addition, the sprinkler system went out when the power went out, so the greenhouse plants died as well. Paul rounded up donors and volunteers and reopened the Botanical Garden in March 2006, a mere six months after the storm.

Paul and his son have just pulled out of our driveway when I walk over to my computer to listen to his songs out of curiosity and courtesy. With all he's had to do with his mother's flooded home, his son's flooded school, and the flooded Botanical Garden, when has he had time to write songs? And release a CD?

When I see Paul a couple of weeks later, I tell him that he should give out a box of tissues with his CD. I tell him how I sat at my computer listening to his Katrina songs over and over, how I burst into tears when I heard "My Hometown New Orleans" for the first time and felt the "...pain of my hometown. Somebody's mother, somebody's brother, somebody's friend you'll never see again, never be with again. Life ain't easy in the Big Easy anymore."

August 2007

I'M ASKED TO join an international workgroup to develop an oral chemotherapy patient teaching tool for global use, and the group decides to meet in New Orleans. There is still considerable interest in how Katrina has affected our city, and the group would like a tour.

It's been nearly two years since Katrina. We drive around the Lower Ninth Ward, the area hardest hit by flooding, and it's still a scene of astonishing desolation. Where houses once stood, only concrete foundations remain. A few of the houses are still standing, all hollowed out, with the rescuers' markings still on the front. I explain what the markings mean and we pass a few houses where the numbers one or two appear, which mean that bodies were removed from these homes. The woman from Turkey says it looks worse than Kosovo after the war.

November 2007

THERE'S A POSTCARD from my dentist in today's sparse mail. Just below the big smiling face with sparkling teeth, there is a handwritten note saying that I'm overdue for my dental check-up. And apparently way overdue, as I have not been to a dentist in two years. I've been oblivious to the passage of so much time, busy with so many other things. I call the dentist and learn that we're all overdue for our exams, and schedule appointments.

January 2008

THE MEDICAL JOURNALS are reporting the growing body of research documenting the adverse mental health consequences of Hurricane Katrina, and some of this research has focused specifically on children. "Katrina kids" initially reported stress related to physical safety and loss of loved ones, friends, and pets. On-going stressors include residential instability, multiple school transitions, and caregiver mental health problems.

A December 2007 *Mental Health Weekly* study suggests that 45,000 children along the Gulf Coast are struggling with mental health issues. Although it's been over two years since Katrina, 37,000 families are still living in FEMA trailers, and reports of formaldehyde leaching from these trailers are beginning to be publicized. A spokesperson for FEMA responded by saying that travel trailers were never designed for long-term use.

In an NPR series, Emergency Medical Services Director Jullette Saussy notes that cheap drugs have flooded the streets of New Orleans, and teachers and healthcare providers are seeing a rise in suicides, high-risk behavior, and clinical depression among teenagers and young adults. In her interview, Saussy states that the suicide rate in New Orleans tripled between 2006 and 2008 to 42 deaths, and the majority of these suicides were young people.

The Suicide.org organization questions these numbers, noting that the official numbers don't take into account Katrina evacuee suicides that occurred elsewhere and those classified as accidents or accidental overdoses. The organization asserts that the true number of Katrina drug overdoses and suicides will never be known.

February 14, 2008

IN THE EVENING on February 13th, my mother said she didn't feel well, collapsed on her living room floor, and died at 2 a.m. the next morning. Sam and I are taking the first flight out of New Orleans to fly up to Albany, New York.

The mother of a classmate of John's is on the flight, and because the flight is half empty, we sit across from one another. Samantha slumbers on the two seats next to me, her head in my lap.

Marie tells me she's headed up to Connecticut again, to take care of her ill mother. She and her two siblings have been rotating being there a week at a time for about four months now.

"No one seems to understand," she says, "that things are not okay in New Orleans even though it's been two and a half years. Things are still messed up for a lot of people. And then on top of it all, you have life. You have all of the ordinary life things, like your mother dying and my mother getting sick. That's all on top of the Katrina aftermath. And then look at all of the people we know who have cancer now, or something bad. You just wait and see; they're going to add 'Katrina' to the list of things that cause cancer."

March 15, 2008

RICH COMES HOME and tells me that his partner Bobby has decided to quit working up at the Bogalusa LSU hospital. The Metairie practice has come back sufficiently for him financially, and he's worn out from working a week at a time up there. With two kids in private schools and with us wanting to help with college, Rich feels he needs to continue working in Bogalusa, but not necessarily a week at a time.

Rich talks to a group of surgeons on the Northshore and discovers that they are interested in forming a group with him to cover the Bogalusa hospital. Starting June 1st, Rich will work in Bogalusa every Thursday and every fourth weekend.

We reminisce about how Rich and Bobby worked two jobs, which required being available 24/7, for two and a half years. It's hard to imagine that *surgeons* needed to work two jobs in order to recover from Katrina. They're not alone by a long shot; the Gulf Coast is full of people who had their livelihoods turned upside down by the hurricane and its aftermath. Many people we know did not have jobs to come back to, and embarked on new careers out of necessity. Some took whatever jobs they could find.

Along the Gulf Coast, people still mark time using the words "before Katrina" and "after Katrina." No one says "before 2005." It's always a statement of life before Katrina, followed by current conditions, and almost always, the current conditions are not as good as people had hoped. It seems everyone has lingering or long-lasting effects of Katrina.

We're still occasionally asked by relatives in other states

why we chose to come back to New Orleans rather than relocate elsewhere, and we tell them we came back because our kids wanted to come home. We also had a house that didn't flood, but is worth a fraction of what it was worth prior to Katrina. There are people in New Orleans who still cannot even give away their flooded homes. Many of us are tied to our debt, not so much our houses.

April 1, 2008

THE BAND R.E.M. releases its album *Accelerate,* which contains a track called "Houston." The opening line of the song is "If the storm doesn't kill me, the government will." Singer Michael Stipe tells *The Sun* that of all of the tracks on the album, this is the one that means the most to him. "Houston is not an angry song, in fact it's filled with sadness. I was writing from the point of view of someone who has barely survived Hurricane Katrina and then has been displaced. Barbara Bush, the ex-First Lady and the President's mother, said, 'So many of the people were underprivileged anyway, so this is working well for them.' Hello, Barbara these are people who lost everything. I know people who lost family members, their homes, everything."

August 29, 2008

"I DO NOT fucking believe this," says Rich as we watch the 10 p.m. news. Hurricane Gustav is in the Gulf of Mexico, headed right for New Orleans. And it's the three year anniversary of Hurricane Katrina.

John has gone with Colin and his family to Long Boat Key in Florida for the long Labor Day weekend. After Katrina, and then Rita, Suzanne had said that they should have gone to Florida in the first place, so this time she happened to get it right by chance since she planned this trip months ago.

Voluntary evacuation begins tomorrow, on Saturday, August 30th, for several parishes around New Orleans. All major highways will have contraflow lane reversal, and over seven hundred buses are being staged around the city to move evacuees. After Katrina, National Guardsmen were trained on how to drive school buses, and chartered buses are being brought into New Orleans as well. People with medical needs will be put on an Amtrak train to Memphis. Newscasters repeatedly warn that the Superdome and Convention Center will not be used as emergency shelters.

We spend Saturday morning fielding the calls from friends and relatives who are asking if we're evacuating. We plan to go up to our farm, which is north of I-12, the non-official line separating the danger zone from the safer zone. We expect high winds and lots of rain, and it's likely our power will go out, but we have a portable generator and ten plastic cans filled with gas.

LSU is scheduled to open its football season in a home game against Appalachian State at 4 p.m., but kickoff is moved up to 10 a.m. so that the contraflow lane reversal through

Baton Rouge can start after the game has finished and fans have dispersed.

We spend Saturday afternoon double-bagging the photo albums and kids' artwork that hangs on our walls. Rich carries it all upstairs and puts it in plastic bins in a closet. Samantha, Rich, and I then scurry around the yard and bring chairs, garbage cans, and pool floats into the garage. I pull the porch rockers inside the house, and toss the doormats inside as well.

In Plaquemines Parish south of New Orleans, Parish President Billy Nungesser flew around in a helicopter and counted the number of vessels and barges that potentially would be a safety issue to people, property, and the repaired levee system. Parish officials called the owners of about 150 vessels and told them to move the vessels or the parish would sink them, and 70 of the 150 were sunk, some by the parish, some by the owners.

New Orleans Mayor Ray Nagin is on TV again, and issues a mandatory evacuation starting on Sunday morning. He calls the category 2 Gustav "the storm of the century" and "the mother of all storms," and declares a dusk-to-dawn curfew. City-assisted evacuation will cease at noon.

Rich and I look at each other. Wasn't Katrina the storm of the century? Just how bad will Gustav be? Perhaps Nagin is exaggerating to scare people and get them out of town.

Rich, Samantha, Buddy, and I drive across the Causeway late Sunday morning. Just like when we evacuated for Katrina, I'm reading the Sunday paper and there's a ton of traffic. We finally make it to our farmhouse and start the shoring-up process.

By Sunday afternoon, 1.9 million people had evacuated southern Louisiana, with 200,000 evacuating from New

Orleans alone, making it the largest evacuation in the history of Louisiana.

Rich is on the B-team at East Jefferson General Hospital this year, and he'll need to go back as soon as Gustav passes. East Jeff and other large hospitals in the New Orleans area remain open, but non-critical patients have been evacuated. Many of the hospitals also have tightened their rules for staff who work at the hospitals during a hurricane or just want to stay there, including prohibiting pets and family members at some hospitals. Nursing homes and other residential health-care facilities also have evacuated their patients following the lessons learned from Katrina.

Rich is the "Thursday guy" at the LSU Hospital in Bogalusa, so he won't need to go up there for another four days. We close the shutters on the windows of our farmhouse, pull out the generator and gas it up, stash bottles of water in our freezer, and hunker down for a long night.

The wind picks up and our satellite TV reception comes and goes. The power cuts off around 9 p.m. and Rich starts the generator. We plug in the TV, a box fan, and the dorm-sized refrigerator we bought specifically for occasions like this. We also have a lamp plugged into the power strip, but turn it on only when needed. I inflated the air mattresses long before the power went out, and they're standing up against the French doors leading to the screened-in porch in back.

"Thank you DISH!" yells Samantha toward the sky when she discovers that satellite TV is still working, although there are periods of time when we have staccato reception.

Rich and I peer out the windows and shine the flashlight around to see what's come down and what's still standing.

We're expecting parts of the roof of the barn to blow off again, like they did in Katrina. Lonnie and Michael, the prior owners, stayed in the house for Katrina, and I find comfort in that. I think the winds here were higher for Katrina, but then again, maybe they weren't. It's another sleepless hurricane night for Rich and me.

Sometime around 4 a.m. Monday morning, the rain starts pelting the tin roof of the house. Unlike prior rainfall, when the sound of the rain was soothing, this rain sounds like someone's shooting a machine gun into the roof. Maybe it's hail. We're all wide awake, and Samantha inches closer to me. Eighty-pound Buddy has awoken and has come to sit on my lap.

We hear the familiar "crack" of big tree limbs snapping and the "pop, pop, pop" of branches breaking off. The wind is now gusting, and we hear a menacing whistle somewhere up near the roof that reminds us of the soundtrack of a scary movie.

The hours tick by.

Light finally begins to spread across the house, and we head to the porch in front to inspect the damage. The barn and its roof appear to be intact.

"One, two, three, four, five," says Rich.

"What are you doing?" I ask.

"Counting trees that are completely down."

He counts to sixteen, and that's just the front of the house. Just like Katrina, it's eerie how the wind has blown the leaves from the trees. Even our Southern Magnolias, which keep their leaves year round, are barren.

We go to the screened-in porch in back. Holy cow, there must be a hundred trees down, and there are many places where the trees have taken down the wood fence we replaced just three years ago.

"I'll get my camera," I tell Rich.

I open the box with the two-burner hot plate that I just bought at K-Mart and plug it into the power strip leading to the generator. I heat water for instant coffee and turn on the TV, but there's nothing but a wavy screen. The rain is still coming down hard, but not as hard as earlier this morning. We move the lamp to the kitchen table so that Samantha can do her homework and I can write in my journal. Rich paces around the room.

We have sandwiches for lunch and play a marathon Monopoly game in the afternoon as rain continues to fall. It's hot in the house, but the box fan helps move the air around. This is nothing like Katrina, so we're not complaining.

We spend another night at the farm, and wake up Tuesday morning to light rain. Rich comes in from listening to the radio in his Expedition and says that the Causeway is still closed because of high winds and that tier 1 workers—and tier 1 only—are being allowed back into New Orleans via I-55 to Airline Highway, the same way that we re-entered New Orleans after Katrina. Tier 1 is comprised of first responders, law enforcement officers, and medical personnel in possession of Tier 1 documents and badges.

Rich pulls the generator back to the barn and moves the big branches blocking the driveway. Sam and I pack up the car and move all of the food that was in the freezer and dorm refrigerator into a cooler. At noon, we head back to New Orleans, and on the way wonder about what kind of damage we're going to find there.

The line of vehicles at the I-55 checkpoint at the Ponchatoula exit must be ten miles long. Despite the warning that only emergency workers with Tier I documents would be allowed back into New Orleans, there are clearly dozens of cars in this line that don't belong here. We inch toward the checkpoint as light rain continues to fall. The heat and humidity are stifling when we let Buddy out to walk around. We haven't moved for twenty minutes, so it is a good time to get out of the car and stretch our legs.

I walk back to our car through the middle of the two lanes of traffic heading south on I-55. A guy in a power truck from Tennessee has his window down and is talking on a walkie talkie or CB radio. I overhear him say to someone—most likely the trucks behind him—that he's heard that it's clear sailing after getting through the checkpoint. The backup is being caused by New Orleans residents who are arguing with the National Guard that they should be allowed back in. Apparently, some have to be escorted at gunpoint to the Ponchatoula exit when they're not allowed to proceed down I-55.

Samantha declares these people "stupid" and is getting agitated from the wait. We continue to inch along and finally—finally!—we reach the checkpoint and breeze right through. And just like I'd heard earlier, we sail on home.

There is a lot of tree damage in New Orleans and once again, just like Katrina, we have to figure out how to get to our house. There's a huge tree down across Citrus Road, and power and cable TV lines are tangled in its branches. We loop around the neighborhood and have to park in front of our house because of the trees and branches lying across our driveway. We also have a big oak tree that has uprooted and has crashed into the front of our house.

We bring everything inside, and after a quick inspection that reveals that the tree on our house is securely wedged on the roof, and isn't likely to come on down into the bedrooms, Rich heads off to East Jefferson Hospital to relieve the A-team, who have been at the hospital for the past four days. Buddy drinks three bowls of water and gets on the couch in the sunroom. Sam and I peel off our shirts and I look for battery-operated fans. The kids had taken them to camp, and I know they're here somewhere.

Because of Katrina, we've all learned the hard way about food spoilage. The number one tip for Gustav was putting everything in the freezer and refrigerator into plastic garbage bags so that if the power goes out, the bags with the rotten food can be removed quickly in one swoop and removed from the house. Too many people remember their Katrina refrigerator experiences when their refrigerators had to be emptied item by item.

The other tip was eating ice cream vertically, so I had Sam eat one side of a pint of chocolate frozen yogurt from top to bottom. The half-eaten carton went back into the freezer before we left. If the frozen yogurt is still mounded to one side after a power outage, the freezer didn't thaw much and the food inside is still good. However, if the surface is smooth and level, that means we lost power long enough for it to thaw completely. Sam does a little drumroll on the counter as I remove the frozen yogurt carton. I pop the top and it's nothing but brown liquid inside. The power is still out and apparently has been out for a long time.

Once again, we have a monumental yard clean-up ahead

of us, and Samantha and I start in the front yard. I've already put in a call to our tree guy, and hope he's got one of those passes so he can come back sooner than the general public. We do what we can do without a chain-saw and bobcat or bulldozer, and head to the pool to cool off.

The pool has become a depository for leaves and branches of all sizes, and Samantha and I take turns using the big net to scoop them out. We sit on the steps for a while in the late afternoon sun, and Sam tells me she plans to sleep in the pool tonight. After a long swim, Buddy finds a place to lie under the azaleas.

Rich honks as he parks at the end of our driveway, pretty much in the street, and we yell to him that we're in the pool. He tells us he's impressed by the pile out front that Samantha and I have produced.

I grill the package of hot dogs that has traveled with us from the New Orleans house to the farmhouse and back again. I give Buddy the rest of the ham and turkey in the cooler, knowing that it may be unsafe to eat in the morning. The ice blocks in the cooler are room temperature now.

Samantha says she feels like she's going to pass out now that she's in the house. She thinks it's hotter inside the house than outside, and I think she may be right. I tell her to keep drinking water, and I remember that I have a few of those disposable ice packs that are activated by popping whatever's inside them. With soccer players in the family, I keep them on hand, and discover I have six of them. Samantha moves hers from her forehead to her throat and then the back of her neck, and leaves it there as she lies on the ceramic kitchen floor in an attempt to cool off.

We sleep downstairs because hot air rises, and we are able to sleep, probably because we haven't slept well for the past few nights. The next morning, I heat water on the gas grill in the back yard and make instant coffee.

Rich leaves for the hospital, and Samantha and I continue to clear the yard. We plunge into the pool every hour or so and go back to work. Each time we go in to cool off, Buddy joins us.

My cell phone rings, and it's Lana, who lives on the next street. She saw Rich go by as she was working on her yard and invites us over for dinner. She and her husband own a tugboat company and have a re-entry pass. Lana tells us that Mayor Nagin has abandoned a staggered re-entry plan and people in New Orleans are being allowed back in, despite the fact that over a million people still do not have power.

We're all sweating profusely as Gordon cooks up the steaks that were in their freezer and thawed at some point before now. Lana has candles lit and music playing from a portable CD player. We eat the steaks, down a couple bottles of wine, and find our way home using our flashlights.

Rich has one of the other guys in the Bogalusa group cover for him on Thursday and heads to the hospital. Sam and I work on the yard some more, and jump into the pool every hour on the hour.

We're working in the back yard when I hear our neighbor's air conditioning unit kick on. I fly into the house and turn on a kitchen light switch and the bulb lights up. By the time I've turned on the upstairs and downstairs AC units and set them to 60 degrees, Samantha has already turned the TV on but to her dismay, cable isn't working. She digs out her DVD collection, finds the discs for the TV series *The O.C.,* and starts watching.

Lana and Gordon come to stay with us for three nights

since we have power and therefore have air conditioning. Although they live on the next street, it takes four days longer for their power to be restored.

Forty-eight people died in Louisiana as result of Hurricane Gustav. The strong category 2 hurricane produced 15 million cubic yards of debris in Louisiana, compared with 26 million generated by hurricanes Katrina and Rita. Katrina and Rita are grouped together because Rita followed on the heels of Katrina, and a considerable amount of Katrina debris had not been cleared when Rita hit.

Gustav can be thought of as a wind event, as opposed to Katrina, which was primarily a flood event. Gustav's wind toppled trees, blew off roofs, and left 63 of 64 Louisiana's parishes without power for several days.

September 13, 2008

A MONTH LATER, Hurricane Ike hits the Texas coast near Galveston, killing 74 people in Texas and Louisiana. Most died from carbon monoxide poisoning after the storm had passed, and eight people drowned. Others died from heart attacks and medical conditions exacerbated by evacuating or riding out the storm. Ike left 2.3 million people without power for several days.

Spatially, Ike was a massive storm. As the system neared landfall, Ike's hurricane force winds extended 120 miles and tropical storm force winds extended 275 miles from its eye. The large wind field was also to blame for Ike's 10-20 foot storm surge, which pushed debris as far as 20 miles inland. Ike sent a storm surge into the same areas along the Louisiana coast that were hit by Rita just three years ago. The fishing camp in Holly Beach that my friend's family had just finished rebuilding was once again destroyed.

Hurricane Ike was the third costliest weather event in American history, behind Hurricanes Katrina (2005) and Super Storm Sandy (2012), and caused over $30 billion in damages in the United States alone. With AIG failing two days later, Galveston Island fell off of the national news, and there were no big fundraisers to help them rebuild.

December 11, 2008

THE FIRST SIX homes built by Make It Right, the foundation started by the actor Brad Pitt, are ready for their homeowners to move in. The homes were built to LEED platinum certification in the Lower Ninth Ward and had their first endurance test when Gustav's 105 mph winds blew through. Built to accommodate high-water events, the houses are raised at least five feet, with foundations resting on piles driven thirty-five feet into the ground. The houses also have rooftop escape hatches, just in case.

Completion of the houses reignites the national debate about rebuilding in low, flood-prone areas such as the Lower Ninth Ward. Many question if the money would have been better spent building on higher ground.

April 2009

I ASK THE mother of one of John's friends how she's doing. Her family has been repairing their flooded home for almost three years.

"We have Chinese drywall," she announces.

The television news pops into my mind, which has shown photos and video of tarnished door knobs and hinges, corroded air conditioning condensers, and sizzling light switches, all linked to Chinese drywall. More than 500 million pounds of drywall from China were imported in the first six months of 2006, and much of it was used along the Gulf Coast as people repaired their homes or built new ones. The drywall that was made in China was manufactured using a process that is different than the drywall manufacturing process used in the United States. Chemicals used in China are thought to cause a chemical reaction that corrodes metal and gives off a rotten-egg stench. Lawsuits contend that the Chinese drywall is emitting sulfur, methane and other volatile organic chemical compounds that are ruining homes and harming health. It's estimated that 34,000 homes have Chinese drywall, and the number may be higher since many homes were built or repaired with a mixture of Chinese and domestic drywall.

September 2, 2009

THE GASTROENTEROLOGIST IS wiping his eyes as he comes toward me. The colonoscopy didn't look good, he says, and he thinks Rich has colon cancer. The biopsy comes back and sure enough, it's cancer and Rich needs surgery. No less than ten people tell us it's a "Katrina cancer," caused by "Katrina stress."

Rich's recovery gives us time to talk about how we're still not out of what we call the Katrina, Rita, and Gustav holes, which were compounded by the 2008 stock market crash. I tell Rich it's like the whack-a-mole game at Chuck E. Cheese's. Just when you get your head above water for a moment, you're hit back down—and in our case, stay down for quite a while. Sam will hopefully head to college next year, and John two years after that, and we're not sure how we're going to help pay for it all.

We're not alone in our financial worries. Everyone we know still feels that they are in recovery mode; no one says they've fully recovered. Most emphatically state that they'll never fully recover from the repeated battering, which is as much psychological as it is physical. People talk about repairing their houses, only to have them damaged again by yet another hurricane. The cost of insuring our homes has skyrocketed, and some find their homes uninsurable. On the everyday level, we are still affected by the hurricanes despite the passage of time.

December 10, 2009

SAINTS' COACH SEAN Payton is the lead plaintiff in a 591-page class action lawsuit against Knauf Plasterboard Tainjin Company, a Chinese company that manufactured drywall believed to be corroding homes and making people sick in Louisiana and Mississippi. Payton and his family moved out of their house and then systematically took it apart. They took photos of the corrosion and then stored the damage in a warehouse, where the Chinese manufacturer was able to inspect it. Just over 2,100 people along the Gulf Coast have signed up to be a part of the suit. As of March 2015, the suit is still in litigation.

December 28, 2009

I'M AT OUR house in New Orleans when I get a phone call from the man who does the pest control up at our farm. We had a major mouse problem in the barn when we first moved in, and since then, Mike has been checking the barn every month for rodents and pests. He calls to say that one of the French doors on the back of our house is slightly open and has a broken pane of glass, and he thinks our house has been broken into. He's called the police and they're on the way.

After the 75-minute drive, I arrive to find two sheriffs' cars, the sheriff's department crime scene van, and a red pickup truck in our driveway. A deputy tells me they're just about done with fingerprinting the place and I'll be able to go inside in a few minutes. The man with the pickup says he lives just up the road and asks when we were robbed, because he was robbed two days ago. I said I wasn't sure since this is a part-time house for us, but it had to have been in the past three days.

"I knew it!" he exclaims and proceeds to tell me that he knows of two other families that were robbed this week. He says that he was cleaned out; his TVs, computer, his wife's jewelry, and their six guns are gone. "And they totally trashed the place," he adds.

I can only imagine what our house looks like as I'm motioned inside. "Let me know if they tipped your beds!" my neighbor yells.

My first impression when I go inside is that a cyclone has ripped through the house. Someone went into the kitchen, stuck their arms into the cupboards, and swept the contents out. The floor is covered with pots, pans, cans and boxes of food, and broken glass. Lots of broken glass.

There's also broken glass in the living room, by the back door where the people broke in. The deputy tells me he snipped a section out of our area rug because it had blood on it, presumably from bleeding that occurred after breaking the window, and it's going to be DNA tested. He says everyone in our family will need to be DNA tested and fingerprinted to rule us out as suspects. The living room TV and DVD player are gone, the TV and Game Box console and the stack of video games in the bedroom are missing, the laptop computer is gone, and the $200 I kept in a sock drawer is gone too. The beds have been stripped of their covers and the mattresses are flipped at odd angles.

I tell the sheriff's deputy that a neighbor is outside and

that he described his house in the same way ours looks now, including the flipped beds.

"They do that to find guns," the deputy tells me. "How many you missin'?"

I tell him we don't own any guns.

"You shittin' me?" he asks in disbelief and tells me that most people around here keep a gun or two under their mattresses. The deputy tells me there's been a string of burglaries just like ours, during the day when people are away, and the houses have been ransacked.

"A lot of people around here made a ton of money hauling debris from Katrina and then Gustav last year. That work is all done, so now they're burglarizin' for money." The deputy takes down information about what's missing and gives me his card. "People always find that there are other things missing, too, when they get around to cleaning up and get to thinkin' about it."

I walk with him back outside and my neighbor runs up.

"Well?" he asks.

"Yup, it's just like you predicted. Kitchen is trashed with everything on the floor and a ton of broken glass everywhere, and the TVs and computer are gone. We had a little cash just to have it on hand and that's gone, and the beds are tipped."

"How many guns they get?" he asks.

"None. We don't have any guns," I tell him, and once again get a look of utter disbelief.

I go back inside and take pictures with my iPhone to show to Rich and the kids. There is so much glass on the kitchen floor that it's impossible to avoid, and it crunches under my feet. I wonder how I'm going to get everything cleaned up.

I decide to turn on DISH radio to listen to some 70s music while I clean up the mess, but as I walk across the room, I am reminded that that the TV is no longer there. I look for the old AM/FM radio and CD player that we keep in the hall closet and find that it's gone too. I start my "additional stolen items" list and get to work with the broom and dustpan.

It takes two hours, but the house is finally cleaned up. Oddly, one pillow from the bedroom is missing its pillowcase, and then I realize the burglars must have used it to haul away their bounty. I take the bag with the broken glass to the trash can, and sit at the kitchen table to make a list of things I need to replace. Not a single drinking glass or coffee cup remained intact, so I drink some water from a Tupperware container and survey the near-empty cabinets.

When I first saw the damage, I was in disbelief, and as the day has worn on, my shock has turned to anger at whoever did this. Stealing is one thing, but why smash and destroy everything? And the little TV, the one that my parents sent us money for, has been taken. The reminder of my parent's generosity and a symbol of our recovery is gone.

I'm ready to head home and call Cheryl to tell her about our robbery.

"Pawn shops!" she says.

"What?"

"You need to go to pawn shops soon, like today. They might have your stuff there. I'll go to the ones around here in Slidell and see if they have your TVs or computer." I tell her the sizes and brands of the stolen electronics, and Cheryl says she'll call me if anything turns up.

I stop by a pawn shop in Covington on the way home,

but our things aren't here. I ask the clerk if there are other pawn shops in the area. He says that there's one in Hammond and the "big one" in LaPlace, so I head toward Hammond on I-12 and plan to circle on down to LaPlace on my way home.

Cheryl calls to tell me she's had no luck finding our things in Slidell, and says that she told the pawn shop people that her son left his clarinet on the bus and was looking for a replacement. She said she didn't want to seem suspicious asking about specific brands of TVs and computers.

I go to the two pawn shops on my route home and say that my son left his laptop on the bus and I'm looking for a replacement. Although both shops have multiple TVs and computers, none are ours.

At dinner, I pass around my iPhone so Rich and the kids can look at the photos I took. Our daughter notes that the clock radio/CD player next to her bed is not in the photo of her room, and we add it to our list. John rattles off the names of the video games that are gone from his room, plus the two controllers and console. When Rich swipes through the photos of our room and closet, he adds that our binoculars are gone. Several days later, we notice that our deer camera was stripped from a tree out back.

I'm superbly annoyed that so many things were stolen from us and start to wonder where they might be. Cheryl suspected that the thieves are looking for easy, fast money and came up with the idea that our things might be at pawn shops by now, which gets me thinking of other ways that things could be sold quickly, for cash with no questions asked. Garage sales!

I find this week's issue of the *Timberland Adviser* online and see that four garage sales are scheduled for the weekend in the Bush and Bogalusa area where our farmhouse is. Looking at the classified ads also gives me an idea, and I write an ad for a cash reward for information about house robberies along Highway 21. The ad first appears online and then is published in the print edition, in the section titled "miscellaneous," right under an ad for deer sausage.

I jot down the four addresses where garage sales will be held, enter the addresses in the tax assessor's website, and learn who owns the properties. I take those names and enter them in the Google search box. Three do not produce any more information than already known, such as address. However, the fourth name produces several Bogalusa *Daily News* article links, including an arrest for robbery three years ago. The ad for this garage sale lists a TV. Bingo! I've found our thief.

On Saturday, Rich and I fill our travel mugs with coffee and make the drive up to Bogalusa, which usually takes about an hour and half but this morning takes over two hours because of the speed restriction on the 24-mile Causeway Bridge. Heavy fog has closed one of the two lanes on both the north and southbound spans, and the speed limit has been reduced from 60 mph to 35 mph.

We drive to the garage sale where I know for sure we'll find our TV—and our thief. A slight drizzle has started, and as we pull into the driveway, we see small children running to place black trash bags over rows of little worn shoes they've placed at the edge of the driveway. There's a table toward the back that has a dozen or so clear vases that come with generic flower arrangements, and an assortment of knick-knacks are on the ground beneath the table. A man asks if I'm looking for anything in particular and I say a TV. He waves me toward a sagging porch where a console TV in a heavy oak cabinet has been placed. It probably dates back to the early 80s. "It works," he says.

"That's a bit bigger than what I had in mind," I say. I look over the pitiful merchandise spread out across the lawn and driveway and immediately feel ashamed that I was convinced that this poor man was our robber. It looks like this family is barely surviving.

I spot a dusty ceramic bird among the knick-knacks and peel off the two dollar tag. I tell the man I can't find a tag on the item and ask if he'll take twenty dollars for it. It's two dollars he tells me. I hand him a twenty and say that it is worth much more than two dollars and I don't want to take advantage of the situation, that twenty dollars is a fair price.

"Whatever you say ma'am," he replies.

Our ad with the reward for information about the robberies did not generate any responses, and all of the things taken from our farm were never recovered.

February 7, 2010

SOMEONE CHANGED THE lyrics of the song "Party in the USA" to "Party in the MIA," or airport code for Miami, and the song is being played loudly, and over and over again, at the Winn Dixie grocery store down the street from our house. A group forms near the banana bin to dance and high-five each other, and the group grows and grows until practically everyone in the store, young and old, is dancing with us.

Shelves with chips and snacks and beer are almost picked

clean, just like they were before Katrina, Rita, and Gustav, but this time, it's a joyous clean out. The Saints are playing in their first-ever Super Bowl game in Miami tonight.

I get some ham and turkey at the deli counter, and get a "Who Dat!" and big smile from the woman behind the counter as she hands the baggies to me. The music is interrupted when the store manager comes on the overhead loudspeakers to let people know that the Budweiser truck has just arrived out in front, and they're unloading beer there. I flashback to Hurricane Gustav in 2008, when I went outside the store to the Kentwood truck for water, and everyone had worried, drawn faces. As I head outside today, I see a totally different scene that can only be described as pure jubilation.

The Saints have won a franchise-record thirteen games and are taking on the AFC champion Indianapolis Colts for the 2009 NFL championship game. In the playoff games, both teams placed first in their conferences, and it's the first time in sixteen years that the number one seeds of the AFC and NFC are playing in a Super Bowl game. Super Bowl XLIV is the Saints' first-ever Super Bowl appearance and the fourth for the Colts.

The entire city, even the elderly and the wee ones, are dressed in black and gold, and people are honking their horns as they drive. Quite a few cars have Saints' flags flying and lots of houses, like ours, are decorated with shiny Saints' wreaths and banners. Although Mardi Gras is next week on the 16th, my purple, green, and gold wreath has remained on the shelf in the closet. I don't even like football all that much, but find myself infected with the spirit of this Saints' season.

People in New Orleans and Saints' fans everywhere are

either having, or are going to, a Super Bowl party tonight. The local TV stations have pre-empted regular programming to show parties that are in progress locally and those that are being held in other cities where Katrina evacuees now live.

On the way to our friends' house, we go through the drive-thru daiquiri shack to pick up gallon containers of frozen margaritas. Along the way, we see groups of cars clumped in front of houses. People are already setting off the fireworks they've been hoarding since New Year's.

The game isn't starting for another hour, but our friends' house is full of people and the dining room table is laden with food. An extra-large Mardi Gas king cake is on the sideboard. There's a big box of Popeye's chicken and a big bowl of Ambrosia. The woman who made it says that she makes it only on special occasions, and this occasion sure is special.

When the game is about to begin, the living room becomes stuffed with kids sitting on the floor, and adults gather around on the couch and folding chairs that have been set up around the perimeter of the room. Black and gold pompoms and those horns that are obnoxious any other time other than tonight are handed out to everyone in the room.

One of the kids says that he won't be able to sleep tonight if the Saints win the Super Bowl. Another runs by and says it's like Christmas, only better.

The adults watching the Super Bowl are all sitting on the edge of the seats, beer in one hand and pompoms in the other. The kids are nervously sliding around on the hardwood floor, figuring out where the best place to sit might be. We watch the kick-off and the kids start blowing their horns pretty much nonstop until one of the dads says stop that commotion right now, we can't hear the TV.

Down 10–6 at halftime, New Orleans successfully recovers an onside kick on the second half kickoff, and subsequently takes the lead with Pierre Thomas' 16-yard touchdown reception. The Saints are playing well, and defeat the Colts by a score of 31–17, our first ever Super Bowl win.

The game is over, and Drew Brees is holding up the Lombardi trophy as confetti falls.

People from the houses in the neighborhood spill out onto the street. Car horns are honking wildly. Fireworks fill the sky with color, and kids are running around yelling, "Who Dat!" at the top of their lungs.

People will later say that this win came at a time when the people of New Orleans, whether living in New Orleans or being a New Orleanian at heart, needed it most.

February 9, 2010

SCHOOL IS CLOSING early today for the celebratory parade to recognize the Saints' Super Bowl win. Pretty much all of the businesses in New Orleans have closed early, and the topic of conversation is where to park near the parade route, which will start at the Superdome, go down Howard Avenue, wind around Lee Circle to St. Charles Avenue, turn onto Canal Street, and end just past the Convention Center. Only a Super Bowl win can upstage Mardi Gras in New Orleans.

We've all been wearing our black and gold a lot lately, and wearing it proudly. It's going to be cold tonight, I tell the kids, and John squeezes his Number 9 jersey over his winter jacket. We get bundled up and head out at 3 p.m. for the 5 p.m. parade.

We take Airline Highway, the "back way" to downtown New Orleans. Once we're on the road, it's clear that people are driving into New Orleans every which way, and the roads are once again gridlocked, just like they were for Katrina, Rita, and Gustav. We finally make it to the parade starting point near the Dome just before 5 p.m. and miraculously find a place to park.

As the parade is getting organized to roll, the United States Marine Corps Reserve band plays the unofficial Saints anthem, "Halftime (Stand Up and Get Crunk)." In between each song they play, someone in the crowd starts the "Who Dat" chant and everyone lining the streets chimes in.

Float after float come down the street. Saints players wearing their jerseys, the coaches, and team owner Tom Benson roll past us. We lose count tallying up the number of marching bands that go by. The crowd is easily twenty feet deep here and helicopters fly in the air overhead. Sean Payton is on the last float, kissing the Lombardi trophy and blowing kisses to the crowd.

We were planning on meeting Cheryl and Wayne and their boys here, but they're stuck on I-10 still trying to get in to New Orleans. Rich calls and says he's had to park a mile up the street, almost to Carrollton. I tell him that we're near the guy holding a big sign that says "Happy Lombardi Gras" and he joins us to watch the tail end of the parade.

There was no official count of how many people attended, but radio station WWL estimated the crowd along the 3.7-mile parade route to be 800,000, despite it being so cold that New Orleans enacted the city's freeze plan that night. According to *The Indianapolis Star*, 11 fans greeted the Colts at the Indianapolis airport when they arrived home.

April 7, 2010

I'VE WEEDED THE vegetable garden on the farm and collapse on my lounge chair to have lunch and rest up before tackling the flower gardens. It's a brilliantly beautiful day.

My cell phone rings, and Samantha tells me that she's been awarded an academic scholarship from the University of Georgia, her number one pick for college. I am so happy for her that I start crying when we hang up. Finally—*finally*—our kids are having more happy times than sad.

May 28, 2010

SAMANTHA IS GRADUATING from high school today, and puts on her floor length white dress with its two inch straps that received official school approval last week. She pulls her hair back so my sisters and I can secure the ring of flowers on her head, and she wears long white gloves for the first time in her life. Mercifully, the outdoor graduation ceremony is at 7 p.m. to avoid the beastly heat.

Each of the girls walks down the courtyard path in the front of the school, carefully navigating the dozens of candles in paper bags that light the way. A spotlight is on the alcove above the front door of the school, where a statue of Jesus stands with open arms. Many of the cars going by toot their horns when they see the outdoor ceremony, and people yell congratulations from the streetcars as they pass by.

April 19, 2011

VANNA WHITE, PAT Sajak, the 2,400 pound wheel, and the *Wheel of Fortune* crew are back in New Orleans to film fifteen episodes of the show. They were in NOLA just before Katrina struck, and evacuated before taping all of the shows they planned to tape. In a televised interview, Vanna says she's happy to see the city in such a great state.

August 29, 2011

IT'S THE SIXTH anniversary of Katrina, and still an emotional time for people along the Gulf Coast. The house across the street from us has been torn down, and an empty lot remains. The house on the next street where the college boys lived was bulldozed last year, and there's an empty lot there now. The house where we found Jack inside just days after Katrina, is gone. Two houses in the neighborhood are being raised up about four feet off the ground.

We've said good-bye to many people as they left New Orleans and continued their lives elsewhere. We've also said hello to the influx of people, many of them young and optimistic, who want to be a part of the rebirth of the Gulf Coast and have joined our communities. When people now ask how we're doing, I tell them that it's a new normal.

"It's very bad in Schoharie," my father tells me on our weekly Monday morning phone call.

"What do you mean?" I ask, now that he has my full attention. I sit down at the kitchen table with my coffee.

"Hurricane Irene," he says. He tells me that my hometown of Schoharie is under water. I can certainly relate and my heart sinks.

Schoharie is located in upstate New York, about forty miles west of Albany. The town is older than the United States, and got its name from the Mohawk Indian word for floating driftwood.

Schoharie is the county seat for Schoharie County, and has a courthouse and county offices, a school, a jail, a quarry, and several small businesses. The historic Parrott House restaurant has recently reopened, and the Glass Bar is still going strong. Schoharie used to have a grocery store but it closed years ago, and like many rural towns, Schoharie is a town without a stop light.

In 2002, David Letterman searched for a small town to parody, chose Schoharie, and bused 475 people, which pretty much equaled the entire town population, to his show. Letterman poked fun at small town life, and said that Schoharie is so small that it has to share a hooker with Cobleskill, another nearby small town. Footage of Biff Henderson milking a cow and visiting a goat farm were shown during the late night show, and the people from Schoharie enjoyed their time in the spotlight. In return, the village of Schoharie named a road after him, Letterman Lane, which leads to the sewage plant.

My father tells me that he talked to Dale and Kim, who own a dairy farm perched on the hillside above the Schoharie Valley. The power's been out, and Dale has no way to milk the fifty cows, except by hand. Their lower fields, with corn about ready to harvest, are under water and filled with debris. There are new tires in his fields, and Dale speculates that they came from Lenny's tire shop outside of Middleburgh, five miles away. Dale says he's lucky though, because other farmers have had their cows and livestock swept away by the floodwater, and he still has his.

Dale also tells my dad that the Bridge Street bridge has water flowing across the roadway of the bridge. The house where my grandparents lived stands in eight feet of water and the garage is now across the street, busted apart and splayed among several trees.

Facebook and Google are a lifeline for those of us with ties to Schoharie but are no longer living there. Social media allows us to obtain information and updates about relatives and friends in the area.

As I'm searching for information on my computer, I watch video footage of New York Governor Andrew Cuomo taking a helicopter tour of the Mohawk and Schoharie Valleys. The shots of the flooded homes and farmland get me crying. Cuomo says the amount of damage is devastating and will get worse before it gets better. He then characterizes Irene's impact as a tale of two New Yorks, a downstate that was spared and an upstate that was ravaged. Officials had expected that New York City and its suburbs would be the worst hit, but the opposite has come true. Cuomo says Mother Nature always wins at the end of the day.

In the eleven counties of the greater Capital Region, well over 100,000 homes are without power. The eastbound side of the Thruway from Syracuse to Amsterdam is closed, as is the westbound side from Amsterdam to Little Falls. Countless roads are impassible because of flooding or washout. The tiny village of Prattsville has pretty much been washed away. Many houses there have been pushed several feet off their foundations, and some have floated down the road.

A National Weather Service spotter reports that the Old Blenheim Bridge spanning the Schoharie Creek had been washed away. The 210-foot-long bridge, built in 1855 using only hand tools, was the longest wooden single-span bridge in the world. I pull up photos of the bridge on my computer, and think back to the many happy times that our kids skipped across that historic bridge on one of our drive-abouts through the countryside. It's hard to believe it's gone.

On Tuesday, I learn that a few shelters have been set up, and one of them is at the Gallupville Lutheran Church, where my parents were married and I was confirmed. From what I can tell on Facebook, people are getting to the shelters mostly via four wheelers or walking because so many of the roads have either washed away or continue to be flooded. People are worried about the Gilboa Dam, which provides water to New York City residents, and there are unconfirmed reports of water overtopping the dam. There is concern that the dam may break and send torrents of water through the already flooded valley.

I'm trying to figure out what I can do, how I can help.

I spend the day reading Facebook posts from other people who, like me, are wondering how to reach people in the hard-hit areas.

I find the phone number for the Gallupville Lutheran Church online and place the call.

"Hello?" asks the timid voice.

I tell the man who I am, and he says oh yeah, you're one of Charlie and Gloria's girls. I tell him that I'm calling from New Orleans, and he tells me that the phone hasn't worked in three days and when it rang just now, he actually thought it was God calling, or maybe a short in the phone lines. He says over and over again that he can't believe he's talking to somebody way down in New Orleans! I ask how things are going there, and he says about two hundred people are coming in to eat, usually three times a day, and they are low on food and not sure what they're going to do. People are sleeping on the pews, too. There are two people there from the National Guard, but the roads are still flooded or washed away. There's so much devastation in upstate New York that even the National Guardsmen do not know when additional food and water will arrive.

"What do you need?" I ask. I'll figure out a way to get it there.

"Well, we really could use some potato peelers."

Potato peelers. Seriously? Okay.

"What else?" I ask.

He gives me a wish list: extension cords for the generators, contractor-grade trash bags, bread or rolls, and some mops and pails. And fresh fruit would be really nice. I tell him I'll see what I can do.

I call my sister Karla, who is the Office Manager at Harvest Church in Clifton Park, and use my iPhone to patch in my other sister Erica. I tell them my plan.

"I'm in," Erica says.

"Count me in," adds Karla.

On Thursday, I take the 6 a.m. flight to Washington National and then take a flight to Albany. I take the DC flight so often for work that a flight attendant recognizes me, and we chat about where I'm headed. She tells me her aunt lives in Iowa, so she knows how bad these floods can be.

Erica picks me up at the Albany airport just before noon, and we wait in the parking lot of the Desmond Hotel for Karla and her church crew to arrive. They pull into the parking lot a few minutes later in a quad-cab pickup pulling a twelve-foot-long enclosed trailer. Paulie, the pastor's son, is at the wheel and another man from the church sits in the other seat in front. Erica and I join Karla in the back seat, and we set off for Gallupville.

We are not sure if we'll be able to get there, but we know the back roads, so we're optimistic. The potato peelers, extension cords, and mops and pails along with an abundance of cleaning supplies are in the bed of the pickup. The trailer is filled to the gills with racks of bread and rolls donated by Freihofer's, cases of fresh grapes, cantaloupes and blueberries donated by the Albany Regional Food Bank, and bottled water and huge bags of carrots and potatoes donated by Harvest Church.

We take the back way to Gallupville, cutting across Larry Hill Road from Delanson, and take the curvy county road down to Route 146, which has been gouged out and is now closed. At one point, Paulie says he has no idea where in the world he is, and I tell him not to worry because my sisters and I know exactly where we're going.

We cross an ancient bridge on Sellick Road that withstood the wrath of Irene's rushing waters and find it interesting that this old bridge held up when newer bridges did not. The dirt road intersects with another dirt road, and we climb up over a hill, and wind around until we drive down into the valley.

It's a warm day and people are congregating outside of the church. They look surprised to see us pull into the parking lot and ask if we're the Red Cross. We later learn that the Red Cross will arrive at this shelter three days from now, or nearly a week after Irene has been here.

Everyone's excited to see fresh fruit and bread, and especially the potato peelers. You'd think I was handing over bars of gold when I bring them into the kitchen.

I look around the meeting room and see the familiar face of despair among the adults. Kids are running around all grimy and sweaty. Word gets around fast that I used to live around here and now live in New Orleans. People come up to thank me and say that I must know how they feel. Yes, I tell them, I do know, and that's why I'm here.

On the way out to our truck, we're told that they're now able to get food and water across the swollen and still raging creeks in the area by using a rope and pulley system to send plastic bags across. No wonder they wanted only contractor-grade bags.

We wonder if we can make it to the town of Schoharie and

head in that direction. We crisscross our way there and drive down Main Street. Erica said that she's heard that only Schoharie residents are being allowed in, but there's no checkpoint and no one stopping us. The water has receded, and thick brown mud covers everything in sight. Every home and business has a water line that is four to five feet from the ground, and as we get closer to the lower areas, the water lines are even higher. Homeowners are beginning to haul their belongings out, and furniture and household items are being stacked at the edge of the street.

On my way here, I wondered if I've become desensitized to seeing everyone's life out on the street but seeing the debris piles still brings tears to my eyes. No one else in the truck has seen this kind of thing firsthand, and they are silent and gasping as we make our way through town.

Even in rural America, flood damage is devastating.

The pews and Bibles have been pulled out of the Presbyterian Church, built in 1795. The bar stools from the Glass Bar are out on the sidewalk. Several mattresses are stacked outside of a bed and breakfast. Every house and business has a pile of soggy, mud-caked debris.

We turn down Bridge Street, where a wooden swing set has traveled into the intersection, and are in utter shock at how bad our grandparents' house now looks. The water line must be six feet high, and it looks like part of the house is off of its foundation.

We continue on to Middleburgh where we see Pinder's barn still on fire. We heard it was burning, but it's so odd to see nothing but acres and acres of water where farmland once stood, and see a barn burning in its center.

On September 26, 2011, an uncharacteristically somber David Letterman tells viewers that the little town he joked about back in 2002 now has $30 million in damage from Irene, and 80% of the 275 homes and businesses need repair, hopefully soon before winter comes. He asks for donations and displays the address for the Schoharie Recovery Fund.

Irene made its ninth and final landfall in Brooklyn on August 28th in 2011, and transitioned into a tropical cyclone that hit Vermont and New Hampshire the next day. Throughout its path, Irene caused widespread destruction and at least 56 deaths. Damage estimates throughout the United States were $15.6 billion, which made it the seventh costliest hurricane in United States history.

February 12, 2012

THE LAST FEMA trailer in New Orleans leaves the city today, almost seven years after Katrina. The trailers had popped up everywhere. Miss Dee Dee had one in the back yard of the house directly across the street from us, and a large mobile home park sprouted up in a field next to the Coke plant in Elmwood, half a mile or so away.

According to FEMA, the response to Katrina and Rita was the largest housing operation in the history of the United States. Transitional housing, consisting of small travel trailers and larger mobile homes, was provided to 92,000 families throughout Louisiana and 44,000 in Mississippi. As the last of the trailers rolled out of the city, Mayor Mitch Landrieu remarked that "another page has turned in New Orleans' post-Katrina history."

Originally, the trailers were supposed to house residents for a maximum of eighteen months. However, five years after Katrina hit the Gulf coast, 860 families in Louisiana and 176 in Mississippi still lived in FEMA trailers.

Beginning in 2006, FEMA began auctioning off some of the no-longer-needed trailers, often for pennies on the dollar. Some were sold to individuals, and some were sold to dealers in lots as large as 20,000 units. Many were priced under a thousand dollars, a steep discount from the original cost of a trailer, estimated to be about $15,000 for a travel trailer and $30,000 for a mobile home.

Fox 13 News in Tampa Bay, Florida, scoured sales records and found that RV dealers and mobile home parks across Florida bought FEMA units over the years, but the news crew was not able to locate anyone willing to talk about it. They surmised it may be because of the well-publicized problems with formaldehyde leaching from the trailers, which now must be disclosed, or perhaps it's because of the great deal that the dealers received—at the taxpayer's expense.

The *New York Times* reported that during the BP oil spill cleanup in the summer of 2010, some of the FEMA trailers were re-purposed as temporary housing for cleanup workers, despite their lack of government-required warning paperwork, and in some cases, the presence of formaldehyde in the trailers.

March 13, 2012

ALTHOUGH IT IS almost seven years since Katrina, groups of volunteers continue to help rebuild the city and the Gulf Coast. Most are faith-based groups, or youth or college groups doing service projects. Many of these groups are making annual trips.

I got a call from a woman at the University of Georgia, where Samantha goes to school, saying that a group of UGA students would be in town over spring break to help rebuild New Orleans. UGA parents in New Orleans were being contacted to see if they would like to do something for these students while they were here, and bringing donuts to the worksite was one of the things suggested.

I always get weepy over things like this—students spending spring break doing service projects rather than tanning on a beach somewhere. Of course, we'd like to do something while the UGA students are here.

Rich and I take the group out to dinner at Mandina's, a classic New Orleans restaurant on Canal Boulevard. Rich orders the massive seafood platter when he sees that the students are gracious guests and are ordering things like a cup of gumbo. We also order several appetizers for everyone to try.

Most of these kids have never seen a crawfish before, or tasted softshell crab or turtle soup. We pass the food round and round the table. I enjoy seeing how they inspect the tiny crawfish, flip them around on their plate, and declare that they look like little lobsters. Down here, I tell them, we eat things that other people exterminate.

May 26, 2012

JOHN'S HIGH SCHOOL graduation ceremony is held at night, under the oaks in front of the school he's attended for thirteen years, except for our time in Houston. The girls are dressed in long white dresses and the boys wear white linen suits. It's hard to imagine how badly this school flooded. A steel beam memorial stands by the walkway where the graduates walk out, the only physical reminder of Katrina.

August 26, 2012

"OH GOOD LORD," says our neighbor as she pulls her garbage cans toward her garage. I'm walking Buddy and stop to chat. "There's another one comin' this way. Isaac. I'm too old for this, too old for this," she says as she shakes her head.

Somehow I've missed the growing intensity of this hurricane and the fact that it's headed right for New Orleans. Late in the day on the 28th, category 1 Isaac, with 80 mph winds, makes landfall in Louisiana.

Rich and I awaken on the 29th to a quiet—and hot—house and realize that the power went off sometime during the night. It's raining and the wind is gusting.

I have my stash of instant coffee ready and peer out the front yard on my way to the kitchen. One of the trees we replanted after Katrina is now toppled over. Big branches cover the lawn. Ugh. Once again I anticipate days of back-breaking work. I'm thinking I'm too old for this, too.

And then I see our neighbor's big pecan tree that has fallen onto our garage and house in back. The back of the garage is collapsed, and the tree is precariously leaning on the flat roof of the sunroom.

Our tree man, who I now know all too well, arrives in the afternoon and uses his bobcat to steady the tree while his crew cuts it up. They are so busy getting trees off of houses that they tell me they'll be back another day to remove the cut-up tree from the yard.

The rain continues to fall, sometimes so hard that our back yard looks like one continuous lake. It's getting hotter and hotter in the house, and the battery-operated fans barely move the thick humid air. I sit for hours scrunched up by a window reading my Kindle and writing in my journal, but at times, the sky grows so dark that I need a flashlight. Every now and then, I turn on an old boom box that we've kept for occasions like this and listen to the news. The city is shut down, Louisiana Governor Bobby Jindal has declared a state of emergency, and only emergency crews are allowed on the roads.

Prior storms gave us confidence that our power would soon be restored, but that's not the case with this hurricane. I'm so glad that our kids are both off at college and not going through this. Isaac has caused $2.39 billion in damage and 41 people have died in its path through the Caribbean and United States.

There's not much more that can test a marriage than heat, humidity, crappy food, darkness, and boredom. It should be the perfect set-up for a romantic interlude, but Rich and I aren't even talking.

Why are we living here, in a city below sea level? Why do

so many hurricanes seem to come this way? Why do we pay so much for flood and homeowner's insurance, and why do the insurance companies pay out so little? Why do we keep going through the destruction and repair process over and over again? Isn't it time to leave New Orleans?

September 27, 2012

A FEDERAL JUDGE gives a $42.6 million class-action settlement to Gulf Coast recipients of FEMA trailers who assert that they were exposed to hazardous formaldehyde fumes while living in the trailers. Over 55,000 residents of Louisiana, Mississippi, Alabama, and Texas participated in the suit.

Air quality tests of forty-four FEMA trailers that were conducted in the spring of 2006 by the Sierra Club found formaldehyde concentrations as high as 0.34 parts per million, which they described as a level nearly equal to what a professional embalmer would be exposed to on the job.

In February 2008, the Centers for Disease Control and Prevention released its report that found that hundreds of trailers in Louisiana and Mississippi had formaldehyde levels that were on average five times greater than typical indoor levels found in traditional wood and brick houses. Formaldehyde in the trailers has been linked to skin rashes, headaches, nosebleeds, and respiratory disorders, and is classified by the National Cancer Institute as a known human carcinogen. The long-term effects of formaldehyde exposure are unknown.

September 30, 2012

THE FINAL DAILY edition of the *Times-Picayune* newspaper has arrived at the end of the driveway. New Orleans is now the largest city in the United States without a daily newspaper.

The paper has been published since January 1837 and will now be published tri-weekly on Wednesdays, Fridays, and Sundays. Along with its website, nola.com, the paper was a lifeline for information during Katrina. The *Times-Picayune* was awarded the Pulitzer Prize for Public Service in 2006 for its Katrina coverage, and four staff reporters also received Pulitzers for their breaking news reporting, making it the first time a Pulitzer had been awarded for online journalism. Following Katrina, columnists like Chris Rose wrote about his Katrina experiences, eventually publishing some in the book *1 Dead in Attic.* Other columnists helped rebuild cherished recipe collections wiped out by Katrina. Dan Gill's gardening column told me when to plant and what to plant. John pretty much learned to read by reading the Sports section.

October 27, 2012

MY 26-YEAR-OLD JERSEY niece, as I call her, says she never thought she'd be calling us for hurricane advice, and asks how she should best prepare for Hurricane Sandy headed her way. She considers us the experts and in some ways, we are. I tell her to bag everything in her refrigerator and freezer and eat half a container of ice cream vertically so she'll be able to tell how long the power goes out. And then drink a bottle of wine.

Her apartment is upstairs, so her things should be safe from flooding. However, they'll be drenched if the roof blows off. She's scheduled to fly to Orlando for work today, and she's glad she's able to leave. She tells me she remembers our stories and photos all too well.

Hurricane Sandy, also known as Superstorm Sandy, first made landfall in Jamaica, and then strengthened and hit Cuba as a category 3 hurricane. Early on October 29th, Sandy weirdly made its way up the eastern coast of the United States and came ashore just northeast of Atlantic City. Sandy affected twenty-four states, including the entire eastern seaboard from Florida to Maine, and west across the Appalachian Mountains to Michigan and Wisconsin, with particularly severe damage in New Jersey and New York. Its storm surge hit New York City on the 29th and flooded streets, tunnels, and subway lines. Many people lost power for days, and damage in the United States was estimated to be $68 billion, making it the second costliest hurricane in United States history (only Katrina has surpassed this amount). As Hurricane Sandy made its way across seven countries, 286 people were killed along its path.

My niece's apartment was spared any damage, but she was surrounded by devastation for months. Whitney said she was one of a few "lucky ones." People living in the housing development next door had sewage water swirling through their houses in addition to the floodwater.

December 25, 2014

THE KIDS ARE both home for the holidays, and we sit on the floor by a Fraser fir decorated with ornaments made by the kids or acquired on our vacations. Every ornament has a story behind it. We even have one for Jack Russell Terror, out of respect, because he was a part of our family for a while.

We open Christmas presents, and it's a happy time for our family. Hurricane Katrina seems so long ago now, but as its tenth anniversary approaches, we're starting to talk about it more often. For some people, though, the memories and wounds remain. When I mentioned Katrina to my eye doctor, he swung around on his stool and said, "I can't talk about it."

New Orleans is home for our kids, and our kids love it here. Both want to come home to New Orleans to work once they've finished college. Despite all they've been through, they can't imagine living anywhere else.

Rich and I have questioned staying here, and my sisters still ask why I insist on living in a swamp. Reason number one for me is that people here are polite and inherently nice to one another. I like how I'm still called "Miss Lisa" at the age of 56, and how people greet you with "How you doin' baby?" I'm tempted to write "Who Dat Nation" on forms asking for my nationality. I like how taking a fast food order is a conversation opportunity, and how there's no hurry here. I've met a woman who calls our house asking for Jeannette. She keeps transposing Jeannette's phone number and calls us instead, and we talk for a few minutes anyway.

NOLA love is a really strong force here, and is the reason that so many of us New Orleanians returned to the homeland. Three-fourths of the people in New Orleans at the time of Katrina were born here, and most had never lived anywhere but here. Love of New Orleans doesn't just happen here, it stays with you long after a visit and you carry it with you, wherever you go.

New Orleans is the land of Big Ass Beers, and Hurricanes from Pat O'Brien's. And Hand Grenades, but you have to remember that one will get you through the weekend, and two will get you in trouble. There really is this thing called "Southern Hospitality," and it's here in NOLA. New Orleans welcomes everyone with open arms, and as the saying goes, "Come as you are, leave different."

I like how people here "pass a good time" and celebrate anything and everything. We dance when people *are* looking and don't care. We love our crawfish boils, our music, our drive-thru daiquiris, and our history. The spirit of New Orleans keeps us coming back, hurricane after hurricane. New Orleans is our home and where we want to be. Songwriter Paul Soniat couldn't have said it better when he wrote, "There's no city like it anywhere, anywhere at all."

My Hometown New Orleans

So shed a tear for New Orleans, but don't you cry too long.
We got work to do, we got lives to build.
Bring back the magic of New Orleans.
Come Mardi Gras time, throw beads to you.
You know we'll cook you up some gumbo too.
New Orleans music will fill your ears.
So wipe your tears, it may take years, but we'll be back.
Bring back the magic of New Orleans.
Bring back the magic that is New Orleans.
No city like it anywhere, anywhere at all.
And if you're looking for me, I'll know where I'll be.
My hometown New Orleans.

Lyrics excerpted from "My Hometown New Orleans," written by Paul Soniat.

Epilogue

IN HIS 33 years at the National Hurricane Center, Director Max Mayfield had never called local government officials to personally warn them about an approaching storm. He called the governors of Louisiana and Mississippi and the mayor of New Orleans on the evening of August 27, 2005, and remembers saying that Katrina was going to be a defining moment for a lot of people.

Hurricane Katrina was the largest and third strongest hurricane ever recorded to make landfall in the United States. An aging and neglected levee system and a slow disaster response have been blamed for the high loss of life and extensive property damage. Ultimately, 80% of New Orleans and large portions of nearby parishes flooded, and the floodwaters did not recede for weeks. A report by the American Society of Civil Engineers states that had forty-three levees and floodwalls not failed, and had the pump stations operated, nearly two-thirds of the deaths would not have occurred. Katrina's storm surge and winds also devastated towns along the Gulf Coast. Total property damage from Katrina was estimated at $108 billion, nearly four times the damage inflicted by Hurricane Andrew in 1992.

Katrina's final death toll is believed to be 1,836, with 1,577 deaths occurring in Louisiana, 238 in Mississippi, and 21 in other states. However, this number has been disputed and may be as high as 4,081 when indirect deaths and excess deaths compared to pre-Katrina death rates are factored in. What is not disputed is the fact that 705 people who were reported missing as a result of Katrina were still missing and unaccounted for in 2014.

In 2009, an analysis of 1,100 deaths caused by Hurricane Katrina in New Orleans and St. Bernard parish found that those who died had two things in common: they were older in age and lived near the levee breaches in the Ninth Wards and Lakeview and Gentilly areas. Forty percent had drowned; 25% died from injuries, including carbon monoxide poisoning; and 11% died from heart and other conditions exacerbated by stress and lack of access to medications and medical care. Nearly 85% were older than 51, 60% were older than 65, and almost half were older than 75. Gender did not have a role in the Katrina deaths; 50.6% of those who died were male and 49.3% were female. Of the 818 fatalities for which race was listed, 55% were African-American, 40% white, 2% Hispanic and 1% Asian-Pacific. The race of 35 of the victims is unknown.

In 2008, 31 unidentified bodies were buried in a $1.5 million monument in the Charity Hospital Cemetery, originally known as Potter's Field and the resting place of the unclaimed, many of whom died during yellow fever and influenza epidemics. From above, the New Orleans Katrina Memorial has the shape of a hurricane, and at its center or eye, there is a carved stone marker with a dedication to all who suffered or died during Hurricane Katrina. Stone benches surround the marker, and six crypts made of reflective stone form an outer spiral of the memorial.

Many Katrina stories have been told, and some have been published. There are accounts from within the Superdome, stories of rescues and rescuers, investigative reports of medical care and the disaster response, and even stories written from a pet's point of view. Some of these are conflicting accounts, and further investigation has revealed that in some cases, events purported to occur either did not occur or were greatly exaggerated or distorted. However, there were also things that occurred and remain disputed, and the truth will never be known.

While some Katrina stories have appeared in print, and some have been fictionalized in televised shows such as HBO's *Treme*, many more Katrina stories remain in the memories of those affected by Katrina. Some of these are being recorded for perpetuity. The Roy Rosenzweig Center for History and New Media at George Mason University and the University of New Orleans organized the Hurricane Digital Memory Bank (www.hurricanearchive.org) in 2005 in partnership with many national and Gulf Coast area organizations and individuals. The memory bank received the Award of Merit for Leadership in History, and is the largest free public archive of hurricanes Katrina and Rita with over 25,000 items in the collection. The memory bank includes first-hand accounts, on-scene images, blog posts, and podcasts, and allows the people affected by these storms to tell their stories in their own words, which as part of the historical record will remain accessible to a wide audience for generations to come. The majority of the stories were contributed by children and teenagers and often begin with the words, "I don't know where to start." Some are completely analytical (e.g. we went from X to Y and then moved to Z), some are philosophical and reflective, and note how the hurricanes revealed strengths they never knew, and some are memorable simply because of their subject matter. For instance, there's a photo of an MRE captioned with, "I lived on MREs for about three weeks. The best one to eat was the Meatloaf with Gravy. I would advise people to stay away from the Black Bean and Rice Burrito."

One of the most interesting Katrina stories is about the three Duke University students who "just did it." The boys wanted to get to the New Orleans Convention Center, where no one else seemed to be going, and find a way to get people out. They had a press pass, shirt, and business card from a TV station, were waved through a security checkpoint, and were surprised to find that they could drive right up to the Convention Center. They took three women and a man who had been trapped in a tree and bitten by fire ants to Baton Rouge, and if they'd had more time, would have taken many more. When interviewed by CNN, one of the boys said, "The overarching question that we had was, how did we get in there, we've never been to New Orleans before, how did we get in there where these people have been stranded for four, five days with no food and water, living in a lawless anarchy environment, how did we get there in twenty minutes in a Hyundai Elantra?" Another of the boys noted that, "A lot of people, including the people at the Convention Center, weren't trapped by hurricane damage, they were trapped by red tape."

The blame game following Katrina continues until this day. What Katrina revealed is that in 2005, the United States did not have a prepared, coordinated disaster response plan for handling a large population of people and/or large geographic area. Probably more than ever before, in part because of weather events such as Katrina, Rita, Irene, Sandy and others, we Americans no longer just assume we'll always have electricity and water and heat and all the goods and services we've taken for granted. We're now more aware that no one is immune from experiencing a disaster and its aftermath, whether it's a fire, tornado, earthquake, flood, or snowstorm.

New Orleanians also now are aware that levees and floodwalls, no matter how big or sturdy, cannot provide guaranteed protection against overtopping or failure. The National Academy of Engineering and the National Research Council note that levees and floodwalls should be viewed as a way to reduce risks from hurricanes and storm surges, and not as measures that eliminate these risks.

The world will long remember 2005 as the year of the hurricane, when so many hurricanes occurred that the A-Z alphabet was exhausted and subsequent hurricanes received letters of the Greek alphabet to identify them. Names like Andrew, Katrina, and Sandy evoke disturbing memories for those of us affected by hurricanes bearing these names. An international committee of the World Meteorological Organization has the authority to retire hurricane names if the storm is so deadly or costly that future use of its name on a different storm would be inappropriate for obvious reasons of sensitivity. When this occurs, the offending name is stricken from the list and another name is selected to replace it. Hurricane names that recently have been retired include Andrew, Mitch, Ivan, Katrina, Rita, Gustav, Irene, and Sandy.

People have asked me what it was like to go down memory lane almost twenty years after the '95 flood and almost a decade after our Katrina and Rita experiences. And why now, some have asked.

In my travels around the United States to review cancer centers for a certification program, I've been asked about New Orleans and Hurricane Katrina when people learn where I live. Several people told me I should write a book, and it was only after someone said that I should write things down for my kids—and their kids—that I seriously considered writing. Not to write a book, but to record what happened.

In November 2014, I pulled out my journals, photo albums, old newspapers and magazines, and the books that were so quickly published in Katrina's aftermath, and sat down on the floor with them. The history of our family as well as a blip of American history lay at my feet. With Buddy's head in my lap, I read through my journals—which still have the power to make me cry—and then studied the photo albums.

First, there's John in his playpen, with Samantha stacking plastic cups on his head. Then there's his playpen, submerged in three feet of dark water against the backdrop of the tipped-over living room furniture. Photos of the construction crew ripping out the sheetrock and insulation. Rich tossing my grandmother's broken china into the debris pile. Photos of the water line circling our house.

The album continues with carpet being laid down, walls being painted, and how the most precious holiday gifts in 1995 were the photo albums made by my mother and sisters to replace those I'd lost.

I look through photos taken on the Gulf Coast long ago. The kids are tiny in the early photos and are busy shoveling in the sand. To protect them from the sun, they're covered from head-to-toe in more clothing than many kids wear in the northeast in the wintertime. In a later photo taken in Biloxi just two weeks before Katrina struck, Samantha is lying on the sand while John rides the waves on a boogie board.

My family looks young and hopeful in August 2005 as they stand at the back of Rich's Expedition, packed with our two dogs in their crates. There are photos of the kids doing their homework in the dark in the motel outside of Brookhaven, not knowing that their school had already flooded. There are photos of motel rooms, the gridlock on the roads, and then the destruction.

The devastation is profound, both in New Orleans and along the Gulf Coast.

The photos are too much for me, and several times I have to slap the album closed to take a break from them.

I listen to Paul Soniat's CD *Below the Water Line* and wipe away tears.

The photos of John and Samantha on the beach in Galveston lift my spirits. I remember it as the first time they were relaxed and actually smiling for the camera. Then there's John standing in Wal-Mart, holding the gingerbread house kit close to his chest, and Sam with her purple comforter set.

The next photo album has photos of our first Christmas and Hanukkah on the farm, with presents under the cardboard tree drawn by Sam. Then, my garden grows and flowers bloom in the photos, followed by shots of the kids happily bouncing on the trampoline.

I come across a close-up shot of Jack the Russell Terror and show it to Buddy. He narrows his eyes and drops his head back down on the ground as if to say he's glad that bad boy is gone.

There's the photo of the lone sunflower growing in the debris that I saw each day as I drove John to school.

The big FedEx plane, bringing the beloved penguins and otters back to the Aquarium of the Americas.

There are pictures of soccer and football games, and birthday parties and proms. A Super Bowl win and Mardi Gras parades. High school graduation pictures, and photos that capture moving into college dorms. The kids are smiling more now in these pictures, that's something I notice as I study these photos taken over time.

Our albums are the repository of our family's history, and I think about Generation K, the Katrina kids. What will they remember? Will they remember? I also think about our collective American history and wonder how Hurricane Katrina will be remembered far into the future, after those of us with firsthand memories of Katrina are gone.

Our Gratitude

I WOULD BE remiss if I did not thank the many people who helped our family after Hurricane Katrina. Although the floodwaters have receded from our collective memories, your kindness will never be forgotten. There are not enough words to express our gratitude to our families (my parents, my sisters, Rich's brother Rob, and all of our extended family members), our angel Carol, soccer Coach Ross, the Rudy family, and the staff and faculty at Spring Branch Middle School in Houston. Special thanks to Cheryl Backes for finding us an evacuation motel and to Suzanne Rusovich for finding our Houston apartment. Thank you to Paul Wabnig for making us laugh and to Paul Soniat for making us cry. We needed to cry and your music helped us heal. Thank you to the Oncology Nursing Society Board of Directors, who sent care packages that strengthened our spirit and reminded us that we were not forgotten. Special thanks to "Santa" at Deutsche Bank for the Wal-Mart gift cards that made our first post-Katrina holiday merry and bright. Thank you to Harvest Church in Clifton Park, NY, Freihofer's, the Albany Regional Food Bank, and Pastor DeBartolo and his son Josh for helping Schoharie County following Hurricane Irene.

On behalf of the people along the Gulf Coast, I also want to thank everyone who helped in Katrina's aftermath.

To the man who went to church in Rockwall, Texas and took the shoes from his feet and placed them in the Katrina clothing collection box, we thank you.

To the little girls in Chicago who set up a lemonade stand so that girls from New Orleans could attend Birch Trail Camp in Wisconsin, we thank you.

To the electrician who left his family in Camp Hill, Pennsylvania for six months to help restore power in New Orleans, we thank you.

To the countless faith-based, high school, college, and community organizations who helped people along the Gulf Coast gut and repair their homes, or build new ones, we thank you.

To the animal lovers and rescue organizations who saved our beloved pets, we thank you.

To those who opened their arms and offered their homes, we thank you.

To the multitude of schools and colleges that offered admission to displaced students, we thank you.

To the many nations around the globe that sent aid, we thank you.

The stories of kindness are endless and inspiring. We thank you for your compassion and generosity.

A Family Update

SAMANTHA, WHO AFTER Katrina repeatedly said that she would never, ever, *ever* become a nurse or doctor, entered medical school in the fall of 2014. John is a third-year civil engineering major determined to improve New Orleans' levee system. Rich remains free of colon cancer and continues to work at the LSU Bogalusa Hospital and his private surgery practice in Metairie. I've continued to work as an oncology nurse and travel the United States to conduct certification reviews of cancer centers. Buddy is now 12 years old and still goes swimming in our pool every chance he gets.

Significant flooding remains in the Lakeview area, eleven days after Katrina.

A house in the Lakeview area, 41 days after Katrina.

Refrigerators with rotten contents are gathered in an apartment complex parking lot, awaiting disposal.

Water lines indicate the receding water levels.

Debris piles accumulate outside of flooded homes.

The debris pile on West End Boulevard.

The Mississippi coast, January 2, 2006.

Highway 90 along the Mississippi Sound.

CPSIA information can be obtained
at www.ICGtesting.com
Printed in the USA
LVOW04s1442101215
466281LV00016B/734/P

9 780996 232708